Solitudes

From Rimbaud to Heidegger

Marc Froment-Meurice

Translated by
Peter Walsh

Foreword translated by
Douglas Brick

STATE UNIVERSITY OF NEW YORK PRESS

Production by Ruth Fisher
Marketing by Theresa Abad Swierzowski

Published by
State University of New York Press, Albany

Printed in the United States of America

For information, address the State University of New York Press, State University Plaza, Albany, NY 12246

Library of Congress Cataloging-in-Publication Data

Froment Meurice, Marc.
[Solitudes. English]
Solitudes : from Rimbaud to Heidegger / Marc Froment-Meurice ; translated by Peter Walsh.
p. cm. — (SUNY series, Intersections)
Includes bibliographical references (p.).
ISBN 0-7914-2524-X (pb acid-free). — ISBN 0-7914-2523-1 (ch acid-free)
1. Philosophy in literature. 2. Alienation (Philosophy)
3. French literature—19th century—History and criticism.
4. French literature—20th century—History and criticism.
I. Title. II. Series: Intersections (Albany, N.Y.)
PN49.F7313 1995
809'.93384—dc20 94-49400
CIP

10 9 8 7 6 5 4 3 2 1

Solitudes

SUNY Series,
Intersections: Philosophy and Critical Theory
Rodolphe Gasché, Editor

Contents

Fore-word

Before entering the outskirts of these "Solitudes" of saying, I must attempt to prevent a misunderstanding that might arise simply from the idea of passing "from" Rimbaud "to" Heidegger. There is no progression and perhaps not even a passage or transition in the proper sense of the word. We cannot pass from one to the other, as from one frequency in the electromagnetic spectrum to another. Not only are they not on the same wavelength and do not speak the same language but, even if Rimbaud had spoken German,[1] nothing says that he would have been heard by the thinker who, nonetheless, dedicated the whole second half of his existence to "approaching" the world of poetry, through thought. Still, Heidegger recognized elsewhere, with the poet of his choice, Hölderlin, that "to each other they remain unknown," the tree of poetry and the tree of thought, as two neighbors in the same forest.[2]

Conversely, it may be affirmed that Rimbaud, who put medicine and philosophy in the same bag, "old-wives remedies and popular songs" (*Oeuvres complètes*, p. 95; hereafter *OC*), was not recognized in the several, admittedly uncertain and belated, pages,[3] that Heidegger dedicated, at the invitation of Roger Munier and following René Char, to the "clarification" of two sentences of the letter "of the Seer." The hiatus is quite striking and goes far beyond the simple difference of languages, though it does pass through that difference. But the difference is less between German and French, which Heidegger mastered better than he would care to admit, than between two *worlds*: to say it rather bluntly, between the modern world and the Greek world revisited in the Heideggerian fashion. Between the sentence, "Poetry will no longer make action rhythmic" and Archilochus's fragment on the *ruthmos* that supports men, the gap is not only of two millennia. The possibility, evoked at the end of Heidegger's short article "Rimbaud," of a destruction of language—and thus of poetic speech itself—by technology's seizure of language, can this possibility be harmonized with the demand expressed at the end of *A Season in Hell*: "We must be absolutely modern"? Does it not rather manifest a blindness (which is not properly Heideggerian) toward that modernity which has not *yet* appeared in all its dimension of, let us say, caesura?

In other words, in going from Rimbaud to Heidegger, the risk is less that of "delivering philosophy over to poetry," as Alain Badiou recently wrote, than in delivering poetry over to philosophy, even if the latter has since then deposed the very name of philosophy. It is true that "Heidegger's thought takes its power of persuasion from being the only one that captures what is at stake in poetry, i.e. the destitution of object fetishism, the opposition of truth to knowledge, and finally the essential disorientation of our epoch."[4] But this is precisely its essential danger, which Heidegger himself had in mind when he wrote that the "good" danger was being in the neighborhood of poets and the "bad," philosophical production: a danger of *capture* inherent in all thought insofar as it grasps, even if not in a strictly conceptual form.[5] Thus it is not because the "age of poets is finished" that it is "*also* necessary to de-suture philosophy from its poetic condition," but rather because such an "age" has not (yet) come and because it will not come as long was philosophy, by capturing "sense," releases us from *thinking-poetically*, with a hyphen that is less a suture than a trans-figuration. It is also true that to speak of an age of poets makes no sense, if by that we mean a grasping of power, like the slogan from 1968: "all power to the imagination." In fact, the age of poets coincides with the epoch in which "there is no Present," in which poetic speech is reduced to extreme impotence and abolished as a "historical power." In this sense, the age of poets was finished before it started, insofar as it denounces itself as the absolutely unpoetic age of the "numerous unrestrained languages" (Hölderlin) that saturate contemporary space with proliferating and ventriloquistic significations. Nevertheless, and in a reversal that may seem to be a simple stylistic figure, we must agree that *modern* poetry—in broad terms, born in the collapse of poetic power as described in Rimbaud—goes *hand in glove*, intimately, with such an epoch of refusal, precisely so that its determining relation with such a planetary obstruction inaugurates its reign, a reign marked more by disarray and destitution than by pomp and circumstance of an *undivided* domination.

I repeat: the risk is not in delivering philosophy over to poetry; this would be like delivering a mountain over to a mouse. The risk is rather that of smothering the mouse. As Heidegger wrote in the "Prefatory Remark" to "Remembrance of the Poet,"[6] perhaps every clarification of poetry, especially a philosophical one, is a "fall of snow on the bell," which would send it out of tune—that is, would irremediably alter its own singularity, its timber or tone. Besides, we might ask ourselves whether this dream of transparency or absolute purity, expressed in the interpreter's wish to efface himself before the pure presence of the poem, is not only impossible and utopian but illusory and deceitful. Does it not conceal a desire for *identification*, which is really only a masked strategy of capture and appropriation? Does Heidegger purely and simply efface himself before the pure presence of Hölderlin's poem? We might well doubt it, but not in order to reestablish an "objective" view of Hölderlin, finally cleared of philosophical glosses or scoria, so as to beatifically contemplate the poem in its "pure presence." For that pure presence is itself chimerical, if it signifies an object-like being-placed-before. No poem, whatever it may be, and certainly not one of Hölderlin's, is an object, and, if it is a matter of "letting it be," of letting it present itself, this does not mean not touching it except for occasional dustings. On the contrary, we must touch it if we wish first to be touched by what it addresses to us, its speech, which is never anything other than an address, an envoy—and thus the announcement of a *common* sense, a sharing of sense and senses. And this "work" (in quotes, for this work, if it works, does so only in the sense in which wood is said to work) is what Heidegger calls hermeneutic. Trans-parence, "appearing-through," is never immediate. It is a passage, a transition, from one *to* the other and vice versa, so that not only the original, passing through the "mi-lieu" (mid-place) of interpretation (or trans-lation), "comes back" to us transformed, altered, but *we ourselves*, comparing ourselves to the original, lose our original and always immediate definition so as to become "strangered," transfigured. We cannot pass from philosophy to poetry or even from one language to another as from the main course to dessert: the crossing is perilous in a completely different way; it is an ordeal, that very *ordeal of the stranger*[7] which already contains all of ex-perience. An ordeal that is not content with transforming the language of the other, but one that also transforms our own language, that is, fundamentally, *everything*. Such is the experience of the "salutary danger" that carries us into unknown outskirts, exposing us to the infinity of finitude, to the experience itself. Heidegger writes, "To experience something means to attain it along the way, by going on a way. To undergo an experience with something means that this something, which we reach along the way in order to attain it, itself pertains to us, meets and makes its appeal to us, in that it transforms us into itself" (*Unterwegs zur Sprache*, p. 177, hereafter *UZS*; trans. as *On the Way to Language*, pp. 73–74, hereafter *OWL*).

We experience this with Rimbaud as well as with Heidegger, with Nietzsche or Hegel as with Mallarmé or Trakl. But who is "we"? Precisely those who, in and through the experience of what touches and transforms them by its contact, are constrained to ask: "Who are we?"—and not only: "Are we poets? Are we philosophers?" As if "poet" or "philosopher" was a sufficient response, a sufficient determination of an identity or state, even a civil one. In response to this question we can only vacillate, hesitate, and defer every answer; we have become the Deferred Ones of an unknown thing that conceals itself, and we decline the question and thus continually incline even more—not so much toward a prudent retreat as toward always more daring breaks.

By *we* I mean something other than a subject, and even less "I," even if I happen to write it occasionally, through impertinence or a revolt against the dictatorship of the academic impersonality conventional in philosophy; "we" is that being touched and *altered* by the experience, made different, but in such a way that finally we exist as ourselves, and we *alone* exist—finite singularities by and through the experience, the crossing or transition, or even the "transcendence," from one *to the other*; although nothing says that in this passage there is elevation, ascension or, conversely, decline or disappearance. Each time it "must be seen," as they say, and undoubtedly, above all, touched.

❁ ❁ ❁

Solitudes, formerly this word designated wild, deserted places, far from everything, where the "world" that Christian theology earmarked as "temporal" stopped, and where that of the hermit began, that of the vagabond, the prophet and the bandit, all those separated from the human community, but who nonetheless felt, by their very distance, the reign and fullness of the "world." Their existence did not take place in a limitless void, but deployed itself within the very confines of the world, on its fringes but always at its *horizon*.

Solitudes, here we find also the echo of "soil," a word that does not come from "sole" (*seul*), however, but from "threshold" (*seuil*): that which carries and maintains the opening of the break and thus allows us to *pass*. Such is the strange "position" held here—one I would rather call *deposition*: the risky step is firmest and best grips the soil by breaking away, from one bank to the other. Walking always implies an excess, if only in tearing itself from the soil, which then and only then is the soil that supports. Thus they are solitudes but not confinements: from solitude to solitude, as from one locality to another, by nearly invisible paths that each traveler must make out each time, and nearly reinvent, so fragile and often effaced are the indications, the marks that signal them. And yet, this is no trail-trial: there is no game to track, no treasure to discover at the end of the trail, and perhaps there is not even a goal. What is important is not that we get something or somewhere, but rather that something gets to us and, on the way, transforms us. Then we are no longer solitary, even if what gets to us is not somebody else, a companion with whom we can make our way. It may seem like a nothing, a pebble on the side of the path, the trill of a bird perched on the neighboring larch, but that is already everything: the call *to* the world.

Solitudes, in the plural, not solitude, and especially not that of an *ego* isolated in its interior pseudo-world; solitudes, like the coming into the world of places, of events, each time singular, irreducible to the common place where nothing ever happens, because they are signed by the unique trait of the finitude of experience. Solitudes and finitude: of being, of thought, of the poetic.

Solitudes also because, in each case dealt with here, it is a matter of the always singular experience and speech of those solitaries to whom something has happened. Obviously it is insufficient to say that something happened to them—after all, something happens to everyone, at least once in one's life; and that does not say *what* happened. But, paradoxically, the essential is not *what* happens, not, at least, if we imagine it like a thing in general, a *quid*. The essential is not the essence, but the existence: at least that is the common experience of all who have experienced, not the "same" thing, but something that touched and transfigured them. This something may well be "existence" itself, in the form—for example—of "there is no Present—no, a present *does not exist*."

This book starts with that experience. In the preceding quote from Mallarmé the negation insists and redoubles itself, but this does not make an affirmation, as in the logic of double negation. "There is no Present" does not deny the existence of the present as one might deny the existence of a thing: "there is no table," for example, or even, "there is no God" (if God is, nevertheless, still a thing). For the Present exists only in its separation from every "real" existence. The Present cannot be posed like a table nor can it be denied, since it is not a thing or, if you like, a being "there-before." Its "essence" is not comparable with that of a thing or of any entity; it is given as a nonessence or the break from every essence: existence.

But perhaps this way of speaking is no longer permitted, or rather, it is always possible to translate a poetic experience into philosophical terms (essence and existence), but then it must be known that such a translation is less a treason than a capture and thus an occultation, a return to the deafness or confinement that during two or more millennia characterized the philosophical position in relation to the poetic experience. But to what extent it is possible to disengage oneself from such a closure or cage is not at all obvious, considering that the poets were the first to be trapped in the snare, ceding to the enchantments of the philosophical sirens—to reverse a "poetic" image so often used by philosophers to qualify poetic sorcery. For example, Mallarmé, since now we are dealing with him, consciously "built" his thought, as he himself wrote, on a patient and repeated reading of Hegel.[8]

So I return to the decisive debate on the relation between poetry and thought, on the "suturing" of philosophy to poetry, to remark that this suturing really has taken place, but in the other direction, before the one Alain Badiou "denounces" in the Heideggerian approach. Perhaps the age of poets is finished, but what poets are we talking about? I remark that if that age really starts with "their prophet, their anticipatory look-out," Hölderlin, as Badiou writes, it is because he was the first who was not one of the great German thinkers "in addition," but a thinker in his own right, as a poet—and above all a thinker of the poetic experience (such is the sense of Heidegger's awkward expression "poetry of poetry"). The proximity of philosophers like Hegel or Schelling was not limited to the years of the "*Stift.*" This proximity continued to act throughout the poet's all too short lucid "existence." Hölderlin's famous letter to Böhlendorf (December 1802), in which he expressed his joy at seeing the "philosophical light" around his window, suffices at this point to show that the philosopher is not an occasional companion for the poet nor even a crutch for difficult moments when "inspiration" has broken down. Rather, he is the essential friend, the fellow way-goer, even if both stay "on separate mountains."

One can undoubtedly say the same for the six other "crucial" poets who mark the age of poets for Badiou: if I omit Pessoa and Mandelstam—simply because they wrote in a language that is absolutely foreign to me—Mallarmé, Rimbaud, Trakl, and Celan, if they did not have 'living' philosophers for companions, can nonetheless hardly be fully understood without the more or less deaf proximity of the philosophers: Hegel for Mallarmé, as I have already said, but also Nietzsche for Trakl, and . . . Heidegger for Celan (no matter what one might say to remove Celan from that incontestable resonance and no matter what their "actual" encounter at Todtnauberg may have been).

Rimbaud's case remains atypical—at the heart of a "collection" of beings who themselves are strongly atypical. But precisely because he represents the greatest break from philosophy and its grasp upon the age of modern poets (though it is not difficult to read in *A Season in Hell* the traces of the first modern philosopher, Descartes) it is necessary to attempt, through thought, the great break—to go to Rimbaud "as poet" is indeed crazy.[9]

It will be said that philosophy has nothing to gain, on the contrary, that it has everything to lose by risking a step toward literature. It would lose everything and more than everything: its identity, defined by the rigorous limits internal to its way of thinking. Literature, like philosophy, admittedly works on "letters" or words, but it does not care about the "truth," which passes (with reason) for philosophy's own proper aim; thus, literature (and therefore poetry) and fiction pass for identical. (And yet, what of the last sentence of *A Season in Hell* "and it will be permissible for me *to possess truth in body and soul*"? Is not the word *truth* the same as in the title of the *Discourse on Method:* "of rightly conducting one's reason and seeking the truth in the sciences"?[10] Is not truth *one* and the *same*?)

Thus, only when philosophy renounces the rigor of its method and mode of thinking (by concepts and not by simple words, though they are difficult to distinguish and though "truth" is, above all, a word), only when it has lost every hope of setting itself up in that universal knowledge of the truth would it incline toward literature, for lack of an object (if this expression is permissible) or in order to regild a coat of arms that has been rather tarnished thanks to the advances of science (which, nonetheless, philosophy made possible).

This situation is well known, and I do not intend to discuss once again the relations (usually conflictual but always complex) that philosophy has had with literature, on the one hand, and, on the other, with science or the sciences. Let us simply remark that the very word *poetic*, especially as a substantive, was first philosophical—Aristotle's *Poetics*, for example—and that poetry has always already been invested by philosophy, even if in the (ambiguous) mode of Platonic "exclusion"—ambiguous because the exclusion can be pronounced only after a prior inclusion, in the form of that violent appropriation that I have called *capture*. This can be read in the single word *poiêsis*, which originally was not poetic at all, since it does not appear in Homer, where the word is *aoidos*, "the singer." Plato was the first to invest the word *poiêsis* with what might be called its "technical" sense (*poiêsis* originally designated all sorts of activities, like the fabrication of furniture, and had nothing to do with song or poetic hymns, and we must put the word *technical* in quotes too, if it comes from *technê*, another word that has had many philosophical [mis]adventures). *Poiêsis*, defined as "creation" or "making to be," then becomes the name of an ontological procedure!

But, although the word *poetry* is originally philosophic, the "thing" precedes philosophy, not only in time, but because it is situated closer to the origin, that is, to language. Herodotus says that Homer and Hesiod gave the Greeks their gods and hence their identity as a people. But this gift is also a limitation, and thus Nietzsche thought that Homer was the "fatality of Greek cultivation, for [he] by centralizing made everything level."[11] Nietzsche only repeated what Plato and even Heraclitus had never stopped saying: poetry, as fabulous or mythic speech, must be hunted out of the *polis*, not for a lack of depth, but for its excessive influence. Obviously "desuturing" is not a new watchword. It characterizes the origin of the philosophical enterprise. The myth is dangerous because it exercises a power more Draconian than any dictatorship in the formation or education of a people and its identity, its "image." It fashions that image, as arche-type, and in this precise sense its fiction is redoubtable, less because it might be a lie than because it effaces the contours of the true and the false by situating itself in the heart and at the origin (*archê*) of what makes it possible to delimit and say the Truth: language itself, which, from a certain point of view or nonview, is the original *Myth*, the speech of the Origin and the origin of speech (Heidegger notes all its power in the German word for "legend," *die Sage*, which echoes the verb *sagen*, "to say"). Once arrived at the limit of thought, where it can no longer say, in the form of "statements," what is addressed to it to think, philosophy itself must have recourse to "myths," particularly at its beginning (Plato) and at its end (Nietzsche). For, at the limits of philosophy, this enigma always arrives: the relation that binds being and language in a single point and even in a single word (*logos*). If language is originally poetic—such is the thesis or the hypoinfra-thesis that Heidegger defends in the Turning—the "de-suturing" (of philosophy from poetry) is absolutely impossible; or, if it takes place, it would announce a strange mutation of language, that is, "destruction" pure and simple (Heidegger thought this too, but without being able to clarify it completely).

❁ ❁ ❁

In reality, if one proclaims the age of poets to be "finished," this implies that one does not want to believe that the age of philosophers is finished. It is really rather tiring to hear, for more than a century now, that philosophy is "finished," and from the very ones who were the "great" philosophers of their age, starting with Nietzsche who, since 1872, predicted the arrival of the "last philosopher" and including Heidegger, of course, who made it almost a refrain. We think of Hegel, who in his *Lessons on Aesthetics* was the first to speak of the end of art—a proposition that today appears absurd, considering that Modern Art had not even been born at the time! But we might also, and more profitably, think of Hölderlin who was truly the very first to speak of the end—the end of the hymn. The end, not as what comes *after*—as we understand it, sad knights of *post*-modernity!—but as what precedes and opens into precisely something other, an *other beginning*, another grasping. "For, if it is over, and the day ended," Hölderlin wrote in the *hymn* "Germanien,"

> Only as from a funeral pyre henceforth
> A golden smoke, the legend (*Sage*) of it, drifts
> And glimmers on around our doubting heads
> And no one knows what's happening to him

"No, nothing here I'll deny and ask no favours," says the preceding verse: the end is that essential hour of *doubt*, in which "no one knows what's happening," precisely because something unknown, something other, is happening to him. The end, or evening (Trakl), "transfigures sense and image," starting with that of evening itself, which becomes a twilight in the double sense of the falling evening and the awakening dawn.

To say that philosophy is finished is not the same as crossing it out, taking it for an outmoded item so as to finally "get on to something else," to repeat Hegel's words, which, precisely, speak of the commonsense reaction when faced with death. In other words, on the one hand, this means that philosophy is *not* infinite, no more than art or the hymn are infinite; above all, this means that it has *attained* itself, as that experience of the finitude (and thus the openness) of what has been addressed to it to think—Being, if one insists. This finitude is, in every way, an insurmountable limit—one cannot get on to something else (except Being, beyond Being, there is . . . nothing), and yet thought cannot experience that finitude, and therefore itself, except by exposing itself to that properly unpresentable, inaccessible "something else." That is why thinking too must experience death *as death*—that is, as what no one can get beyond.

In this sense—which we could almost call *positive*, if it were not beyond all positivity and negativity—we would have to admit that the philosophers who have gotten to this point, to the point of experiencing that end, are rather rare and that, on the contrary, for the greater part of those who concern themselves with philosophy, it is not (yet?) finished (finite). That they still believe it possible to develop "systems" infinitely is not a good sign, not a good manifesto *for* philosophy. It is rather a sign of blindness or simply of inexperience: it shows that even today there are people to whom nothing has happened. To whom it has not even happened *that* nothing is happening anymore or that a Present does not exist.

Even if we do not entirely share the analysis of Philippe Lacoue-Labarthe, who brings out all the possible consequences of that "insurmountable limit" assigned to philosophy, we must recognize not only what I would call its almost excessive "logic," but its incontestable greatness. As he himself says, "The renouncing of the voluntaristic *habitus* [the will to philosophy] necessarily maintains itself in the form of a heroism in the *modern* sense of the word, which is indeed that of Baudelaire or Benjamin, for example. This means that it is, in effect, a resistance that is involved."[12]

The *modern* heroism comes out clearly in *A Season in Hell* with even more force than in Baudelaire, it seems to me, in the form of that farewell to poetry that must be understood as the supreme poetic experience of the "absolutely modern" age (of the end of the age of poets). The farewell makes the epoch endure like the hard and nearly endless night of the "there is no Present," but, as a poetic farewell, it also and above all causes one to pass over; it permits access to the truth, it makes everything turn, even one's head, in that turning which is the end that *happens* (to us). "And at dawn, armed with an ardent patience, we shall enter the splendid cities" (Rimbaud "Farewell," in *A Season in Hell*): the splendor that illuminates and transfigures the city, let us assume, is nothing other than the "golden gaze of the beginning" piercing by and through "the somber patience of the end" (Trakl).

But, "while we're waiting," it will be said—while we are waiting for that end to come to us—the situation, especially that of the "philosopher," in such a time of misery in which the question continually comes up "what good are philosophers?" (And the poets? Let us not even talk about them: they are not even an endangered species anymore, they have completely disappeared, become the Disappeared themselves), this situation really seems quite impossible, the Impossible as such. The philosopher can no longer philosophize as if nothing had happened to him (and to us)—whether what happened is called Auschwitz or "the death of God"—and, at the same time, he is deprived of all aid, of all recourse (and of all return). So that all he can do is persist "in" philosophy, knowing full well that he is speaking and thinking in the void, suspended on a coming that has already struck him with an inter-diction, that has already cut short his speech before he could even *take* it up. An impossible situation, an untenable position, in fact. That is precisely its virtue, if I may express it in a "triumphant reversal" (Mallarmé), as silence and destitution were formerly held as virtues, as virtualities richer than abandoning oneself to what passed for realities in this world. Solitudes are not consolations for the desolation of the planet, they are the only supportable soils, since they are the thresholds that support the break in which the brokenness of the Present carries itself.

The philosopher's position is untenable, since, strictly speaking, there is no longer a philosophical position, nor even, absolutely, any position that holds. Considering that the proper business of philosophy is to expose the thesis of Being (and hold itself there), and that it has even exposed this as the *absolute position* (Kant), then it is necessary to imagine the case in which this thesis has been posed and that philosophy having thus accomplished its task no longer has any thesis to expose, nothing therefore other than the continual turning over, inside the same now closed field, of "positions" that would be merely infinite variations—and thus to which nothing happens—on the same theme. This situation is actually untenable, because no living thought can deploy itself in the closed air of a prison, however gilded and infinite it might be. The air of freedom is more vital to it than anything, as Nietzsche clearly perceived: "Philosophy . . . is a voluntary living amid ice and mountain heights."[13]

However, such an existence is impossible at present, perhaps because it remains marked by precisely what forbids it to be free or to experience freedom: will and voluntarism. That is why, now more than ever, and forever as now or never, the relinquishment, the dispossession of the will (and above all the will to philosophy) appears as the paradoxical demand of the thought that renounces the very word *philosophy* to return to the solitude and poverty "of its provisional essence" (Heidegger, *Letter on Humanism*)—of an essence so precarious that it can no longer even say *what* it is nor if it is an "essence." In fact, it no longer poses itself, but deposes itself, as it deposes every will to (self-)position.

Solitudes or Depositions. The word has a double or triple sense, a properly speculative word, thus still philosophical, but insofar as philosophy, whether it likes it or not, is a river of language whose source can be nothing but mythic. Above all, *deposition* speaks of discharge, of a sovereign for example, his dethronement, and in this sense it responds to the gesture of relinquishment by which philosophical power, of the concept for example, is discharged of its prerogatives. But to make a deposition is also a "positive" act: is to testify, to make a testimony. But of what? First and foremost, of the fact that a position is untenable, or that there is no Present (or, in Heidegger's vocabulary, Being is not). But one who makes the deposition, the "authentic" witness does not try to re-create the entire event; one limits oneself to reporting what one knows (what one saw), what happened to one, to oneself or to another. The event always precedes the deposition, as the accident does its report.

Nevertheless, the event, what happens (to us), must *call* forth a deposition, a saying that makes present, reconstitutes, as faithfully as possible, what happened. But how can we make present the "there is no Present"?

To declare the intention of this book: what is at stake is a constant break, of language as well as of thought. The fault of a fore-word (avant-dire)—and I expressly do not say "*avant-propos*," for every proposal or matter can be apropos, whereas nothing can really be pro-*posed* as an alternative solution or even as a change—is that it ventures beforehand what it can only expose by default. By default, I mean, of (ex)position. Thus beginning with the default of "matter" but also of "form": of language. Hölderlin speaks thus of *Gottes Fehl*, "default of God," as the only thing that can support the speech of the poet and come to his aid in the destitution where he lives. In the same way, the German word *Not*, before being "distress," is a call, an invitation to enter always farther into the abyss where the God dwells. Not hidden or absent; in the same way, to awake Being from its Forgetting is not to make it present, to make it come out from an enigmatic absence. Being can no more be presented (or re-presented: posed) than it can be absent. It has not retired someplace, to the basement or attic, to a place apart from which it would be proper to flush it out in order to bring it back to light. For it was always already in the light, it is even there that it has been deposed (or drowned). Being is not exposed like a secret or even like a question (to be dealt with); it is no matter for an exposition, however brilliant or profound.

Elsewhere, Hölderlin speaks of the default of sacred names. But if they are lacking, this default is nothing that can be corrected, nothing that obstructs the way, even if it be the way of the Sacred: on the contrary, such a default opens the way for a liberation of speech, delivered from its task of exposition or representation, liberated for an experience other than that with the gods who are present, the Greek gods now "flown."

With the default of the Present, *all* is in default, above all, proper names, starting with those for saying (presenting) the default itself. Thus *default* or *fault* or even *abyss* are not appropriate names. Nonetheless, they call us to think what, at the heart of their impropriety, necessitates—a speech, for want of everything, for want of words. *Poetic* is also a name for the lack of a proper name—which has always already been improper. Not only because it is originally a Greek word, like *philosophy*. Nothing guarantees that in passing from Greek to German, where *poetic* is said in a completely different register (*dichten*), we shall have taken a step back toward a greater originality. For, in the last analysis, the German word already refers back to a Greek root (*deiknumi*, to show). Is the Greek horizon our *insurmountable* limit? And yet, we *must* transgress such a limit, and perhaps it even calls out for transgression. But Heidegger recognized the impossibility of any passing over, simply because the will toward passing over is constitutive of the beginning (Meta-physics), and it has been reinforced over the centuries, just like the forgetting to which it is intrinsically linked. The epoch prescribes it to us: we must be absolutely modern, an absolute demand founded in its own absoluteness (what I here refer to as autodeliverance), that is, founded on the abyss. We must be absolutely modern, for lack of being (so).

Passing over, transgression, and even, conversely, retrogression, a step backward: it comes to the Same. Here again, Heidegger experienced it, although he never actually said it—probably because it cannot be said as easily as one confesses one's sins. So what remains? Nothing? Perhaps—or, nothing but remaining, apart or on the "line" of division, the line of the default of present, of accomplished nihilism, always broken, never traceable except in an infinite re-trace, a *re-treat (retrait)* in the sense in which Derrida, tuned to the French language, understands the word. Of itself, the retreat or break calls for a deposition, above all, of presence as position. A present does not exist, that is, it exists only as a break, the ex-sistence of which we are less the depositories than the Deposers, the "witnesses," the "place-holders." We witness, but what we see above all is that it breaks away—and thus makes a place, gives way. If a Present existed in the same way as a table or any other being, nothing could take (a) place and, further, nothing could happen—that is perhaps what is starting to happen to us, in the effacing of Difference, in which we are implicated parties as "placeholders of nothing." (Heidegger, *What is Metaphyics*?)

"When [will be] the harvest of the abyss?" asks the poet, he who can say "I dwell in a pain"[14]: the pain that is, the brokenness, opens the dwelling and maintains it apart/open. When is the harvest or gathering of what remains rending, what forever defers its coming, at least as long as that rending trait is not even shared, endured, but forgotten like the Hand-of-the-Present (*Main-tenant*) that maintains everything *inclined*, one toward another, and thus exposed, in the finitude of the "infinite inclination" (*unendliche Innigkeit*, Hölderlin)?

When? Never, as long as a Present (*Main-tenant*) does not exist? And at present, what present remains to us? Nothing but its want? But this want, as improper as this word is, must truly be presented, if not represented. And so it is: to a present that defers or retracts its coming, a speech that is cut off (cor)responds. Or rather, the one and the other harvest each other in the same inclination, that, so to speak, of declining the invitation and thus of simply declining their name: solitudes held in common, of the unpresentable present, of the forbidden-unspoken and cutoff speech. The same experience of retreat: just as the Present escapes from the will to (re)presentation, so speech refuses the will to expression and signification. Or rather: speech does not speak, is not meaningful (*parlante*, speaking), except when left to itself, in its solitude, in a relinquishing that Heidegger calls the "resonance of silence." And similarly with the word *present*, which speaks of giving—being and time in giving—but a giving that can never present itself to itself, which declines only the other toward which it inclines, so that everything would follow that inclination and thus be open. Such strong language (*écarts de langage*) is led up to by the experience of language itself, as the dwelling of Being, that is, of the break (*écart*) which can never present itself except by default, in the impropriety of the names in which speech "delegates itself in foreignness" (Hölderlin), speech that is itself the ordeal or experience of the foreign, of the default of proper names.

It is necessary to repeat that this experience of the default of names, that is, of the property of language as a power that sends everything in the infinite inclination, has taken place, that it happened, and that we can even say precisely *when*, without its being a question of date, and that we can say *where*, without having to take out our surveyor's instruments. And yet, a paradox that slaps all postmodernity in the face: even though we come afterward, we still cannot say that it has happened to us.

Thus, although in this book the same words of the same poets, from that age of poets that has been quite correctly declared finished, continually return, this will appear to be nothing but the ratiocination of a halfwit, a halfwit incapable of escaping the horizon—already passed over, since finished—in which he has confined his cultural "references." To which it would be tempting to answer that there is no question of producing references, as if for previous services, and that the experience of these poets who were the first to endure the essential disorientation of our epoch cannot be produced as a reference, as something to hold on and refer to, and even less as a cultural reference. It is also tempting to reverse the objection or to subvert it by proclaiming long and loud that the experience in question really does call *the* reference into play, insofar as what is at stake is the rapport with Being, thus the possibility of having a rapport with anything whatsoever, and finally, even the possibility of carrying "oneself" (*"se" porter*), of having a carriage (*un port*) or a posture. Thus it is, thus and not otherwise, with those soils on which we support ourselves, as well as we can, more faltering than ever, searching for a port of call (*un port d'attache*), and yet always more detached, unanchored, and drifting from place to place: whether it be the city itself become un-quiet, ravaged, and decomposing as far as it covers all the soil with its diffuse network, or whether simply the landscape (*paysage*) somehow vanishing into a nature itself denatured or scaped (*dépaysée*), what is always at stake is what is closest, most "concrete," if we do not hesitate to use a word that generally serves marvelously as a guillotine for those heads "in the clouds," the philosophers, not to mention the poets, reputed to be unreadable, so that no one any longer feels any need to read them.

Yes, it is always tempting to respond with scorn to misunderstanding and ignorance, always strong in its rights, the rights of "common sense," which is nothing other than a single sense (or a "one-way"), in the comprehension that comprehends only itself and its "self-evidence." But this temptation must be resisted, especially in the desert in which each of us is, at present, "for want of everything" or for want of a true common sense, in which the Crowd declares itself to be—the whole of mankind. For want of a world and of that sharing-division that makes a world of a whole.

At present, before and above all, before the very existence of a whole common sense, the sense of a community is lacking or the least shared, even where there is a call to "solidarity" or consensus. It was no simple play on words that made Camus say, solidarity-solitary.[15] Whereas the masses (or mass) isolate(s), solitudes create solidarity, solidarity with the common-place, the commonplace of dislocation or delocation from the place as well as from being-in-common. To say that this being in common dislocates itself or that the *place* for a being in common deserts us is, by the same token, to say that a present does not exist. Which is also the same as saying nothing can be done anymore, or that the community—whether philosophical or poetic, let us say "literary"—can no longer put itself to work (or in works), like that stage, for example, on which Spirit appears to itself *as* the theater of operations. This, however, is not purely negative, even if, in the eyes of the perfection of being-in-work, the appearances are always "against us." The work is experienced as a refusal, unachievable, and this impossibility is equivalent, as Mallarmé so well expressed it, to a *suicide*: "suicide or abstention, doing nothing"—such is the only possibility left to us in a time when there is no Present. And yet, doing nothing is not nothing—not pure do-nothingness!—it is even already all, but different from totality or anything-at-all; it is a doing, but different from acting toward a goal and "effective" results; it is an operation, but in the sense of opening rather than producing. It is dwelling at the very heart of what is reserved, what delays; fundamentally, it is to begin to think, if all thought *begins* only in a suspense or suspension (of itself) and a being-close (to [or of] the thing itself, which slips away). Philosophy starts like this—when that to which it stays close slips away, thus the sense of the word *being*—in the suspens(ion) of astonishment, *touto to pathos*. And the abstention that Mallarmé speaks of is so far from being nothing that it allows him to risk the great Work: "What was it? That's hard to say: a book, quite simply, in many volumes, a book that really would be a book, architectural and premeditated, and not an anthology of random inspirations, however marvelous."[16]

Nevertheless, even Mallarmé became disenchanted, and like Proust or any of the other great Moderns, he could not finish his Book-Cathedral; he would have "to prepare his book with meticulous care, perpetually regrouping his forces like a general conducting an offensive, [and he would also have] to endure his book like a form of fatigue, to accept it like a discipline, build it up like a church, follow it like a medical regime, vanquish it like an obstacle, win it like a friendship, cosset it like a little child, create it like a new world":[17] a sublime dream, but already one from a different time, the time of the Cathedral builders and the community present to itself in and by the Work, just as the body and blood of Christ in communion are there through the bread and wine. That time still exercises its fascination even today. It feeds all the nostalgias, just as it makes the modern works in which such a dream is *incarnated* incapable of being anything but nostalgic, for, as the very title of Proust's *Recherche* indicates, that time is "lost,"[18] and just as we cannot show ourselves the equals of the ancient builders, just so we cannot have the ambition of "creating a world." It is not that we have become more modest—only beggars are modest, said Goethe, or was it Marx? and the time of beggars, like that of knights, is past—something is missing . . . but what? Could it simply be a world—a Present?

Nevertheless, it is inexact to speak of failure if we must qualify Mallarmé's enterprise. *A book that really would be a book*: hidden beneath this seemingly tautological formula lies a true challenge, an outrageous demand, analogous with the infinite work of weaving, a demand that is always taken up again, which Proust *took* right into his death bed. "A book that really would be a book," in one sense, is always impossible, for it would imply a "world that really would be a world," a present that really would be a present. The Book represents nothing other than that: "*it is*, the title of an interminable study and series of notes that I have here, under my hands, and which controls even the deepest part of my soul," as Mallarmé writes in a letter.[19] This study is revealed to be infinite because, in a manner that Maurice Blanchot has brought into relief quite well, the Book remains *to come* (*à venir*), and it can never stop at "some last point that consecrates it"—except to be declared closed and terminated in advance, that is, inexistent. It is vain to regret the absence of the Book (such as Mallarmé dreamed it, as they say, but that can never be anything but dreamed), for it is only thus, as the unpresentable and unaccomplishable, that the Book "is." In one sense, it can never come to light—appear to itself like that glorious Day of self-presence—and in another, it always remains pro-mised (placed before), but promised as self-reserving, forever deferring its coming, discernible only in the "blanks" that are no less sweet to compose than the tracing of words.

❁ ❁ ❁

For reasons that are clear and have nothing to do with false (or even real) modesty, I do not claim to have written "a book that really would be a book." In philosophy, the last attempt at a Book or Treatise was also a "failure," in its own way, and its nonaccomplishment is a deposition for an infrangible finitude, an impassable idleness: *Being and Time* was, one the side of works, the last attempt (and perhaps also the last temptation) of this century, nonetheless fertile in "works." Since then, although Heidegger did not write in accordance with random inspirations, he wrote only "collections." Collections that seek less to *totalize* works—though occasionally succumbing to that temptation—than to get under way: *Wege, nicht Werke*, "Ways, not works," Heidegger said of what is improperly called the "complete edition" (*Gesamtausgabe*), now in the process of being published; improper because they are not the complete works but rather a collection, in which, as in every collection, a selection was made. But, even more important than this incompleteness (which nonetheless makes one dizzy, to think of what a real complete edition would have been, considering the number of projected volumes) and independent of any "critical" question concerning the criteria of selection, what should be retained is the very idea of the impossibility of *works*, in the proper sense of the word: thus I cannot but share Lacoue-Labarthe's report when he writes that Heidegger's work "belongs almost entirely to the sphere of commentary, and by his own admission, he did not produce a 'work' in the sense in which tradition has understood the word" (*HAP*, p. 12; *FP*, p. 14).

In this sense, not only is this book not a work, but because it is almost exclusively a commentary on that "work" which is not a work, it is a commentary on commentaries, which seems to condemn it to the subordinate and, at present, much discredited rank of gloss. A gloss that cannot even claim to clarify a (barely) original text, no more than to acquire the honorable status of objective critique, since it deliberately rejects all the scientific criteria of clarifications and relates, for example, all paths—from Rimbaud—to a single one—to Heidegger—which, in addition, according to the "uncontested" popular opinion, is a "path leading nowhere." In fact, is this not an attempt to relate everything to Heidegger, under the guise of a modern "Poetics," and is this not pseudo-Poetics, which has even abandoned the name, merely a sneaky, roundabout fashion of imposing on the French philosophical scene the return of a philosopher believed to be forever banished (by the Nazi "affair"—I shall return to this)?

To which I could respond, once again quite easily, too easily, with scorn: what is this, really, that you keep repeating? What is this famous "French philosophical scene"? And in general, what is any philosophical scene? A theater made of representations. On this stage, ideas, theses, positions are exposed, even launched. The scene can be empty or loaded, the play brilliant or debilitating; one can improvise one's part or, on the contrary, enjoy one's seated position as spectator—even though "engaged"[20]—most often, whether the text is known or not, the scene is (de)termin(ed)/ated, and nothing can ever happen. The only thing that could really happen is to close up shop and the curtain. But it is to be feared that this will never happen, because it has already happened, and that is why one can replay at will, in whatever order or disorder one wishes, the winning combinations: yesterday Marx-Nietzsche-Freud, today Kant, who is making his return like an old diva who can never make up his mind to "bid the stage adieu" . . .

No, Heidegger cannot return to the scene, rest assured, the Great Lights of Reason, finally restored, will not be tarnished by the disquieting dissonances or shadows of the Old Man of the (Black) Mountain! For only someone who has played a role can return to it. But Heidegger, in some way, retired from the stage before truly making his entrance. Whether he retired after a false entrance or about a quid pro quo (concerning the nature of the theater of operations) can give ample material for reflection, for us who come *after*, and who no longer know precisely *where* we are, on which foot to dance, who have perhaps even forgotten our lines and are reduced to stammering and stammering again, *nur lallen und lallen*, as Celan would say.

To understand this "voluntary retreat," as Mallarmé wrote, as not being the result of ill (or well) placed pride, as coming from farther away, from the very place where *all* takes place and where all is lacking, that is what we are obliged to do, if we do not wish to be simply the survivors or players in a (hi)story that is *finished/finite*. In this (somber?) history, scorn is no longer fashionable—or, as Baudelaire already said: "to insult the Masses is to lower oneself"—and it would be time indeed to be turned over to the soil and its rugged solitudes: the scene is no longer the scene, so to speak, since the tragedy happened, but in such a way that it exploded the walls of the stage, exceeding itself as no longer in any way being re-presentable. It is the event "beyond-tragedy" of Auschwitz; it is the extension to the entire planet of the theater of philosophical operations, total mobilization in the name of the ideologies of Power; in the very name of Power alone, the only ideology that can take the blow (*coup*) (and the cost [*coût*]). It is also, and by the same token, the transformation of everything into simple-scene, the world into images and exorbitant orbits, the perpetual show of "worldviews," the transformation of faces into simple fashion statements. And many other things still, next to which the philosophical scene has become a simple country scene, amid the grotesque but touching appeal of outmoded dress, of tics and old-fashioned stuff, less lovable however than the "stupid paintings, door panels, stage sets, side-show canvases, shop signs, popular prints" of a poet (Rimbaud) who found the "celebrities of modern painting and poetry derisory" (it is true, at a time when the pomp of official art was dominant, now rehabilitated in the vast catchall of the postmodern museum). The scene no longer has a proper place: it is everywhere and nowhere. Above all, it is close, right here, here also "the gods are present," that is, the idols or simulacra, which, soon enough, will do without us, doing without philosophy as without poetry, because they will no longer need to be spoken or thought.

❁ ❁ ❁

I would like to have given a less decided turn to this fore-word, less to avoid frightening the reader by the abrupt and savage character of these *Solitudes* than to preserve his or her freedom, to impose nothing on him or her in advance that might, not alter, but perform his or her vision. At least to leave every freedom to see what was at stake here, and what does not expose itself but deposes every form of mastery (and information) in not letting itself speak, except at the limit: once again, the eminently uncomfortable position of a thought that risks extinguishing itself for lack of words before even having found them. Thus it is always at the point of dismissing itself, of giving "itself" its freedom, without, however, being able to accomplish this last gesture, for lack of a place to return or turn about, even if only provisionally, in the guise of a shelter. Nothing then remains but the erring, that is, the experience.

So where are we at? Do we know? And shall we ever know? Perhaps we may hazard the following: we dwell in parting, on that improbable line of division, almost entirely effaced, which might well resemble a twilight, either dawn or dusk, and which, nonetheless, resembles nothing, does not separate day from night or vice versa, but rather night from night, or day from day—the same from the same. Such is the place: the petrified threshold, as Trakl said. A threshold that no longer allows passage but retains, by solidifying itself on itself, a self that is nothing other than a break from itself or the "pain." A threshold that deposes every possibility, the threshold of the Impossible. ABGESCHIEDENHEIT: a secession, a scission that recollects itself in itself—in nothing, the coffer of nothing, or death as death.

Or the abyss that flashes through the dead time of the present deserted by its radiant past and a future that delays, remains indefinitely on the threshold of its own expectation. But the empty time is that of the "at present," of the desert installed in (the) place of the departing dwelling, the long time of profound boredom, which perhaps at its limit will return from its extreme annihilation? Nothing is less sure, however, and it is possible that Heidegger, here as elsewhere, gave in to the sirens of eschatology. It is true that the experience of the limit is that of place, of its tip and of its clearing. "The Evening changes sense and image," perhaps. But this change cannot be due to a celestial mechanism, a pure and simple reversal of sense (or direction), an irreversible and radical transmutation. The Evening does not automatically become a radiant Morning: and death is not converted into "Being" unless it is presupposed as negative. In that place where there is no longer any position, neither is there any *Umstellung*, any "trans-position." And if there is a conversion, it will be of everything, starting with the sense of evening—or of the sense of sense (of Being) as time. It is as evening, as the deposition of sense and image that it turns, and turns on itself, or better, "in" itself: in its "*Disparêtre*" (disappearing-being).

All of this continues to be obscure. Indeed. The obscuring of sense is also a destiny of the evening in which we find ourselves, of the epoch which, nonetheless, does not stop believing in the dawn of a glorious Day and proclaiming it with blinding evidence. Obscurantism is denounced with as much vigor as at the beginning of modern Times but with even less clairvoyance than that which caused Descartes to say that he could walk in the shadows only by feeling his way like a blindman. Two centuries ago, while all of Europe was governed by despots (even if they were "enlightened"), the great thinkers saw the light—Rousseau, Kant, to name only two who, for the first time, sketched the foundations of modern political thought concerning freedom. Today, when we nevertheless enjoy (at least formally) a democratic regime, all is lacking to us for a genuine *experience of freedom* (Jean-Luc Nancy) and not simply of freedoms (plural). That Heidegger rejected modern democracy should immediately make us think as much about the thinking of Being as about the aforementioned democracy. It remains for us to explain why and how our century, the most barbarous of modern Times, has been incapable of "producing" a more profound—and more abyssal—thought: this would at least risk throwing us into the "abyss" of perplexity as to the nature of our present. It is true that no thought is born "of" the century but always either against it or out of step with it, if only apparently. But this movement seems to have become accentuated during the course of History: where Descartes, despite everything, participated strongly in the "spirit" of his time, Hegel, Nietzsche, and finally Heidegger continually broke away from theirs.

I have said, at the end of this book, that it will not be possible to "turn the page" (close the wound of "Nazism") until we have been able to think Heidegger against himself. This is not a sophism or an evasion so as to save Heidegger, despite it all, from disaster (the more than political disaster, affecting everything "for want of everything") and thus to establish for ourselves a safe territory in which we can peacefully occupy ourselves with "pure" thought. On the contrary, one of thought's *vital* necessities is at stake: as long as we do not succeed in thinking *thus*, against (*contre*) Heidegger's thought but also in the same *region* (*contrée*), we shall not yet be thinking, in the sense of what *that* thought, and it alone, calls *thinking*. To think "against" does not mean to renounce. Besides, how can we rid ourselves of such a thought if we do not put another (essence of) thought to work? But, as I have repeated (though it cannot be demonstrated, nor does it need be), the possibilities of the philosophical scene have been exhausted, and in any case, with such ersatz, we cannot face what immediately exploded the framework of the scene and the mise en scène.

To think against means rather to approach, to get right up against—but still remaining on guard. Keeping watch. For the abyss is there, it is opening. And the harvest is not easy, precisely because it is so close.

> Not without wings may one
> Reach out for that which is nearest
> Directly
> And get to the other side.
> But here we wish to build.
>
> Hölderlin, "The Ister"

(trans. Douglas Brick)

Notes

1. And Rimbaud learned nearly every language, with a disquieting taste for the most exotic dialects, but only after abandoning his own, the *poetic* language he had forged for himself, not the French that "they" speak.

2. See Heidegger, *Poetry, Language, Thought*, p. 13; hereafter *PLT.*

3. Text translated in *Cahier de l'Herne "Heidegger"*, pp. 109–111; cf. *Aus der Erfahrung des Denkens, Gesamtausgabe* 13, pp. 225–227; hereafter GA 13, pp. 225–227.

4. Alain Badiou, *Manifeste pour la philosophie*, p. 54.

5. See Heidegger "The Thinker as Poet," *PLT*, p. 8: "Three dangers threaten thinking. The good and thus wholesome danger is the nighness of the singing poet. The evil and thus keenest danger is thinking itself. It must think against itself, which it can only seldom do. The bad and thus muddled danger is philosophizing."

6. *Existence and Being* (p. 234).

7. *Epreuve de l'étranger:* the title of a book by Antoine Berman, borrowed from Heidegger's commentary on Hölderlin.

8. See the letter of 3 November 1883 to Charles Morice: "We have been so retarded in our thought that I have spent no less than ten years edifying mine." Mallarmé the thinker is no less a poet than Mallarmé the poet is a thinker. Everything lies in the relation to language.

9. As René Char writes in his presentation of Rimbaud (*Oeuvres complètes* [Paris: Gallimard, 1983], p. 729).

10. Descartes' *Oeuvres et lettres*, ed. André Bridoux [Paris: Gallimard, 1953], p. 125.

11. Nietzsche, *Human, All Too Human*, vol. 1, p. 262.

12. Philippe Lacoue-Labarthe, *La Fiction du politique* [Paris: Christian Bourgois, 1988] (hereafter *FP*), p. 19–20; *Heidegger: Art and Politics*, trans. Chris Turner [Oxford: Basic Blackwell, 1990], hereafter *HAP*, p. 6.

13. Nietzsche *Twilight of the Idols*; cited by Heidegger in *An Introduction to Metaphysics*, pp. 12–13.

14. René Char, "J'habite une douleur," in *Oeuvres complètes*, p. 254: "Songe à la maison parfaite que tu ne verras jamais monter. A quand la récolte de l'abîme?" These two sentences were quoted as epigraph to the French edition of *Solitudes*.—Trans.

15. Albert Camus, "Jonas" in *L'Exil et le Royaume*, in *Théâtre, Récits, Nouvelles*, ed. Jean Grenier (Paris: Gallimard, 1962), p. 1654.

16. Mallarmé, letter to Paul Verlaine, 16 November 1885, in *Selected Letters of Stéphane Mallarmé*, p. 143.

17. Marcel Proust, *A la recherche du temps perdu*, vol. 3, p. 1032.

18. The title of Proust's *A la recherche du temps perdu* (usually translated as *Remembrance of Things Past*) means, literally, "in search of the lost time"—Trans.

19. Mallarmé, letter to Vielé-Griffin, 8 August 1891.

20. Raymond Aron, *Le spectateur engagé*, English trans. as *The Committed Observer*, trans. James McIntosh and Marie McIntosh (Chicago: Regnery-Gateway Books, 1983).—Trans.

1

There Is No Present

Suicide or abstention, to do nothing, why?—Time, unique, in the world, since, because of an event I will have to explain again and again, there is no Present—no, a present does not exist.[1]

"There is no Present": an assertion that never fails to inspire surprise. It violates every good sense that seems to know about the present—that it exists—and that it is the only thing of which we may be certain: inasmuch as we ourselves exist. Each of us, whether in the confines of some dreary dungeon or in the open air, is in the presence of that which is: concrete walls or the battle blue sky. The human being, withdrawn into the uppermost solitudes, remains within the presence of a present—even if it be that of an absence. Moreover, it would suffice to simply turn on the television to see, with one's own eyes, the infinite wealth and richness of the present: for it is spread out throughout the entire world and is there at every level of life, from the microscopic amoeba to the nuclear warhead. Though it is unclear whether there will be a present the day the world explodes.

In addition, this good sense would add that the present is that and only that which is or exists—if only because the past no longer is and the future is not yet . . . present. And here, once and for all, the philosophical tradition would fortify this good sense, even though it itself remains the arch enemy of common sense. For philosophy has, from its very conception, conceived the present (the "now"), as the normative measure of the existence of time. Only that which now is—that is, is present—is. To be sure, the definition itself would call attention to the tautology involved here. But good sense as such, rarely requires us to take a closer look.

Now the poet, like the simple quidam (which the poet is at bottom), would never ask himself what either time or the present are. He never asks the philosophical question, par excellence, of essence. Rather, he would merely ascertain the nonexistence of some thing, commonly called the *present*. But is this truly an ascertainment—an established fact? Certainly we could have an affadavit drawn up by some official notary who would note, with his own eyes, that a chair is missing from the table. But—and here we must emphasize the *but*—the present is never simply a piece of furniture. It can never simply be absent such as the absence of a spoon from a place setting. Indeed, no one has stolen it; and, if it has dissappeared, it has not gone elsewhere—to some other place—setting. And then, can we even speak of it as being lost in the same way as Proust speaks of the "Searching for Time Lost" or *Remembrance of Things Past*. This, of course, would signify that once upon a time, in a place far far away, there was a present (time); but which, at present, no longer exists. The very formulation of this loss is already aberrant insofar as it must call upon the present to explain its nonpresence.

"There is no Present;" the very sentence seems suicidal. Simply because the present, by definition, names everything that is. A thing is able to not be present, and, at the same time, not be nothing: thus it becomes a memory, myth or image. But the present, if it itself is not (present), swallows everything whole with non-being. Could it be then, that this declaration by Mallarmé represents nothing more than the very culmination of nihilism?

On the whole, such a thought would correspond with our image of the poet madly in love with nothingness, with some small suppressed thing of naught, with the resonance of empty space and every other absence.[2] This, of course, on condition that we know of what this "nothingness" speaks. Nothingness, after all, signifies that which is not. However, we must ask from whence comes such negation? Is it anterior or posterior to nothingness? And who is able to validate its validity or force—perhaps even its "Being?" Who, in such a sentence, could speak here and assert, "There is no Present"? The poet? Indeed, but in asserting such nonpresence, must not he himself be present? Perhaps—perhaps—he also signs his nonpresence and thus the very sign of suicide?

As we have already remarked, the present is not a thing. We can neither place it before us for our admiration nor remove it if it happens to be loathesome to us. Is it then, nothingness—like the thing of naught or like the abscenity of every fork or chair?

As soon as we think to seize this strange "thing" that is the Present, we fall deep into a hole. For these words that compose "There is no Present" are themselves present—at least insofar as we may read them. But the word that would assert the opposite is unable to render present that which it articulates. Such difficulties have always been present in philosophical thought: for, if the present names that which is, then it itself is (in a certain sense) "nothing." It is nothing with respect to something present. And if the present names that which only "is" in time, then time itself is determined, at the very beginning, as a notion of temporality; that is, Being as presence. This inextricable cirularity gave birth to *Being and Time*.

Certainly, Mallarmé was not a philosopher. Therefore, we must renounce, once and for all, the application of our "philosophical" scapel. For the appellation of any so-called nihilism may very well turn against the one who articulates it. We must be satisfied with a reading without prejudice: we must remain naive. And rightly so. For Mallarmé, to explain (in spite of everything) this "event" that constitutes the want of any present, spoke of a naive traveler who imagined himself deep within a tunnel. "From without, like the cry of space, the traveler hears the distress of the whistle. 'Probably,' or so he would convince himself, 'we are traveling through a tunnel—the *epoch*—at long the last one, stealing under the city before the all-powerful station of the virginal central palace, which wreathes.' The underground will endure, O impatient one, your train of thought to prepare an edifice of high glass, swept with the wing of Justice."[3] The image of the tunnel was not entirely rejected by Mallarmé. Rather, he simply wished to warn the impatient traveler (i.e., the modern human being, who is always in a hurry and forever hateful of wasting time), that the "underground will endure." In every case, it is a question of time. Perhaps there will be an end to the tunnel, or a way out. (Here we think of the cave in Plato's *Republic* and the manner in which presence is perceived: the escape from darkness and the emergence into the illumination of day.) Yet, and this is the essential point, at present, "there is no Present." *At present* means at this time or the epoch in which "we" are. Thus, with this notion of epoch, we would glimpse that sense which must be given to the want of any present. It is possible that Mallarmé had in mind the original meaning of the Greek word *epochè*, which signifies a pause or suspension. And yet, he never really needed to have recourse to this etymological root. The epoch refers to a time that endures longer than a single moment—longer because it is more *stable*. The epoch remains more stable even when the times themselves are unstable and revolutionary. This is so because a higher identity rules over the epoch. It is a law or destiny that gives to every event, as to the whole of humanity, its character, its special stamp and mark.

The epoch is still ours. And here, let us underline that which is peculiar in the tale told by the traveler. It is precisely the use of the definite article with the word *epoch* that strikes us as strange. Clearly, this is not an anatomized discourse on history, laid out, etherized, upon the table. It is not a course on pathology whereby a postmortem is performed and every epoch is tagged accordingly: Antiquity, Middle Ages, Modernity, and so on. Nevertheless, a certain view of History is implicated—but not as an object. On the contrary, History itself is the "subject" of the experience and this directly implicates the subjectivity of the traveler. Let us note, precisely, the preeminintely historical terms in which the traveler speaks. He travels through the epoch "as" he might travel through a tunnel. In other words, he takes the train and hopes to arrive (perhaps on time?) at the end, which, naturally enough is called the *omnipotent palace*. At the time (during the latter half of the nineteenth century), train stations resembled royal palaces, and hence the name *central palace*. Moreover, train stations were the heart and lungs of the city. And such tunnels were contemporary with the railroad. In a conference given at Oxford, Mallarmé wrote: "Nature takes place and to it we shall not add: save for some cities, railroads and a few other inventions that form our means and production."[4] The particular epoch is definitively one of means and production—and from it we would coin the term *materialism*. Yet this materialism is no longer that one by which we are daily beaten over the head, neither with an ideological club nor any other instrument of punishment. We cannot simply say that everything is material. Rather, we must see that everything we would add to "Nature" and that everything one might realize—including oneself as laborer or personnel or the human resource—is constituted as means—as *technè*.

Is there nothing more than this then? . . . But it is precisely here that the poet would rise up and rebel. It is precisely here that there is . . . nothing: "We know, confined in an absolute formula, that there is only what there is. However unrestrained to spread, under pretext, the decoy, would accuse our inconsequence, refusing the pleasure we want to take: for this *beyond* is the agent of it and the motor I would say if only I wasn't loathe to effect, in public, the impious disassembling of fiction and consequently of the literary mechanism, in order to display the principal piece or nothing."[5] There is only what there is: a rather ex-acting tautology in which we see the mark of Western nihilism or what Heidegger called the *oblivion of Being*. For if such is the case—and it could be otherwise only with great difficulty—then there is nothing left of Being. In other words, there is no Present. There is only what there is—whether such being is natural or manufactured (*techne*). The rest (that is, the "other thing," the "beyond")—is nothing.

It is not certain that Mallarmé has rescued this "nothing" by simply giving it the role of "principal piece" in the literary mechanism. Yet the mere fact of speaking about such a mechanism or about any machine (one totally dissassembled to display its "motor"), exudes a subtle influence over such a materialistic epoch. And we might ask whether pleasure itself (already similar to the "pleasure of the text" that is so dear to the modern critic), is sufficient to bring into being that which is not? More specifically, by putting into production the "poietic" process as defined by Plato? Furthermore, we wonder if this process is able to be determined as fiction?

But this question would carry us far away from where we should remain at present: "There is no Present." Nevertheless, by referring to the epoch and the return to the literary process, we understand that much better the need to differentiate between the present-as-now and the present of presence. That is, when Mallarmé speaks of there being no present, he does not mean that there is nothing or that at present, nothing is. But rather, that this "now" is a false present or a present without presence. Plato said as much when he referred to the visible world or world of appearances as a phantasmagorical nothingness—as a world of "idols." Presence wants a present in such a way that it is not one: it is a "nonbeing" or *mè on*. At bottom, Mallarmé's formulation is quite similar to the one formulated by Rimbaud. "The true life is absent." Here it is sufficient to substitute the word *present* for *true life*.

At the same time, this want constitutes the only possible present offered to the human being: *the epoch*. The epoch is one of "distress;" it is the midnight of the world—and the disapp-errance of the present: it is the epoch of the oblivion of Being. Certainly, other images may also come to mind. Yet it suffices us to cite that page of Heidegger where he comments on the following line by Hölderlin: "Long is / The time, but the True comes into / Its own."

> Long is the destitute time of the world's night. To begin with, this requires a long time to reach to its middle. At this night's midnight, the destitution of the time is greatest.

> Then the destitute time is no longer able even to experience its own destitution. That inability, by which even the destitution of the destitute state is obscured, is the time's absolutely destitute character. The destitution is wholly obscured, in that it now appears as nothing more than the need that wants to be met. Yet we must think of the world's night as a destiny that takes place this side of pessimism and optimism. Perhaps the world's night is now approaching its midnight. Perhaps the world's time is now becoming the completely destitute time. But also perhaps not, not yet, not even yet, despite the immeasurable need, despite all suffering, despite nameless sorrow, despite the growing and spreading peacelessness, despite the mounting confusion. Long is the time because even terror, taken by itself as a ground for turning, is powerless as long as there is no turn with mortal men. But there is a turn with mortals when these find the way to their own nature. That nature lies in this, that mortals reach into the abyss sooner than the heavenly powers. Mortals, when we think of their nature, remain closer to that absence because they are touched by presence, the ancient name of Being. But because presence conceals itself at the same time, it is itself already absence. Thus the abyss holds and remarks everything.[6]

It was necessary to include this rather long passage from "What Are Poets For?" simply because it makes clear (though perhaps not within the visible spectrum of light) the want of any present already perceived by Mallarmé. Heidegger—indeed in deference to Hölderlin, but also striking out on his own—relates the want of any present to the want of any god. Something Mallarmé never did. Yet both are very similar in their perception of the epoch. Like Mallarmé, Heidegger preached patience: we must not yield too quickly to the illusion that we see the end of the tunnel. The underground shall endure, o impatient one—and shall endure that much longer simply because we believe we have finished with it and its "distress." This is no accident—such as a sudden eclipse of sense—but a destiny that will endure: long is the time as is the tunnel. And we, perhaps, have only come halfway.

Heidegger spoke of a possible turning. But this can occur only if the "mortal" takes his place in "his proper being." The epoch is only able to turn if we ourselves engage in the turning. Yet this turning does not lead to a place of rest. Rather, it leads directly to the Abyss, or at least within its proximity. This is possible because the human being (contrary to the God) is closer to the want or absence; because we are concerned with and care for presence. Perhaps this strange way of reasoning would appear to be a dialectical detour. But, in fact, it is nothing of the sort: to be concerned with and to care for presence does not mean that we ourselves are present. On the contrary. If the question of presence concerns only mankind—and it does, for we have very few texts written by the hand of God or scratched in the dirt by some hoove or paw—it is because mankind in a sense, is deprived of presence. We are in "need" of it; but this is not some simple need that might be satisfied by going to market. No, it is a need that Heidegger thought in terms of a double-appropriation. For this reason, he would call man—*Dasein*: the man of Being inasmuch as the Being of man. Being itself (presence) is in need of Being-there that it may appear as such. Consequently, when this "need" is experienced as a simple necessity (that is, one among others: shelter, food, clothing, culture, and coffee), then, we might say, obscurity has reached the stratosphere. In the same spirit, Heidegger "defined" *Dasein* by a radical negativity and finitude before having replaced this term with the even more neutral word *mortal*. The human being, closer to nothing in his or her "identity," desires presence that much more and thus is that much more concerned with it. But because this presence is suspended—which is the very definition of the epoch—it is itself already an absence. Hence, this "There is no Present" constitutes the only possible presence. It is from this possibility—and only from this possibility—that one is able to find a pathway to one's proper place.

Quite honestly, I have developed this line of thought without having entirely subscribed to it. Without having bought into it. Indeed, I would like to know what provoked it and made it necessary. And what could possibly justify it "at present." And what could unsettle it—because it must be unsettled. Yes, it is necessary if only because we hardly wish to be swallowed by an abyss . . . more mysterious and, above all, more insensible than our present pain. Today we are no longer able to *believe* that a long wait shall be sufficient. Nor do we believe that the "long time" will be able to turn about once it has reached its halfway point. Nothing authorizes this logic of extremes—save the eschato-logical.

The eschatological is the logic of the worst: of the apocalypse, which literally means the un-covering. Yet at the same time, nothing is able to unsettle such a logic because it rests upon a belief. There is a religion of thought, or at least of Heidegger's. Whatever he may have said concerning the onto-theological structure of Western philosophy—from Plato to Nietzsche—he still slid into the same old rut as Plato. For Heidegger, the "present" world of modern technology constitutes the utmost oblivion of Being—of presence. The "true life" or rather, true presence has withdrawn itself; but where or when—we do not know. Was it from the time of the Greeks? Or perhaps the future? Or both? Still, such representation would still be possible (though nontheologically) if Heidegger had not identified "true" presence with the presence of God and, by way of consequence, the want of any present with that of any god. That this god no longer has anything to do with the god of metaphysics—with the demiurge of Plato or the Absolute Spirit of Hegel—does not prevent it from being modeled on the same model. That of the whole and full presence of a thing to itself. And this want, regardless of what Heidegger may have written with respect to the abyss (*Abgrund*) of Being, remains just that: a want. Of course, it is one that may—and even ought in a certain respect—turn wholely and fully around.

Nevertheless, the want of any present cannot be fully explained by the want of any god. Even in the spirit of Hölderlin, it is not sufficient to simply rue the "evanescent" gods, who, "at that time / [were] truer." The gods had "their" time and now their time is come: we must not wait for some new generation of deities. Neither nostalgia nor constant expectation are able to endure the intensity of the present age; neither can endure this time of want—this solemn and *sacred* night. But what exactly is it that is missing that makes our time one consumed with the Present? In the sixth stanza of the poem entitled, "Bread and Wine"—and thus before the seventh that says, "We've come too late," and asks, "What are poets for in a time of distress?"—the poet speaks of a want, but not the want of God:

> Where are they? Where do flower the Glorious, the
>   Feat's Crowns?
> Thebes has long since faded and Athens too.
> The illustrious arms no longer clank in Old Olympia.
> Nor roll the chariots in their aggressive game. . . .
> Why the silence of these old and sacred theatres?

"Where are they?"—Here Hölderlin does not call solely to the evanescent gods; rather, he would first address himself to the people: those who, to receive the Immortals, to be worthy of them, would lean upon one another in "powerful order." And thus uplifted, they would erect their sound cities and noble temples. These peoples (the plural was mandatory for Hölderlin), are the Greeks; these ancient craftsmen who lived upon a land that was itself "contructed" (fourth stanza). Thebes, Athens and Corinth are not mere names that represent a local and picturesque color or even a simple recollection of "antiquity." The Greeks really were the ornamental crown of the great and ancient Feat: they crowned the Feat, that is, the ceremonial visitation of the gods, precisely by celebrating their role as divine host. In Ancient Greek, crown or *stephanos* signifies that which wreathes and thus gives contour and countenance and even configuration. The walls of the city or Acropolis are never those of a prison. They are a limit (*peras*) that gives place to and opens up. Such was how the Greeks experienced presence in its essential finitude. Likewise, "the aggressive game" (*Kampfspiel*) has little to do with what we call *war*—which, as it were, is nothing more than an anonymous slaughter whereby the battle is fought with human means and human material. Heraclitus called *polemos* the "father of all"—the very one by which and with which each man was measured. Here each man would discover his limit and thus his proper place. The *polemos* revealed who was mortal and who immortal; who was a master and who a slave. Meeting face to face, the Greek athletes were no longer concerned with the sport of it all: in fact, they never entered into competition as such simply because the best (*aristos*) would always win. They stood face to face to find their identity. Each sought, by a combination of audacity and limiticity, not only to save face—but to find it. It was in this way that the Greeks entered into the presence of presence.

Entire peoples confronted one another in the same way. Oftentimes we stand with remorse and look back upon the Greek city-states that exhausted themselves with their futile feuds. We lament that they never knew how to handle and dominate the heedless and rebellious ones! That they were never able to unite and thus impose a universal empire such as the Romans were to later establish with their *pax romana*. And yet, the universality of Roman "civilization" already carried with it the poison of imperialism—a poison that had infiltrated even the splendrous democracy of Athens. For here we must not forget that Athens imposed its "democratic" empire with terror, deportation, and the random massacre of its indigent population. To be sure, the *polemos* soon lost its spirit (we wonder if it ever had it) and thus its great feat.

And what was this great feat? That men should meet the gods and with them stand shoulder to shoulder and face to face—just as did the many peoples to build their cities. Still, what do we really know about this great feat; this bold factum? Do we see the silence through the clamor of celebrations and through the uproar of the persevering festival? Is it possible to arrive at such a feat without the peoples? And are there still such peoples? Is there even a many-headed multitude?

Can we speak of the whole of humankind as such? A certain Stephanos Mallarmé would tell us the following: "There is no Present, no—a present does not exist . . . the Whole of mankind wants to disclose itself, for want—of everything." That there is no Present because "the Whole of mankind wants to disclose itself" seems to be a gratuitous assertion. Yet it is one that corresponds rather well with the contempt and arrogant attitude—the supremacy—that the poet was supposed to have felt for the ignobile vulgus. Indeed, this particular image of the poet seems to be supported by "public" opinion—including criticism. To illustrate the aristocratic attitude of this "prince of poets," one often cites the text that bears the title, "Artistic Heresies: Art for Everyone." We must remember though that it was the time of Marx and social upheavel caused by modern industrialism. Nevertheless, Mallarmé seems to have snugly wrapped himself up in that Parnassian doctrine of "art for art's sake." Even the conclusion he comes to at the end of his text is convincing: "The hour that now sounds is serious: culture is carried out by the people and great doctrines shall go out about the world. If there be any vulgarization, may it be that of the good and not of art. And may your efforts never lead to such a deformed thing—to the *poet worker*—so sad it is for the artist of the race."[7] Despite this awful word *race*, Mallarmé does not show himself to be against the common people. In fact, he even quotes, quite notably, the words of Baudelaire: "To abuse the multitude is to humiliate oneself." Mallarmé protests, principally, against the outrageous and nonsensical idea that began to grow in the minds of his contemporaries: "to think it indispensable to teach poetry in the schools." For, he believed, such teaching would irresistably lower "poetry to the rank of a science."

Hölderlin, on the contrary, believed it was necessary to teach poetry. At the beginning of his *Remarks Concerning Oedipus*, he wrote the following: "The lack of any modern poetry is most certainly the fault of the school and of the trade. Unfortunately, the way that he [the poet] must walk cannot be calculated or even taught; and then, once it has been learned, it is not always able to be repeated—safely and practically—again and again." Yet between the time of Hölderlin and that of Mallarmé, the concept of science had collapsed. Even if Mallarmé still had in mind the idea of science as Absolute Knowledge—a Hegelian idea that very few poets had at the time—his contemporaries referred to something entirely different: the ideology of a progress that levels everything not positive—everything that is unproductive such as art. For example, poetry being valuable only as a technique for the production of "beautiful" language. Between this "technique" and the *technè* or *mechanè*—the height to which Hölderlin wished to elevate poetry—there is a gulf. When he spoke of the "regulated rules" of the Sophoclean tragedies, by this he did not understand a totality—rigorously codified or not—of literary recipes and mechanisms. Moreover, the regulated rule necessarily needed to be allied with "the living sense—which can never be calculated"—and which no technique could accomplish. It is for this reason, considering the current state of affairs in both our schools and our own culture, that we would do well to follow Mallarmé's advice. We might consider teaching the art of reading and writing before attempting an "analysis" of literary works: because for the ordinary illiterate, such works shall remain but dead and decayed letters strewn across the page; they shall remain an object of disgust.

We can continue our critique of "vulgarization"—even though the latter consists less in casting pearls before swine than in transforming the pearls into something swiney. Metaphor we extend to the entire domain of art: for has not the institution of the museum had, for an immediate consequence, the transformation of living works into objects secluded from sense, that is, from their "presence"?

But this is not our sea of troubles. Though if it were—we would need to interrogate the status of the work of art at a time when presence expresses itself in a way other than as a work or even as a thing. In all actuality, Mallarmé abandoned at a very early age his "aristocratic" notions. So much so that he did not deem "Art for Everyone" dignified enough to include in his collection of prose, as has mentioned Henri Mondor. Yet is it only because he blamed it for "the somewhat invective tone which he was careful not to use from the moment he was master of his style?" Is it simply a question of style? Does "Art for Everyone" constitute an "important, if not surprising, testimony to his precocious artistic convictions and to the firmness with which he was to conform to them?" Or does this judgment itself—this question—simply testify to the blindness of criticism? A criticism that refuses to see that Mallarmé overturned all his "artistic convictions"?

Fortunately, Mallarmé did not merely write minor texts that he threw, as it were, into an oubliette and that were only later exhumed by his pious disciples. Quite notably, he wrote "The Restricted Action" in which he disclosed, for lack of a better word, his *political* position. The following would be the best way not to read this text: as a justification written, a posteriori, by the poet in his inner sanctum—by a poet whose mind had already assimilated the aristocratic contempt for everything that emerged from the multitude. It is true that Mallarmé laid claim to the term *aristocracy*—but on what terms? Let us read the following quote taken from "*La Cour*" (The Court): "Aristocracy, why not articulate this term in the presence of the maddening cries of democracy: reciprocity of those states indispensable to the national conflict and by which something stands upright; they clash and interpenetrate, and are without virtue if either one is missing."[8]

There is no aristocracy without democracy; no democracy without aristocracy. "The coin, unearthed from the ring, presents both heads and tails: the former, a serene figure; while the latter, a universal and brutal figure." Such is the *double state* of politics, which may very well be analogous to the "double state of every word." Perhaps here we hear the faint echo of Heraclitus's *polemos*? To speak of aristocracy without uttering democracy "consists in speaking ill of the City." And so the reciprocal relationship is true—yet this we refuse to see. How strange indeed our sightlessness that makes a mire out of our "democracies"—how "foul!" (to use the expression used by Rimbaud in his poem "Democracy").

Let us repeat, but this time in French, what Mallarmé wrote: "Il n'est pas de Présent, non—un présent n'existe pas. Faute que se déclare la Foule, faute—de tout." If there is no Present, it is not the Crowd's fault; it is for want *of (de)* a Crowd. In French, the word *faute* has a totally different meaning when followed by the preposition *à* or *de*. In the first case, the Crowd or, as here translated, that is, interpreted, the "whole of mankind" is guilty. In the second case, which here, following the French syntax, is the correct, the want of present is not due to the Crowd; on the contrary, there is no Present *because* the Crowd is wanting or, at least, cannot disclose itself.

This minimal difference changes everything, and we wonder if criticism has not been a bit too hasty: instead of attributing to the poet a fictive contempt for the Crowd, the critics should first be less contemptuous for the syntax. Mallarmé, who described himself as a "syntaxist" (*syntaxier*), wished to be understood even by children, provided that these knew French syntax. As for the accusation of being "obscure," the same accusation that would be later leveled against Heidegger, Mallarmé once responded: "In effect, the danger is equally great, whether such obscurity comes from the poet or the reader."[9] Before going directly to the meaning, we—readers—have still to learn the basics in every language: I mean, syntax, the systematic order that gathers each single element of a particular language to constitute an organic "whole" and not a random collection of letters and "significations." These never are the primordial elements and can emerge only as the results of the *binding* act of syntax.

Thus, not only is the "Whole of mankind" not nothing, it is "everything." And it is precisely because this everything is wanting—let us call it the great de-feat—that there is no present. But why does the Whole not disclose itself? Because—and here we enter into a certain circularity—it is the want of any present that prevents the Whole from disclosing itself.

If the whole of mankind does not disclose itself, it is because the Whole is wanting. It is the Whole that wants to speak properly (properly speaking) and wants to properly disclose itself. (The capitalization of *Whole* like, in French, *la Foule*, indicates that it is an entity of which we speak and not a haphazard and heterogenous gathering of individuals). Yet how could it disclose itself and with what word? The Crowd has seemingly spoken up and simply taken the word—as it once took the Bastille—though, in all actuality, that which it has taken, it does not have. And thus the silence of the sacred theaters of old is perpetuated unto the present—even if this silence sinks away into the noisy noise of the media. Defeat, but no victory. The want of any word is also the want of any present (and of any presence). Only the poet dare say what the Crowd would disclose:

> This haggard crowd! claims: We are
> The sad opacity of our future ghosts.[10]

At present, we are the absence of any present: "our Future ghosts," specters that will come—back (*des revenants à l'avenir*). Contemporaries, we shall never be—not even of ourselves: "Naive is he who would himself proclaim his own contemporary; deserting, usurping with equal impudence, when the past ceased and the future would delay or when both would intermingle with perplexity; always with an eye on covering up the a-part."[11] Disrupture—what I call the a-part—is another way of specifying the present when it is wanting; when it is trapped between a past that is "fled" and a future that would delay.

However, we must take care. The poet is not fundamentally different from the crowd. Perhaps he is its condensation and incarnation; its deification and "coronation"—that is, if we remember the "ornamental crowns of the ancient feat" that were the Greek peoples. "Crowns," but only insofar as they were wreathed with a holy Word. For this reason, when the Crowd does not disclose itself, the Crown, that is, the poet grieves. He dwells in mourning; abstention ("to do nothing") is equal to suicide; withdrawal from the multitude is not proper to the poet as it is to an umbrageous and prideful personality who refuses to intermingle. The poet does not withdraw from the time in which he lives, rather time itself withdraws as does the Whole of mankind. This time that draws away—the epoch—remains our own. It was Nietzsche's too and to it he referred as "the desert [that] spreads." Time of the desert—of the present—which, from itself, deserts; disrupted, beseiged by a lifeless past (of old values, idols, and cadavers of capital) and a future that would delay—desperately. Nothing—nobody—can be his or her own contemporary, even if we still believe to be from "our" time. Even if we read, daily, the daily newspaper—newspapers that each day carry some new news of failing banks, of revolution, dissolution—war!—always in flux; always carried by the current—affair. Here *current* does not carry the sense of "contemporary." Perhaps we are left with only a "sad opacity"; for even the most lucid journalist cannot be but haggard and perplexed before the question of presence however little one may examine the mode of "presence" and so-called current affairs.

And yet, to withdraw oneself from such a day (from the daily world of the newspaper that Mallarmé never stopped interrogating) would be for the poet, "the equivalent of not being." "For me," he once confided to a journalist, "the poet who resides in a society that doesn't allow him to live, is similar to the man who isolates himself in order to en-grave his own tombstone."[12] In recognition of his own solitude, he once claimed: "I believe that poetry is made for the ostentatious display and supreme pleasure of society; one so constituted that glory too has its place—though the people no longer seem to have any notion of it." The religion of art shall be the religion of the future. But only for that society which knows how to deify itself and yet, which, because the Self equals "the principal piece or nothing," deifies nothing. This explains why, for Mallarmé (just as for Nietzsche and Heidegger), the political and social question is one founded in *fiction.* This in no way devaluates the question, because fiction itself is founded in "literature." *Society* may very well be an empty term—"the heritage of philosophers"—and "nothing in fact may exist," which corresponds to "the injunction awakened by its august concept." "To discourse on it is equal to not treating any subject or to silence oneself by distraction": "Nothingness or the irruption into emptiness."[13]

At an interval of fifteen years, the "Restricted Action" responded not to the prose of a young and "aristocratic" Mallarmé who also refused to embrace the inept idea of an "art for everyone," but to Rimbaud's injunction: "Poetry shall no longer submit action to its own rhythm: it [poetry] will be *in advance.*" For Mallarmé as well, "action is not life, but only a way to squander some force—a sort of exasperation." And to this word (by Rimbaud) Mallarmé would add, rather ironically, the following: "But this generation does not seem very concerned—even beyond its lack of interest in politics—with the desire for physical exertion. Except," he would go on, "with the monotony of winding along the pavement between one's shin bones, according to the machine presently in favor, the fiction of continuous dazzling speedway." (We know that the poet preferred sailing to every other sport; however, he was enchanted not so much by bicycles as by their female riders—especially when the wind raised their skirts.) Leaving this sort of primitive action aside, we may ask what does it mean to act, if it does not begin with the simple act of smoking? Let us be serious or philosophers and respond with Mallarmé: "To act, without this and for whoever does not begin with the simple act of smoking, signified, visitor, I understand you, philosophically, to produce over much a movement which, in return, gives you the sensation that you were the principle of it; therefore exist, you: of which, beforehand, no one believes himself certain. This practice encompasses two ways; or, by a will, unknowingly, which withstands a life, until the manifold eruption—to think, that; otherwise, the outlets within reach now within a forethought, newspapers and their whirlwind, determining therein a force in a sense, whatever diverse contradiction, with the immunity of the null outcome."[14] After having played naive, that is, the ape, Mallarmé aped the philosopher—and found along the way, the common-place: the modern world of Cartesian coordinates. To act: to believe one is the cause of an effect which, in return, gives rise to the feeling of having been—the cause. And thus to exist in and of oneself. This is the vicious circle that defines the philosophical and vulgar scene—of "good sense."

However, Mallarmé did not stop here. He discerned an alternative that corresponded to the "double state of every word": "essential"—it was thought as act (to be sure an anticipation of Heidegger!)— "unrefined and immediate." Thus it is only in the press and journalism that we are able to say everything; if only because there are no consequences. It is the medium where everything amounts to the same thing: where the nothingness of the result is obtained already in advance.

What remains to be contemplated: the "action" in question is very soon *restricted* . . . to paper. ("Because contemplation, without any traces, becomes evanescent.") In some cases it is restricted to the Book; in the best of cases, to the poetic "coronation." But the Book needs no one, no subject, no *agent*: "Inasmuch as the author is separated from the impersonalized volume, so too is the approach of any reader. Know then, that between the human accessories, the Book takes place all alone: done, being."[15] This happens in such a way that the "suicide or abstention"—the *to do nothing*—is at the very root of every *essential* action. Here we say, "to do nothing" precisely because there is nothing to do; because it is already *done, being*. In a sense, to stand aside and to be published are the same thing. Moreover, we must remember that Mallarmé was always published in newspapers: he who supposedly scorned such "sewers."

To understand Mallarmé, we would do well to grasp that which Marx called "the positive sense of negation brought back to itself." Although Mallarmé's thought is not dialectical, it is, perhaps, more profoundly engaged in negativity than any metaphysics. Furthermore, in this respect, there is good reason to reconsider the end of the "Restricted Action." Such that it becomes a question of a "triumphant overturning" at the very heart of the "principal piece"—that is, *nothing*. In this way, it would reveal itself under the auspice of an *apparent* alternative—and only apparent. "Restrain yourself," the poet would say, "abstain yourself, withdraw into your Dwelling place, into your own existence and ask yourself" whether "it is not better—only to risk over a total state the least incomplete surrounding, certain conclusions, extreme, about art which might irrupt, like a diamond, in this time forever, in the integrity of the Book—to play them, though and with a triumphal overturning, with the silent injunction that nothing, shuddering in the unscious side of the hour, with the pages shown, clear, obvious, finds it ready; even though this might be another that must illuminate."[16] What is the difference between "risking" extreme conclusions concerning art and putting them into play? None, except that between-times, a triumphant overturning has taken place: one that would "shudder in the unscious hour." This hour that speaks under the auspice of an or: *now or never*. Now never excludes never, rather, it includes it: whereas the "time for ever"—when such conclusions were risked—such a now was excluded. The now that holds, like the hand that handles, is the time of the essential act, when nothing finds the hour ready, when the hour is deferred; and always for the simple reason (the triumphant overturning) that it is the hour of nothing. Or rather, it is the hour of the principal piece, irrupting in the Book, and even in the sentence itself. For, between the word *nothing* and the negation that normally follows immediately after, there are inserted at least a dozen words.

The hour (now or never) is nothing other than the epoch—this epoch in which there is no Present. Indeed, the hour "is incessant as well as never" and is characterized by urgency. And never has its urgent and incessant character been more pressing than today. At the same time, it would incessantly defer itself and refuse its own arrival. It would hold itself—in suspense—just as would the epoch. It—the hour—is the present moment—the now—that holds off and delays. "For whom or what are we waiting?" asked Nietzsche, "The grandiloquent heralds and trumpeting trumpets? And what pleasure in this noise! There is a silence that smothers us; too long have we lent an ear."

Yes, what are we waiting for? The end of the world? The second coming of Christ? Or for nothing and nobody? Are we waiting for—Godot? Heidegger would say that waiting is without object. And yet, in our waiting, we hear the silence that would smother us; this silence that we never cease to silence with our "universal reporting." Such reporting fills in the emptiness of every word, as if it were a septic tank or sewer. "Express yourself!" or so an election poster proclaimed. But what? A self that remains reduced, in advance, to its "daily nothingness"? Again and still, this nothing is to be disclosed; perhaps the Whole of mankind shall have the power to speak it. Still and again, with what word? If speaking is equivalent to the "silent return of a coin to another's pocket"? Could we, if we were to everywhere cease our wanting, and at every hour, cease our speaking and "self" expression, hear the silence that smothers us? And this voice crying in the desert: "The desert spreads?" But "riddle upon riddle! What was once the cry 'The desert spreads . . . ,' now threatens to turn into chatter. The threat of this perversion is part of what gives us food for thought. The threat is that perhaps this most thoughtful thought will today, and still more tomorrow, become suddenly no more than a platitude, and as platitude spread and circulate. This fashion of talking platitudes is at work in that endless profusion of books describing the state of the world today. They describe what by its nature is indescribable . . . "[17]

The risk, most certainly, is great: for it concerns the transformation of the "cry" of thought into a simple "manner of speaking." Even Heidegger, who never cried out, saw his own thought transformed into chitchat and prattle. For example, the prattle that marks the "want of any thought" in rock music and every other "absence of thought!" Let us be careful, then, not to identify the "desert" with everything that emerges from some pseudo-"decline" of Europe or the West and that corresponds to the technicalization of the planet. On the other hand, let us not believe that this desert or decline can be stopped by a simple return to those good, old-fashioned values of humanism or "culture" or to an agrarian society: that perfectly pastoral utopia. No returns, no exchanges. No return whatsoever is possible and this—maybe—is the desert—the exile of the expatriated is merely the first sign of its arid encroachment. It began with the first grain of "occidental" thought and since then, hasn't ceased to spread. Moreover, we are left without the possibility of being able to predict its end—nor is it desirable. How can we arrest the devastation of the earth? What measures could we take: administrative? political? social? Should we organize international colloquiums? But then, how can we take measures against that which has no measure and which destroys all measure? "The desert spreads," even in the shadow of abundance. Nor will it suffice to simply irrigate, as did the Israelis, to turn the desert into a green garden rife with flowers. Furthermore, we wonder whether such a desert could be crossed—in much the same way as the Jews crossed the Red Sea? But such a crossing implies two sides or "shores." Where is the "other" side? Where is the "line," over which we must cross to be saved?—to be welcomed into the Promised Land? Does nihilism have such sides? Are we able to cross over its line (as thought Ernst Jünger)? "In no way is the Line—thought as the sign of the Zone of nihilism brought to completion—something merely placed before man; something that might simply be crossed. Consequently, the possibility of a *trans lineam* gives way as well as does any crossing that might lead us there."[18] We cannot travel through this desert as we might travel over an ocean or through a tunnel; no shore is within sight. In effect, it would appear that this desert has no shore at all: "The devastation of the earth may put man within reach of a higher archy of life; primarily as the organisation of a state of uniform happiness for all men."[19] Or so Heidegger wrote, while thinking of the last man described by Nietzsche: " 'We have invented happiness,' the last men claim, while blinking." Invisible desert or caricature that spreads all the more vigorously because, by itself, it remains unseen or because it would appear as its opposite: as the cornucopia of abundance. And this an abundance of consumption brought within reach of every hand, of everything—including that which is not coined. The Desert: the "there is no Present" that would give itself over as the only present. And from such "giving itself over," every other present is held to be a fiction, myth, or mystification. Here it would be wrong to become indignant, for present nihilism speaks the truth about the epoch: "There is no Present"—while, at the same time, it would deride it.

The Desert—silence of the sacred theaters, though no longer perceptible as such, smothered in advance by the noisy noise of cultural "manifestations." Either on the burning or icy earth, we see the last man—and the last vestige of the dance—leap and bound—man who makes everything look small, for want—of everything. A species that is indestructible, like the flea. This land, this earth stripped of every god and filled with fleas; land without land, without any inhabitants and yet, overpopulated, overexploited, and overequipped.

What is there to do? Perhaps, there is nothing to do. Whether suicide or abstention, nothing to do, why? Why poets in such a desert? Why poets who commit suicide?—Mallarmé, Rimbaud, Hölderlin, Trakl—the list is long, even though each poet did not actually take his own life. Mallarmé once wrote that Rimbaud "cast away his dreams, either by his fault or theirs, and purged himself of poetry." And Mallarmé, his whole life long, continued to dream of the Book; to describe his solitude simply as "the case of a man who isolated himself in order to engrave his own tombstone"—or those of other poets. Certainly this is the aristocratic attitude of a poet who considered the "contemporary epoch as an interregnum"; a poet who refused to "mingle" in it other than by sending, every now and then, "his calling card, a sonnet or stanza to the living; so that, by them, he would not be vilified; especially if they suspected him of knowing they had no place."[20] But such reserve as this was moderated by an even greater secret, by an even greater fear, the incessant temptation to commit suicide: "Victoriously fled, sweet suicide . . . "

Hölderlin also experienced this temptation to commit "sweet" suicide—like the death of Empedocles rejoining the great fire. But Hölderlin fought against this urge and "victoriously fle[d]" this "great transport, eternally hostile to man; this energetic transport that always is en route towards the other world." He came to learn of the turning round of Time, wherewith the want of any god gave comfort. Such was revealed by his *Remarks on Antigone*, and this, under the figure of Zeus's turning into "father of Time" or even "father of the Earth." Yet does a Present open up in such a rending a-part; or in such destitution? "The constant coursing of the hours"—counted, as it were, by a Niobè now become "equal to the desert"—may very well contain the only possible allotment that is vested in whomever stands fast and refuses to flee toward the other world. But also who refuses the meta-physical urge, this desire to transcend, whereby the earth may appear as only a phantom with respect to a "true life," "absent" down here on terra firma.

This flight has opened up the way to the desertification of the earth; and it is against this that Nietzsche vociferously protested. Ever since the time of Plato, the human being has been a stranger upon this earth. But it will not suffice to simply renounce this will to transcend: that thus, we might find our way back, our return. It shall not suffice to worship and exalt the "body" to end our exile. Perhaps, in fact, our first step shall be the renunciation of any will to "return." Perhaps it will be to take care and keep ourselves—"Take care and be there," wrote Mallarmé. But first, we must take care to not believe ourselves already "there," finally there.

Upon this path we must make our stand and stay and, more than ever, keep our guard. Such vigilance, even vis-à-vis the "withdrawal," remained for Mallarmé, a voluntary and almost heroic attitude. It characterized the poet who went unrecognized by his contemporaries and who, without contempt, adopted, certain measures of retaliation or, at least, of outspoken defiance. "To keep oneself," according to the "Restricted Action," while waiting for better days to come—and then, precisely *while waiting* "to publish." On the one hand, this implies a certain consent with respect to the state of things and a certain "wait and see" attitude that is always able to turn into "collaboration." On the other hand, this implies that we are ready with a rather heavy dose of illusion, for nothing assures us that the worst has come to pass. In effect, does this waiting not partake in a general and planetary movement: of firy transport or impassioned nonmovement; this infinite movement by which the epoch exhausts itself in its search for an orbit—forever out of balance and greedy for assurances and absolute certainties? On this decisive point, even Heidegger would disappoint us inasmuch as we would only need to prepare ourselves for an enigmatic "turning of time." A turning we are never able to accomplish with will power alone; for precisely this voluntarism and this "action-for-action's-sake" prohibits our access to Being. Thought itself is of a preliminary order; that is, it is only able to prepare and, even, only able to prepare the preparations for a prefiguration of change. And this change, this small mutation, itself shall be but a small step; unable, by itself, to do anything as long as a "sign" has not come from a "big" step . . . And so, while waiting, we wait . . . It is in this half-heroic posture—and half-grotesque—that the sectaries of the Master find themselves; each one justified in his immobility by the extreme prudence of a philosopher who had not always been as prudent and who, for some time, kicked himself in the pants (without openly admitting it) for having believed the moment come, for having saluted the dawning of a new age, for having been "revolutionary"—that is, horribly hoodwinked. A time, "a Present" seemed to exist; a German present that would have put an end to the confusion, that would have stood up by itself, that would have been on the lips of all the people finally present; a people finally re-united in the same mystical body, the same magical communion: "There it is, we have arrived!"

Returned from such excessiveness and errantry, we now understand that Heidegger remained apart from everything, that he returned from everything, except, paradoxically, from those to whom he (re)turned in the most profound way: the first Greek thinkers. However, at the twilight of his life, he declared: "Only a god can save us." Here he expressed the ground or root of that which must be called a *belief*. And his waiting—even if Being is supposed to replace the ancient gods that have "flown"—resembled much too much the waiting for the Messiah: so much so that we *Moderns* might have difficulties in following such a slippery path. The West—that is, if this word still has a sense; if it is not already overloaded with a pernicious mixture of bad conscience, otherworldliness, and the underworld, and overcoated, as it were, with good intentions—has, as a result of its murderous eschatologies, fallen into discredit. Eschatologies that other peoples pay at their expense and not ours—while we, tortured or serene, assist in the collapse of everything in which we had, some time ago, placed all our hopes: communism, revolution, liberation—ideas that shook the world and continue to shake it—except our own, to which nothing more can happen; our ends of history, our tomorrows which sing all this—this, in which we are no longer able to believe (and for good reason); finally we have unburdened ourselves, more or less, at the expense of others—Africans or Cubans—who are unable to do anything, but . . . who will kill each other for some time to come, without understanding what has happened to them; the fallout of a History that has come to an end—but an end only for *us* . . .

And yet, who are we? Are we those to whom nothing more can happen? Or rather, are we those, unique in our historical position, to whom *nothing happens* or for whom there is no Present? And for whom—because this does happen and because it does overturn *everything*—the possiblity of having an experience is reserved?

Notes

1. Stéphane Mallarmé, "*L'Action restreinte*," *Oeuvres Complètes*, p. 372; hereafter *OC*.

2. This sentence refers to the following one by Mallarmé: " . . . *aboli bibelot d'inanité sonore.*"—Trans.

3. Mallarmé, *OC*, pp. 371-372.

4. Mallarmé, "*La Musique et les Lettres*," *OC*, p. 647.

5. Ibid., p. 647.

6. Martin Heidegger, "What Are Poets For?" in *PLT*, pp. 92-93.

7. Mallarmé, *OC*, p. 260.

8. Ibid., p. 415.

9. Ibid., p. 869.

10. Mallarmé, "*Toast funèbre*," *OC*, p. 54.

11. Mallarme, "*L'Action restreinte*," *OC*, p. 372.

12. Mallarmé, *OC*, p. 869.

13. Mallarmé, *OC*, p. 419.

14. Mallarmé, *OC*, p. 369.

15. Mallarmé, "*L'Action restreinte*," *OC*, p. 372.

16. Mallarmé, "*L'Action restreinte*," p. 373.

17. Martin Heidegger, *What Is Called Thinking*, p. 49.

18. Heidegger, *Zur Seinsfrage*, French trans. in *Questions I*. (Paris: Gallimard, 1967), p. 233.

19. Heidegger, "What Is Called Thinking."

20. Mallarmé, *OC*, p. 664.

2

"We Must Be Absolutely Modern"

"We must be absolutely modern." To be sure, a simple sentence; and yet, we must understand it; and yet, we wonder what the difficulty could be. For example, everybody knows what *modern* means; we need not seek its definition in a dictionary. *Modern* signifies current, contemporary, present. We think of "Modern Times," the modern world, modern society, and modern technology. By extension, (that is, if we were to look in a dictionary), modern is that which is *of its own time*. "This young girl is too *modern* for my taste." This sentence is taken directly from the formidable *Dictionnaire de l'Académie* (1935 edition). *Le Grand Robert* would cite the sentence by Rimbaud and then, one from Gide's *Les Faux Monnayeurs*: "That which will appear, shortly, as the oldest, will have already appeared as the most modern." A sentence that would make visible the modern, in light of the *future anterior* tense. It speaks of the commonplace as nothing more than that "banality" which, according to André Malraux, can never be subdued. Malraux is also cited by the dictionary: "Nothing is able to subdue this banality that, for the man of the thirteenth century, the Gothic was modern."

Notwithstanding, the adjective appeared only a century later. It was taken from the Latin word *modernus*, which itself was derived from the adverb *modo*. The latter had the sense of "recently," "in a short while," or "there is little." When one wished to shorten, even more, the time span—with respect to the moment at which an event took place, but which had nevertheless *already* taken place—one simply repeated the adverb: *modo modo* or "just recently." *Modo* refers to *modus* or mood, and this in the unrestricted sense of measure: the measurement of a field, "good measure" in the sense of moderation; but also, musical measure and melody; and finally, in the grammatical sense of the mood—of verbs.

But why bring up all this? What good can it do us insofar as we already understand the sentence: "We must be absolutely modern"? Moreover, has it not become the catchword of our present epoch? Who, in his or her right mind, would want anything that was not absolutely modern? That was not the latest and most up-to-date model, whether it be a CD player or bicycle? Who would want a secondhand item? Or who wishes to be behind the times (outmoded) instead of being on the *cultural edge* of "progress"? Surely, we must be absolutely modern; absolutely up-to-date and in the know. We must be current. It is even the name of a French magazine (*Actuel*) and an American TV show (*A Current Affair*). In any case, everything must be current, real, modern, *new*—including that which, in former times, only had its reality in God or Being. Yet, we would modernize the mass (perhaps the masses too?) just as we would modernize philosophy. Hence, we go in for the "New Look Philosophers," the "New Look," or quite simply, "The Look." Fashion lays seige to everything; and even has its "philosophical" philosophers: philosophy which celebrates this "era of emptiness" as the triumph of "modern" democracy.

There is a specter that looms over every fashion, something that does its silent work and leaves that which was fashionable old-fashioned. For fashion does not exist but in the future anterior tense: something will have been fashionable (à la mode), yet, is unable to establish itself as a present, for any length of time. It must yield to the everchanging demands of the market, to the stock on hand, or to the idea in head. Walter Benjamin spoke of fashion as the "eternal return of the new" in the form of an erraticism that calls upon the modern to be incessantly newer and evermore "current."[1] That which is current is condemned to *pass away*, to become "surpassed" and hence, out-of-date. It is only in this continual passing and surpassing—this continual handling—that the world of business and business affairs would move. Nor is the political or intellectual domain spared this movement. Books do not escape the vertiginous rapping and ongoing goading of this process. They do not escape the passing fancy that reduces the printed page to have worth only under the *mode* or method of the wrapper. Each week boxes of books are sent to the bookstores, most of which return unopened—like junk mail (or junk bonds) or letters sent to the wrong address—to a publisher who must resign itself to recycle the new books—for which the date of expiration is always being shortened.

It is no secret that the freshness of the book lasts only two or three weeks. Indeed, let us not even speak of images, for which, in any case, the mode of being is immediacy.

Fashion—and here I mean the garment industry as well as the intellectual, for today, ideas emerge from the same movement of clothing and "disclothing"—reveals the methodical return to the *return* or *retro*. Whether this be a return to Kant or the modern style makes little difference, inasmuch as it is a question of the machinery, instrumentation, and source of supply. That is, what Barthes referred to as the "shameful repetition": "Content, ideological schema, the blurring of contradictions, these are repeated; always new books, new programs, new films, new items, but always the same meaning."[2] In effect, fashion (la grande mode) always privileges *the* fashion or mode; and form is always privileged to the detriment of content—but only by reducing, in advance, the form to a wrapper. For only form matters: "sense" is rejected as that which is accidental or superfluous, as that which merely adds a tinge of "authenticity"—a *supplement of souls* so to speak—to the merchandise that, at all cost, must be put into circulation.

If, after all, everything amounts to the same thing; if every "new" product is destined, almost immediately, to be surpassed by another product (whose wrapper is almost identical); if all modernity lives only for the passion of surpassing—then, we must say, that the modern passerby no longer has, in the alienated form of the eternal return of the new, something on to which one may hold. One is condemned to run after every mirage and every apparition that appears and condemned to search for a utopia at which one might stop and catch one's breath. But because it is utopian—forever beyond . . . and always surpassed—this running-after becomes an obsessive chase. And this chasing—ever forward—remains the sign of our illusion, illusion so proper to modernity that we gave it a name and called it *progress*.

But must we hold on to this catastrophic or apocalyptic vision? Must we hold on to this eternal return of the new that overpowers us with modernity—and this, not unlike a precocious and insurmountable asphyxsia? Or rather, in spite of everything, is there an even more violent wind (we dare not say *sacred*—although Mallarmé did), that blows? "And a sacred wind—to speak nothing of history":

Shall it rend us a-part with its drunken wing
This frozen and forgotten lake that lurks under the rime
The transparent glacier of flights that haven't flown![3]

Would the wind of history, whether it be rare or concealed, be just another name for the "virginal, the vivacious and splendid today," that is, the *present*? But a present without any news or any current affair—because these are incapable of "impregnating the past while creating the future" as said Nietzsche. Indeed, they are incapable of breaking through "the frozen and forgotten lake" of the past, and thus unable to free that which sleeps within in its icy state: the "flights that haven't flown"—that is, the future.

To impregnate the past is not simply a matter of heating it up again or defrosting it—as if the past actually existed somewhere, ready to be served like a TV dinner fresh from the microwave. With respect to contemporaneity, the past only exists—or is consumable—as that which is rerealized or recontemporalized or reheated and served like the soup de jour. It is similar to the restoration of an old building—or the Statue of Liberty—whereby the sooty facade—or faded torch—is simply resurfaced. Contemporaneity would gather about everything that lags behind to clothe itself anew. It is the civilization of refuse—of the secondhand ragpicker so dear to Baudelaire.

Yet, if it is a more destructive and thus *truer* (unveiling, perhaps even prevaling) wind than the simple newness mechanically produced today and destined, by tomorrow, to become trash, then might it not be characterized as modern—though in different sense of the word? The will to newness or to news is able to exert itself—radically. For it itself is one of those trade winds of history that irrupts into the world and constitutes our present. Rimbaud was the first to have endured such a wind in all its violence: from the said "letter of the Seer" in which he demands of the new poet, "*anew*—ideas and forms," to the "Farewell" of *A Season in Hell* in which we read: "Yes, at least the new hour is severe." And, of course, we have that apparently simple sentence that we took as our point of departure: "We must be absolutely modern."

Without a doubt, simple. Still, we must comprehend it: we must hear it with our inner ear and understand. And for this, we shall have need of more than just good ears. It is not sufficient "to know" the language, even though this, most certainly, is a prerequisite in understanding. Thus, we would do well to remark where the adverb *absolutely* has been placed. Obviously it refers to *modern* and not *we must*. It is not simply a question of being modern—which, by itself, seems to be a superfluous declaration; for, insofar as we are always already modern, we need not become so—rather, we must be *absolutely* modern. Are there, then, different *modes* or *moods* of being modern? One that is completed and absolute and another that is imperfect—a half-measure—wholly rejected? To be only "relatively" modern is not enough; in fact, it is to be absolutely not modern. In pushing this grammatical analysis to the ontological level (i.e., to its groundwork), there is only one authentic way to be modern—and thus, for us who are modern, of *being* absolutely: it is absolute modernity.

But here, we might object and ask what such an absolute modernity could really mean? Is not modernity, by definition, a relative notion? For even the etymological root bears witness to this: *modo* is an adverb that marks the measure of or the relation to. Nevertheless, could we speak of an "absolute richness" or an "absolute greatness?"

❁ ❁ ❁

> The New is not a fashion, it is a value, the basis of all our criticism: our evaluation of the world no longer depends, at least not directly, as in Nietzsche, on the opposition between *noble* and *base*, but on that between Old and New.[4]

Barthes clearly understood how the modern surpassed the simple phenomenon of fashion. To be sure, we could say that "all times" (an absurd expression) have had their fashions, clothing or otherwise. Yet the modern phenomenon par excellence is that the "new" has become a value and not that there actually is something new. Before the irruption of modernity, every appearance of the new was regarded with suspicion and distrust. Oftentimes it was considered to be a sign of decadence or a softening of the "hard kernel" that formed the moral, political, and juridical basis of a society. Philosophy itself was the first victim of this conservatism that was so proper to the Mediterranean and ancient civilizations. Socrates corrupted the young, but only by undermining the authority of a tradition and the Ancients themselves—an authority that was left in ruins by the profession of his radical "ignorance." Plato was wiser in that he limited parricide to the figure of Parmenides—though we suspect his Sicilian adventure cost him dearly.

With Christianity, we not only saw the rise of a new religion, but one that claimed to be the only "true religion." At this point, the ancient world suffered a second blow—one that was to be fatal. At the beginning of his *Confessions*, St. Augustine is rather indignant with the education he received as a youth; an education that *we* would call *humanist* but that, for *him*, was dehumanizing and barbarous. Here he took cognizance of a violent disruption with tradition—one that he, in fact, wished for—for the way would thus be paved to the city of God. For example, it was not sufficient to simply know how to speak well—which was the very ideal of the tribunal, the rhetor, or the orator who, accordingly, ruled in the public market of the ancient world. Such men spoke well in order to be good men. Notwithstanding, the man who "takes every caution to not say *inter omines* instead of *inter homines*, never thinks of checking his anger as he permanently subtracts one man from a crowd." Clearly, for St. Augustine, it was better to commit some sort of barbarism in the retelling of a "good" act, than to employ a twisted language to elevate base deeds. Later, the divine Marquis would know how to speak in the most eloquent language—language of a civilization already at the height of its eloquence—to relate the *Cent vingt journées* . . .

Nevertheless, if Christian morality thus severed the many centuries of pagan culture, it could not claim to be truer simply because it was newer. St. Augustine—however Christian and however desirous he may have been to destroy all the old "idols"—was not modern: the truth of the Good Word he transmitted had nothing to do with its newness. In fact, Christian theologians would later attempt to demonstrate that Christianity had always already existed—even for the "wise" old ancients who, historically, were utterly ignorant of the phenomenon. Surely, the truth of any word always legitimizes itself in the same way: by referring itself to an atemporal and absolute order. Throughout the Middle Ages, the *reference* remained a constant, not because of some fetish for the Letter, but because such a relationship assured the unity of a world situated upon unshakable grounds. *To increase* the Scriptures, by commentary or by adding to the theological "sum," was to participate in its authority (*auctoritas*), the value of which could not be measured by its character of leaving a trace or monument or cultural "patrimony." Paradoxically, the cult of antiquity *as* antiquity is a purely modern phenomenon: the Holy Word still must be transmitted and interpreted—correctly—by a priest and for an illiterate though eternally living mass without age. The Holy Word is unable to age or be restored to youth—even if it is not absolutely cemented in a "corpus doctrinal." Therefore, it is always revisable.

But would not modernity also justify itself insofar as it has recourse to the absolute? Did not Hegel, who hailed Descartes as the Columbus of modern times, write, "Only the absolute is true or the true is the absolute"? And Descartes, did he not flatter himself with having discovered an unshakable and absolute ground in the *cogito*?

However, the absolute of modernity is not the same: for, inasmuch as it would identify itself with the incessant labor of consciousness appropriating "its" truth, it no longer contains anything of the timeless or immaterial. There is never a thing-in-itself, but rather an absolute that, in effect, would *effect itself* as absolute. For Hegel, the absolute was a result, the product of a slow and painful process of progression toward the absolute. The first movement takes place in, or is effected by, a tabula rasa—what Hegel called *negativity*. The result is such that the ground never originates from the outside (as does the revelation of Truth in Christianity). Rather, the ground would produce itself by itself; it would construct its own foundations in such a way that that which is not constructed upon such grounds—even if it is "true"—is not true—or at least not truly so. "We must make a tabula rasa of the past, for the world shall change from the bottom," or so goes the "Internationale": a song that could be sung as the international anthem of modern times.

Here we might raise the objection that Christianity, at least in its beginnings, made no less a tabula rasa of the past than modernity. But Christianity never explicitly vowed to *change* the world—at the very most, it merely announced the "end of the world." That is, it announced the end of *a* world already in decline—and this, for the simple reason that its truth was located beyond the world, beyond *this* earthly world that represented (as it did for Plato) that which had no place whatsoever with respect to the eternity of the being. Under such conditions, everything that arises from temporality—and by extension, everything that arises from the modern project of transforming the world—cannot have any effect over the essential. To know whether or not we are modern has no importance for an "authentic" Christian. In effect, it can acquire importance only at that moment when Christianity enters onto the highway of historical decline—that of "modernization."

The adjective *modern* reveals the wealth of its meaning only in the expression *modern times*. The German is able to say it in a single word, *Neuzeit* or "the new times." Yet, it is not new with respect to something ancient, or rather, its newness is not exhausted by the fact that it succeeds, necessarily, something else. Otherwise, every epoch could be characterized, *relatively*, by another—by the one that must follow and that, by this gesture, must become modern times. Here, such newness is not relative, but absolute—modernity consisting in nothing more than the following: to expressly will itself as absolutely modern and to think this will as its truth. In it and by it, the *caesura* between the before and after is such that, "The two no longer allow themselves to be arranged as if they were rhymes" (Hölderlin). It is an absolute caesura because it is not determined relatively, but from the inside. It wills itself and posits itself as the decisive moment *with respect to* the before and after, which only then would situate themselves. The caesura does not follow as a result of some outside event qualified *as* decisive, rather, the caesura *precedes* it and makes it possible. Certainly, we could locate certain subsisting elements from the before in the after, thus we might come across the mortal remains of Mediaeval Scholasticism in the work of Descartes. But who could locate and register such remains? Always the one who comes after—the modern person who already inhabits the caesura—because that person was given birth to by such a caesura. Because one would identify oneself with the decisive moment—that by which one is able to make an allowance for that which is already modern and that which is not yet quite modern.

The following poem by Rimbaud, entitled "To a Reason," illustrates this point:

> One step from you and this, the rising up of new men
> and their movement in motion. . . .
> To you the children sing: "Change our lots, sift through
> the banalities, beginning with time."
> We beg you: "Raise up, wherever, the substance
> of our fortunes and our wishes."
> Having arrived from always, you shall go everywhere.[5]

The "reason" here to which we address ourselves, must *sift through the banalities, beginning with time*. It is by reason that the accounts are kept; it weighs, in one sense or another, with each arm of the scale and thus distributes the portions and the parts, the fortunes and the lots. It is the *sieve of time*—the critical moment par excellence that is responsible for the allotment of history.[6]

Yet this critical moment can never be located in a predetermined moment of time—one considered as history itself. Rather, it would continually *move about* according to the uninterrupted progression of this reason which has arrived from always and which goes everywhere—and always further and further away. If modernity is unable to take in the whole of contemporaneity, it is because it is not determined by the contemporaneous moment. It would itself determine—in its *contemporaneity*—the positivity that is auto-position, the "place and the formula" and thus, the moment. It is modernity itself that decides what will be modern and what will not.

Let us repeat once again "our" sentence—this time accentuating it in the following way: *We must* be absolutely modern. Why? Or so we would ask. Why is it necessary and in the good name of what? In a certain sense, there is no answer: *We must* be absolutely modern. So, there would be no reason for such insistence? Perhaps. But only if we understand by "reason" an *exterior* or outside motive. Many years ago, God guaranteed the eternal and everlasting validity of the Law—that is, of the ethical imperatives. But here, nothing would intervene and play the role of guarantor; nothing would order the cosmos and the divine Creation. Nothing authorizes the categorical imperative to be absolutely modern: for modernity would, on the one hand, free itself from all authority or reference point. Yet, on the other, it would free itself precisely so that it might be delivered, absolutely, to itself. To this phenomenon, we give the name *self-deliverance* or *self-delivery*. Moreover, we must understand this in a double sense: first, deliverance with respect to every exterior model, whether this be a transcendental authority such as the Holy Scriptures or a historical one based on the Greek "model."

For this reason we must be *absolutely* modern. And this is why we must free ourselves from the historical models that continue to determine us, more or less explicitly, to the point where we see modernity simply as an *imitation* of the Greeks or Romans. Yet, this deliverance or liberation is not absolute until it would constitute itself as a Supreme Tribunal—of reason, for example—by which everything is subpoenaed and before which everything is made to appear. An absolute moment whose sole ability consists in judging whether something shall be "true" or not; in other words, whether something shall be modern. This moment—from which the very principle of evaluation would emerge and call itself (properly so and modernly so) the *Critique*—is never received from the outside, as was traditional authority. It would form itself from its own bosom and produce itself as being critical modernity itself. The modern does not define itself, relatively, to some heritage; rather, heritage as such gains value only insofar as it has passed through the sieve of the modern critique that is essentially formal.

But once again, let us not align ourselves too quickly to the same new and modern plan. Let us be suspicious of this heirloom. We might remark that Rimbaud's poetic undertaking took nothing that was absolutely modern. Does not *A Season in Hell* pick up again the wish of the "Voyage" that composes the last poem of Baudelaire's *Les Fleurs du Mal*?

> We want, as long as this fire burns within our brains,
> To dive deep into the bottom of the Abyss, Heaven or
> Hell, what does it matter?
> To the very bottom of the Unknown, that something
> *new* might thus be revealed!

Yet this simply means that, in light of Rimbaud's poetic undertaking, Baudelaire appears as the first modern poet. Or, as Rimbaud wrote, "the first Seer, king of poets, a *true God*." Indeed, Rimbaud hardly felt himself *authorized* in his modernity by the Baudelairian legacy. On the contrary, it was Baudelaire who acceded to the dignity of the modern thanks to the undertaking of the Seer. Incidently, this authorized Rimbaud to criticize his "father" for having "lived in an environment that was too artisitic"—and not modern enough. "For the new must be free to execrate their ancestors!" Baudelairian aesthetics leads to the deadly sin of conceiving poetic modernity relatively rather than absolutely. Benjamin notes that, with Baudelaire, "the ancient pretense to immortality was such that one hoped to be read one day as an ancient author: 'that the whole of modernity might so dignify itself to become antiquity.' "[7] Such a reference is deliberately absent from Rimbaud, who, in fact, proclaimed the opposite: "Poetry shall no longer submit action to its rhythm; it [poetry] will be *in advance*."

Nevertheless, all referentiality is not absolutely absent from such a "vision." In this particular case, we see in the "letter of the Seer" that the question is one explicitly concerned with the poetic model of the Greeks: still the imitation of the Moderns. Poetry submitting action to its rhythm in such a way that poetry, "lines and lyrics," that is, "rhymes" was the Action itself—such was the Greek model of poetry; at least, for example in its Pindaric form. It was, according to Michel Deguy, "something (though neither 'thing' nor decor) as *decisive* as the Pentateuch was for the Hebrews; here I mean the enactment of the law itself or laws that were not quite yet 'juridical' or 'constitutional' but rather, a law that inscribed itself or that submitted itself to its own rhythm: *gignoske d'oios ruthmos / anthropous echei.*"[8]

Here, *decisive* is the right word. Even if it is no longer possible to imitate or equal the Greek model, it is still possible to invent another, one that is even more decisive because *absolutely modern*, because it is "in advance." Possible because of a radical *caesura*.

"Poetry shall no longer submit action to its rhythm": if we were to only abide by this one sentence, we would find ourselves before a commonplace in modern times. The evidence is a bit pungent (easy to smell). Poetry, *at this present moment*, no longer bestows a rhythm to action. And action, thus given over to the debauchery of calculation, planning, and programming, would relegate poetry to the status of a snack or hors d'oeuvre: a supplement of the soul, of work, a leftover, as it were, in a world where the word would exist only to be useful—to an action without rhythm. *By the same stroke*—whereby an action acts without acting—language comes to be seen simply as a means of communication. And action is surrendered to the service of that which no longer needs to be poetically rhymed. This *by the same stroke* that would give sign of the sequence remains the only sign of the rhythm that has fled. It is in this sequence that the simultaneous secession of [the] word and [the] action would manifest itself. Action for action's sake—which would self-produce its own productivity and thus its own criteria for "truth," that is, efficaciousness—becomes the dominant value that dominates all of reality. Furthermore, the poetic word—once rhythm and rhyme—becomes little more than the refuse of the reality principle; at least insofar as it is separated and absolutized in "pure poetry." It is for this reason that Rimbaud, before recognizing the "stupidity" and inanity therein, had always to project poetry *in advance*. He had to wipe away the chalk and clean the slate; a gesture in which we see the decisive rupture with all heritage and all former *poetics*. With this rupture, we must *invent* a language "that would be from the soul and for the soul"—thus effecting, though unknowingly, "the miracle of a poetic prose; musical, yet without rhythm and rhyme; and still, with enough subtlety and disaccord to be adopted by the lyrical movements of the soul, to the undulations of reverie; to the summersaults of conscience."[9] Such a language could be only *a-part*; it could hardly have any rapport with the action it claims to have surpassed. Rather, it would address itself to the "soul." In this way, it would stumble, once again, upon that modern principle—though now rewoven by Rimbaud—of a self-delivered subjectivity. Similarily—but differently—without the "lyrical movements of the soul," but always in the same climate of the absolute, Mallarmé would invent the "total" word as utterly foreign to language . . .

In other words, the poetic word would understand itself as an *absolute* language—without any outside referent. It is precisely in this determination that it reveals its absolute modernity. This self-deliverance that constitutes its manner of being—absolutely—implicates a radical recess or hole rather than a present. We are not born modern, we must be it; we ourselves must bring ourselves forward as absolutely modern. The *we must* ex-acts a want (which is the Present insofar as it only exists in advance); and the want, in return, ex-acts a *we must*. This simply means that the modern is never able to establish itself as tradition. It must incessantly turn back upon its initial exigence for modernity—and rupture. And yet, we wonder whether this incessant "turning back" doesn't itself constitute a type of tradition—a new tradition such as Harold Rosenbery has remarked?

> If, by tradition we mean the most complete and faithful transmission, from one generation to another, of an ensemble of ideological [and formal] models, and a certain body of beliefs and styles, then any weakening in this

> transmission must necessarily shake tradition in its foundation. Now the new fact or phenomenon—from the moment modernity would set itself up as the basis by which we judge—is such that this change itself becomes the touchstone of the creative project. That will be creative which breaks with the past. . . . The negation of tradition, now transformed into the search for something new, singular and surprising finishes by installing itself as traditional: there is, to be sure, a certain continuity in this iconoclastic project that, with the repetition of its appearance, institutes itself, in the end, as the tradition of the rupture. As Octavio Paz has remarked, the tradition of the rupture not only implicates this negation of tradition, but also the negation of the rupture.[10]

Perhaps the paradox of this tradition of the rupture is only apparent, originating from an inability to think an absolute rupture. Inevitably, the rupture is repeated every time *it* is necessary—to be absolutely modern. But we must ask: Will this end, "after all is said and done," in the establishment of a tradition? Or would the repetition of the rupture cancel out this tradition, as Octavio Paz believes? Or would it re-enforce its intensity, its poignancy, and even, its tragic character? Tragic and *necessary*? Arising from the ex-acting exigence, the demand, that constitutes modernity as such but that escapes its imperious hand—as long as it originates from an abyss or abyssmal hole?

The objections that we might make to this apparently contradictory notion of the "tradition of the rupture" would originate from a rather peculiar blindness to the modern "fact." Such that this latter does not exhaust itself by, and with, this will to newness—especially inasmuch as it is a will "to be peculiar": a change for change's sake. If, for example, Rimbaud's dream was *to, indeed, change life*—which may seem like an impossibility or empty slogan—just as Marx dreamed, indeed, of transforming the world and not simply interpreting it, then this dream would not only collide with the "Impossible," but also, it would rise up out of it. In effect, such a dream would originate from an original impossibility, or from an ex-acting want that is proper to this particular life: "The true life is absent." Which is a variation of "There is no Present." Here, the question is not only one of changing the old and ancient life—if only because it is already dead from the very moment the modern would speak. "Tradition," in the sense of a splendorous ensemble already constituted—already made—and which merely needs to be transmitted, "in the most complete and faithful way possible," is already a myth. And this, perhaps, is a myth peculiar to modernity—its shadow. The rupture *precedes* and renders possible a "modern age"; it is its re-source and its future. Such is modernity's only "tradition." It is one that is expressed by a "disruption" that is always more energetic and by a critical concern with crumbling foundations and the "dis-ease of civilization." It is a tradition that, in a sense, is other than the pure and simple transmission—*just as it is*—of a past deep frozen in the freezer of yesterday. Rather, it is a tradition in the sense of a liberation or deliverance.

We must be somewhat superficial to see this "rupture" (I prefer the term *caesura*) only as a *negation*, even if this is in the lyrical form of a revolt. The accepted image ("traditional" in the common sense) of Rimbaud as a "rebel," iconoclast, or terminator of everything that was ancient (and thus "venerable"?), can only obstruct our view. For, from the very outset in *A Season in Hell* the poet writes: "I am unable to understand rebellion." In fact, Rimbaud was not modern only because of his rebellion. If we are satisfied in our denial of the established values (such as God, Reason, and so on), we quickly conform to a nonconformism that is as antiseptic and sterile as that to which we are opposed. (In the long run, the avant-garde becomes the ancien regime, just as surrealism became an absurd and absolute dictatorship). Hence, Rimbaud was absolutely modern, not because he was opposed to an institution already in place (thus determining himself relatively), but because he posited himself absolutely. His caesura was a surgical operation only insofar as it was the Operation—the grand opening or putting into operation or putting into abyss of an absolute ground or foundation. This latter has nothing to do with such terms as "positive" or "negative." It is the absolute: the *caesura* opening itself *in the guise of a ground.*

> We affirm you, method! We have hardly forgotten how yesterday you glorified every one of our ages. We have faith in the poison. We know how to give our lives, every day, without reserve.
>
> The hour of ASSASSINS is upon us.[11]

Here we are confronted with a double impossibility: first, how to present Rimbaud as a simple nay-sayer precisely when he would affirm with utmost intensity and inner jubilation. And second, how to speak of an affirmation precisely where it is a question of affirming the end of the world—"The hour of assassins is upon us?" But perhaps this double bind is modernity at its extreme. From this point of view, we are able to discern a rather profound similarity between the word of

Rimbaud and the thought of Nietzsche: in the latter, we find the joyous affirmation of the *Übermensch* in coexistence with the culmination of nihilism as proclaimed by "God is dead."

God is dead and we are his assassins. No, this is not a declaration of atheism, as if it merely claimed, for us, the opposite of faith. We wonder in what way the negation of God's existence could harm Him? The attitude of metaphysics, inasmuch as it would syllogize and demonstrate His existence (and even to speak of His "existence," without knowing whether this has any sense at all: to ask of God whether or not He exists), is already an anticipatory sign of a vulgarized atheism. A God that we would prove—as we might prove a geometrical theorem—is hardly the living God who appears in prayer and fear; in destitution and ecstasy. Moreover, did Nietzsche not add: "It is on account of theology that God is dead?"

Thus the rupture is not a negation, but a *triumphant* affirmation of its own absoluteness. It precedes and makes possible such events as the death of God and the hour of Assassins. It is the very operation of modernity as self-deliverance. Deliverance and not negation. For, every negation is only possible if that which is negatible is given beforehand. But now we must speak of deliverance: liberation of Self as the supreme moment—the liberation of the Critique. Or of method. According to Nietzsche, the proclamation of modern science is such that that which characterizes scientific modernity is the triumph of the scientific method over science itself. Method is that operation by which modernity would auto-deliver itself to itself; by which it would be delivered from every transcendental authority, while, at the same time, grounding itself, absolutely, as this transcendence itself. Nothing escapes method or the Critique—not even "reason."

But, we might object, has not the demand of method always characterized science? For how could a science that remains uncritical with respect to its own foundations retain any value? And Descartes, did he not adopt the Greek word *methodos*? Without a doubt—he did adopt it. As Rimbaud once remarked, "O Science! we have adopted you for everything. For the body and for the soul—the viaticum—we have medecine and philosophy—old wive's tale remedies and songs sung by the folk" (*OC*, p. 95). Yet, how is a word transmitted from one language to another? And, more important, how is it transmitted from one world to another? "Tell me what you think of the translation, and I will tell you who you are."[12]

Method is not without precedent; and science hardly admits of spontaneous generation. Yet the precedents of method were (despite the ingenious invention of mathematics by an "uncivilized people" according to Descartes), to be formulated by this same Plato who did not want to admit "anyone to the study of wisdom who was ignorant of Mathematics." Precedents exist. But they are able to appear as such (as precursors) only for those who come after and who would only then discover the "true" meaning of method. This way of seeing the world—methodically—is so natural for us that anything to the contrary would seem absurd. Yet, for the Greeks, the very notion of Nature revealing herself to the one who makes her speak the *lingua mathematica* would have been "uncivilized" and "barbarous."

In Greek, *methodos* means the pathway or road that leads to . . . Translated into a modern language, method becomes the process that opens up and inhabits a region of research. In the fourth *Règle pour la direction de l'esprit* (in which the primacy of method is outlined), Descartes writes the following: "It is better to never seek the truth of something than to have sought it without any method."[13] With this sentence, the whole of premodern tradition was overthrown in such a radical way, that we—Moderns—have never recovered from it. Certainly, the Ancients discovered valuable truths; beginning, for example, with Euclidean geometry. But because this was accomplished without any method, we might as well consider this knowledge null and void—and begin, once again, *at zero*. (In place of the *places* of Aristotelian physics, we would have infinite space!) With this, the Cartesian—and modern—conception of truth as certitude becomes clear: at the outset, it was not a subjective fact in the order of a belief—even though this latter could be maintained only by the original principle of subjectivity as *cogito*. Rather, this fact would establish itself in the very moment of the critical decision: the true is that which is tightly bound and *enclosed* because it is *disclosed*—analytically sifted. And the sieve through which this would pass is nothing other than the Critique assimilated to "reason." Only this Critique has the power of sorting and sifting out or of evaluation and disclosure, which consequently constitutes the *absolute criteria* of truth.

Of course, we could pretend that certitude is nothing more than a modified figure, secularized, as it were, of Christian salvation. Even Rimbaud discerned in Christianity the "proclamation of science": "But is there not real torment in this that, ever since that declaration of science, Christianity, man *fools himself* proves to himself the obvious, puffs himself up with the pleasures of reiterating those proofs, and can live in no other way! Subtle, silly torture; source of all my spiritual errantry."[14] According to Braque, proofs wear out the truth. Nevertheless, for the modern person, what does it mean to exist? Nothing but this: the demonstration to oneself that one exists. If ever we suspect ourselves (according to Mallarmé), of not having truly taken place or that there is no Present, we must, then, assure ourselves *in advance* of a certitude that certifies nothing more than our own existence: a certitude in itself. The proof, whether it be that of the existence of God or that of the *ego*, remains a vicious circle. It proves nothing *other* than the fact that it approves of itself. Yet, the vicious circle of the *cogito* allows me to assure myself with utmost certainty: it is not doubt that grounds certitude, but certitude that authorizes doubt. To exist in such a way hardly signifies that one must expose oneself to the other (to the world, to other people). Rather, it signifies an incessant return to the self: a return to zero. But is this not, in a sense, to trick—or to treat—ourselves to a farce? Of course, for Nietzsche this was all the better: the tragic farce of modern man is such that he only risks or surpasses himself in order to return, constantly and absolutely, to the same—Self. This farce ends in a society that is absolutely modern. (A trick rather than a treat?) Something truly torturous because it is certain: man is tricked in advance and treated like a rat. And this trick can never be de-feated—that is, itself tricked in its silly and subtle machination—simply because it rests on both the self-critique and self-affirmation. Nothing is more modern than the critique of modernity. It is this that escaped both Heidegger and Adorno.

Diabolic trick? (At least not a very nice one). "I think I am in Hell, therefore I am in Hell." This is no less effective than that other pseudo-syllogism: "*cogito ergo sum*." Both have the peculiarity of presenting the same flaw or irregularity of form: both are only dis-played proofs. In this case, it is a question of the Cartesian *ergo*, though later it would be that of the Mallarmean *Igitur*. "This story speaks to the Intelligence of the reader which would itself stage these things." Everything takes place on the stage of representation or mime. Hence, in a sense, the hell of the *Season* would only be the most dramatized version of the Cartesian pseudo-melodrama in which Satan replaces the all-knowing-genius-God. Notwithstanding, Descarte's text is, at times, as somber and tortured as that of Rimbaud: "Just as a man might walk all alone in the darkness, I resolved myself to move slowly along: to use so much circumspection in all things that, would I hardly advance at all, at least I would be ever so careful not to fall."[15] The slow step of this man, "alone and in the darkness," foreshadows something dreadful and agonizing, something that announces the "harsh night" of the Farewell, where the poet knows himself to be alone ("Not one friendly hand!"). For the first Modern, it bears witness to the utter giving way of the ground, and with it, the community of mortals. Nevertheless, this step in the dark remains guided by a fundamental certitude—that of the *ego cogito*. And yet, it is a black light that does not come from the world—that reveals this world of shadows: "Seeing that I was able to pretend I had no body and that there was no world and no place I could be," wrote Descartes. It was precisely this work of *fiction* that was decisive for the determination of that which would be called modern *reality* or the lack of reality. From that moment on (after Descartes), the poet was only able to repeat: "The true life is absent. We are not in the world." He may have repeated it, but in so doing, he pushed the discourse on method to its extreme: he refused its "circumspection" which, to him, did not seem to be *absolutely* modern—enough. Likewise, when Nietzsche later criticized Descartes, it would be to show himself more modern (Cartesian) than Descartes himself. Method would then become "the perspective with the most value."

❁ ❁ ❁

The search for antecedents (historical, Greek or Christian) is in no way exclusive to modernity. Once again, Rimbaud is an exemplary case. In fact, the *Season* opens up with such a search: "If only I had some antecedent, at any point whatsoever in the history of France! But no, nothing." To be sure, this search has nothing to do with that one which drove Marguerite Yourcenar to turn toward her *real* ancestors. No, Rimbaud felt himself to be so radically uprooted—so modern—that he had to *invent* a genealogy for himself. Subsequently, we find the famous Gallic ancestors that gave him their "bluish-white eyes, narrow-mindedness, and a certain clumsiness in a scuffle." (And yet, for all that, we see nothing of the "butter-colored head of hair.") It was an imaginary lineage—unfulfilled like an unconsummated marriage. "I remember the history of France: the oldest daughter of the Church. I would have traveled throughout the Holy Land; I have in mind . . ." This was a time when Rimbaud had just graduated from the college of Charleville—and when history books had something of a legendary air (for example, they included the lives of the saints). In other words, Rimbaud's remembrance had nothing scientific or critical about it; rather, it was much more of a projection. His narrative begins, significantly enough, in the conditional tense only to continue in the present; not a "historical" present, but an absolute present—without reference. "I remember only as far back as this earthly land and Christianity. And I shall never stop seeing myself in this past. But always alone; without family; even, what language did I speak? I never see myself within the councils of Christ; or within the councils of those lords—representatives of the Lord."[16]

It is this that radically distinguishes Rimbaud from Nietzsche—although in spirit they remain rather close. Nietzsche looked beyond "this earthly land and Christianity;" he looked toward the Greeks and saw the mask of Dionysus. Rimbaud always felt himself to be alone and without an equal, and even without a language ("I no longer know how to speak"). Behind him there was nothing—nothing but a "horrible underbrush" as he would write in the "*Adieu.*" And consequently, there was nothing before him but the unknown; the desert. Nothing behind, nothing before; nothing remained but "now." But "now I'm cursed; I abhor the fatherland."

The fatherland, what could it have been now that it was abhorred, now that it inspired horror? A Hell. Hell, "night of Hell," "harsh night": for such was the alloted allotment. At the same time, the poetic work would struggle against such an obfuscation only to better appropriate it. We must be absolutely modern. We must want the exacting want of the present to dwell within it. This assumption is not a pure resignation, but a *farewell*—a salutation. It assumes the *caesura*, just as we must—as what is necessary. In effect, it is the caesura itself, the "historic night" that bids farewell. And in this bidding, it would liberate itself as a *poetic* farewell.

In other words, the poetic work, in separating itself from the word, would also give itself over—to the word. In this separation, the whole of tradition would move off *and* be moved. The ambiguity here is that of an absolutely modern self-deliverance, which is also that of European nihilism. "The poets found that which remains," wrote Hölderlin ("*Andenken*"). But heritage itself, how can it be founded or established if it does not remain? If it simply slips away? If the poet, who is supposed to establish the human dwelling place on this land, here and *now*, is himself forbidden such a dwelling place? Nevertheless, the poet retains an ultimate resource: he can show (say) the dwelling place that is forbidden. That is, show the dwelling place itself as forbidden. In the forbidding, there flutters a bidding. The peculiarity of Rimbaud's poetic word follows this bidding, while, at the same time, forbidding itself to be poetic. This forbidding-bidding would disclose the re-treat of the poetic word as granted to the retreat of the dwelling place itself. In this way, it remains "rhythm" or the very rapport that would support and sustain humankind.

Recognizing no other authority than the "spirit"—"He [the spirit] wants me to be Occidental"—the poet is doomed to the *impossible*: that which would bid his word come forth and which would forbid his dwelling place. But only if the forseeing eye of the poet is such that it sees the dwelling place as only the "Occidental mire" of a "people inspired by fever; by cancer."[17] Yet, even in this impossibility to dwell, in this eternal return of the "same desert, to the same night," the poet must also see the possibility—utopian, promised and refused all at the same time—of a new day, of a *Morning*: "From the same desert, to the same night, always, my weary eyes wake to the silver star; and the royal ones of life do not move: the three magi: the heart, the soul, the spirit. When will we go beyond the mountains, beyond the shores, to greet the birth of new work, of new wisdom, the end of superstition, to adore—the first ones!—Christmas on this earth!"[18]

A Season in Hell begins in the past tense, "Formerly, if I remember right, my life was a festival . . ." and it ends in the future, "I shall be free to *possess truth in both a body and a soul.*" The narrative hardly progresses in a continuity, but rather breaks apart in fragments, each of which constitutes a *caesura* wherein time is overturned. Each (especially starting with "*Délires II*") is the repetition of a tragic experience: "Hell" or the night that wants any present. The want of any present—which determines the present of the poetic word—carries, each time, the sign of the caesura. The time of old, the Golden Age or imaginary Eden is dismissed, for it has been recognized as a chimera; as "poetic refuse." "*This has come to pass*" would end "*Délires II.*" But it is able to be sent away only as long as its initiatory power has been deferred to a future: a future that has been marked with the want of any present—the "harsh night"—and that, in a sense, has itself been *recalled*. It would always return toward the now (of the forbidden dwelling place) from a future crossed out as a future anterior or from a past already dismissed—such that this present remains that of the rupture of time. And thus, in this way, it would return to nothing. Perhaps even, this return is exiled as the impossible and forbidden. In the guise of a present, *the desert remains*.

The caesura not only determines the moment at which this begins, but it also establishes this moment as irreversible, decisive, and absolute. And this moment is itself nothing *other* (not another present); nothing but the awakening to "truth"—to a pure destitution—brought about by the renunciation of those "pernicious instincts" of return. Of a return to a blessed and "unforgettable" epoch that was once wholly present. It is a paradoxical truth, emptied of all positive content: it is a deliverance, a liberation (with respect to every loss, and hence, to the will to return), but also, a deliverance that delivers nothing other than *the moment of deliverance*. We must be absolutely modern; we must be absolutely—delivered.

Notes

1. Walter Benjamin, *Charles Baudelaire: A Lyrical Poet in the Era of High Capitalism.*

2. Roland Barthes, *The Pleasure of the Text*, p. 42.

3. Mallarmé, "*Le vierge, le vivace et le bel aujourd'hui,*" *OC*, p. 67. This poem has been translated by Roger Fry as "This virgin, beautiful and lively today," in *Poems*, p. 103.

4. Barthes, *The Pleasure of the Text*, p. 40.

5. Arthur Rimbaud, "*A une raison,*" *Oeuvres complètes*, p. 130.

6. It should be noted that the "origin" of the words *critic*, *crisis* and *criterion* hail from the Greek word *krinein*, meaning "to sieve, to sift through or analyze by separating the 'good' from the 'bad.' "

7. Benjamin, citing Baudelaire, "Le peintre de la vie moderne" (*Oeuvres complètes*, vol. 2. [Paris: Gallimard, 1976], p. 695). In this text, after justifying himself for his invention of the word, Baudelaire writes that "modernity" is only the first "half" of art, "the transitory, the fleeting, the contingent," whereas the second half is "the eternal and the immutable." Thus, it can be said that Baudelaire is only "half-modern," that is, in the logic of "absolute" modernity, not at all modern.

8. This text was published for the French translation of Pindar's *Olympics* in the *Revue de poésie* (no. 40, 1971, p. 101). The fragment, taken from Archilocus, is also quoted by Heidegger in a text dedicated to Rimbaud and translated in the following way: "Learn, yet, what kind of relationship bears man." See *Cahiers de l'Herne*, "Heidegger," p. 110.

Heidegger interprets this "in advance" as deliberately nontemporal; that is, as an almost ontological "precedent" of order. This is quite possible. For Rimbaud hardly worried about being at the avant-garde of "progress" and even disclosed his project: "At bottom, there will always be, if ever so little, some Greek poetry." But the suspicion of the philosopher with regard to any modern "fact" lead him to commit a rather radical disjunction that was absolutely foreign to the thought of Rimbaud. "The word of the poet to come—will it be built by buttressing itself against the Rapport (that bears men; the *ruthmos*), thus preparing for man the new dwelling place upon the earth? Or will the destruction of language by linguistics and computer science undermine not only the precedence of poetry, but also, poetry itself in all its possibilities?" For Heidegger, the "*new* dwelling place upon the earth" cannot be modern because modernity is negatively determined by the nihilism of *technology.*

9. Baudelaire, Preface to *Le Spleen de Paris*, *Oeuvres complètes* vol. I, p. 275–76.

10. Jean Clair, *Considérations sur l'état des Beaux Arts*, p. 28. Jean Clair cites the text by Paz entitled, "*Point de convergence. Du romantisme à l'avant-garde*" (1976).

11. Rimbaud, "*Matinée d'ivresse*," *OC*, p. 130.

12. Martin Heidegger, *Gesamtausgabe 53, Hölderlins Hymne "Der Ister,"* p. 76.

15. René Descartes, *Règles pour la direction de l'esprit*, p. 24.

14. Arthur Rimbaud, "*L'Impossible,*" *A Season in Hell and the Drunken Boat*, p. 73.

15. Descartes, *Discours de la Méthode* II, in *Oeuvres et Lettres*, p. 136.

16. Rimbaud, "*Mauvais Sang*," *OC*, p. 95.

17. "It is not that I believe the light altered, the form exhausted, the movement digressive," Rimbaud added in "*L'Impossible*." In his description of the "West's decline," he never gave a common, symmetrical, and complementary place to the belief in progress, as Benjamin thought. "The concept of progress must be based upon the idea of catastrophe." (*Baudelaire*, p. 242). There is, for Rimbaud, an urgency to liberate modernity from those poisons that it would itself secrete—unknowningly. Urgency to be *absolutely* modern.

18. Rimbaud, "*Matin*," *OC*, p. 115.

3

Farewell to Seasons

Every great modern poet has appeared at a historical and critical moment of utter *collapse*—of everything. For such a poet, poetry itself has become critical—has entered into a "crisis" according to Mallarmé—whereas everything else has contracted to an exercise in style, or worse, a profession. At stake—for every great modern poet—has been anything but a game—anything but the play or innocent occupation to which Hölderlin referred in a letter to his mother. The stake at stake has been more than the eternal question of life or death: for, what the great modern poet has sought has far surpassed the personal and subjective aspect of his or her existence. Indeed, the poet has dared to pierce and penetrate the very question of the human being as such: as one who dwells poetically upon this earth and for whom all poetic dwelling is forbidden.

"There is no Present." "We are not in the world": whether articulated by Mallarmé or Rimbaud, such forbiddance (the Greek *mè*), is always the first—and last—word. However, each poet responded differently to this forbiddance. Although Mallarmé absented from the world in a way that amounted to little less than suicide or to an unbearable solitude, Rimbaud bid farewell to the one power that was able to reinvent the true but absent life: farewell to the poetic bidding that, for him, signified a sort of suicide as well, or burial in an inept existence existing deep within a desert that was only too real.

And Mallarmé, too, bid his farewell. Not to poetry; even though he knew the all-embracing Book was impossible. No, he bid farewell to the world. "A poet only ought to be a poet on this earth, and I . . .

I am a corpse, a mere portion of my life" or so he wrote at the age of twenty-three. Mallarmé knew that by renouncing the world, he would also entomb himself as a poet. (Of course, he may have had the satisfaction of having engraved his own gravestone.) Still, Mallarmé's renunciation seemed to sanction the irreconcilable space between the only word capable of "endowing our dwelling with authenticity" and this dwelling itself, kept in abeyance and abandoned to its own inanity—its own un-holiness.

Rimbaud, too, knew that he, in renouncing his one "spiritual task," would sink deep into a desert: first Aden, and then Harrar, and finally, the desert of his pathetic return to a fatherland that disgusted him. And this disgust, mingled with his own sickness and sorrow—the amputation of his leg—pushed him always to depart again. From a somber and solitary hospital bed, Rimbaud, on the day before his death, dictated last words to his sister. It was a dictation that bore witness to an *insane* stubbornness on the part of a poet (or ex-poet) who had assimilated, utterly, the language of the calculating and ratiocinative merchant:

> To the Director:
>
> I have come to inquire if I have left anything on account with you. I wish today to change over to another transport line, to leave this one whose name I do not even know, but in any case I must get passage from Aphinar. All these transport lines run everywhere, and I am helpless and unhappy and I can find nothing, any dog in the street can tell you that.
>
> Please let me know the cost of passage from Aphinar to Suez. I am completely paralyzed, and so I am anxious to be on board early. Please tell me at what time I must be carried on board.[11]

In fact, he was taken on board early the next morning. However, on the hospital registration form (the company whose name he forgot), Rimbaud described his occupation as that of a "businessman" rather than that of a "poet" or "man of letters." (He would have abhorred these latter titles.) Of course, this was entirely consistant with a poetic condition that had been rendered impossible. Nevertheless, Rimbaud was a unique example of someone who was a poet *in spite of* himself. (I would point out that such absolute singularity has since become commonplace.) In spite of himself—though later he would renounce the insufferable "identity" that he had sought at the age of seventeen, and which he would continue to repudiate for the rest of his life. In effect, after his repudiation of poetry, it took many years before he became *somebody*: a certain Monsieur Rimbaud, businessman "extraordinaire" from Harrar and Aden. For *us*, Rimbaud was he who authored *A Saison in Hell.* Yet, for *him*, Rimbaud came into his "own" only by absenting from writing, or rather, by writing nothing more than "objective" and descriptive reports.[2] Suddenly he became *somebody*: someone who had attained a prominent position and stable identity; someone who was, perhaps, the opposite of a poet who (as Celan might have said) *is* nobody. But the poet is "nobody" insofar as he is unable to identify with anybody or any state. Indeed, he cannot even identify with a determined "I"—for "I *is an other.*"

It may be that we shall never know who Rimbaud really was: whether businessman or poet, somebody or nobody. For, the Rimbaud who bid farewell to poetry was far different from the Rimbaud who bid for various commodities; different, also, from the Seer who saw the *Illuminations*. In the last analysis, whoever he ever was, he was always an other. And yet, precisely on account of "him" we are no longer able to know ourselves. In reading Rimbaud, the modern reader risks his or her own identity insofar as one identifies, utterly, with this Other (this *Stranger* with whom Trakl identified). But the modern reader must also beware that such identification is always underhanded; that is, always constitutes a sort of foul play. Thus, the poetic word calls into crisis one's identity (especially the identity of the "person") at the very point of *alienation*.

Notwithstanding, we must not assume that the ensuing identity crisis has deprived the referent "Arthur Rimbaud" of all essential signification. Poetic "alienation" cannot be reduced to an impersonality or parenthetical reduction of the poet's *existence*. It is hardly insignificant that *A Season in Hell* seems, in many respects, to be an "autobiography." (I would point out that we must modify this latter term with the word *poetic*, if only because we can never identify who the "I" is that speaks.) Likewise, several of Trakl's texts, (such as "Revelation and Decline") would seem to be "disguised" autobiographies. On the other hand, as Heidegger pointed out: "Who the author is [of the poem "Winter evening"] remains unimportant here, as with every other masterful poem. The mastery consists precisely in this, that the poem can deny the poet's person and name."[3] Can we not make the same claim for Rimbaud? Did he not disclaim himself as "author" in a way that was so radical and irreversible that, to this day, no one has yet surpassed him? So it is with Mallarmé, who, on May 14, 1867, wrote to his friend Henri Cazalis: "I write to inform you that I am become impersonal; and that I am no longer the Stéphane you once knew.

Rather, I am really an aptitude through which the Universe shall see and develop itself." Perhaps too we should mention Trakl, who, three years before his death, wrote to his friend Buschbeck: "Here is the reworked poem. It is much better than the initial version because it is impersonal and at the very point of breaking into movements and visions."

During his "poetic" period, Rimbaud incessantly inveighed against that which he called "subjective poetry." I is an other: an other that is other than the intensified "somebody" or person that is comparable to the Romantic "genius." "If those old fools who claimed to be authors had found more in the Ego than the false signification, we wouldn't have to sweep up all these old bones and skeletons, which, for an infinite period of time, have accumulated the refuse of their one-eyed intelligence."[4] In effect, we have seen a dearth of "functionaries and writers," but "the author, the creator, the poet—this man has never existed!" For "man has not shaped himself; he is not yet awake; or at least not in the fullness of the great dream." Is this mysticism? Perhaps. But then, what could such mysticism mean? Is Nietzsche's philosophy mystical simply because it refuses to abide by the limits of subjectivity? Mystical?—even when subjectivity itself is somewhat deceptive? And what of Freudian thought? Is it not mystical inasmuch as it discerns, in every work of art, a subject that is itself subjected to an unconsciousness of which "I" am not the master? How (unless we voluntarily blind ourselves), can we not see that the traditional "subject" of a happy-go-lucky Humanism is everywhere tattered and torn and shaken and falling to pieces? Indeed, we experience this latter only insofar as we are *absolutely* modern.

But a broken down, beaten up, and battered subject hardly means that it is nothing. Rather, simply, that it has lost its lawsuit that sues for presence. Perhaps now we can understand Heidegger's distrust of biographical information and his contempt for anything founded upon the well-known mechanisms of modern psychology; that is, anything based on "lived experiences." For, such explanations—which explain everything in terms of "personal history" (including, even, a "stylistic" study of the work of art)—are not only too simple but also too simplistic. Subsequently, the "work" is transformed into a superstructure without life—into a lifeless letter. At the very least, we must needs envisage, not so much the "work," but the poem as word (which both sends and receives), as word that constitutes the only possible *existence* of the poet—word that is the poet's *dwelling life* according to Hölderlin. But we do this on one condition: that we do not yield to the (philosophical) temptation of essence that leads, immediately, to empty and abstract generalities. Can we, as did Heidegger, speak of a *Sister in general*? Which is to say, of a sort of mythical figure similar to the figures of Elis or Sebastian in Trakl's poetry? Can we leave unsaid the unique and singular feature of *this* sister (Trakl's) who, not only physically resembled him (they could have passed for twins), but who also resembled him spiritually, inspiring, as it were, the hymn, "from an imperious need"? Furthermore, can we leave unsaid the question of incest? Whether or not such a relationship "actually" did exist is unimportant; for there it looms in all of Trakl's poetry. From the very first poems (particularly the poem entitled "Fault of Blood") to the final evocation of the Sister, who, with a haunting voice, drove the poet to suicide. And, should we not find it strange that Trakl's family destroyed all of his letters addressed to Gretl?[5]

Not only did Heidegger leave untouched the troublesome problem of sexuality in poetry, he also refused to consider the *material* conditions under which these poems (regardless of their impersonality) were composed. Hölderlin, in his "madness"—his night—literally wrote on anything. Zimmer once noted that "he [Hölderlin] writes as soon as he has something to write, whether on a piece of paper or scrap of wood." In a sense, the poet became poem—and nothing other. And Trakl—if and when he wrote on paper, and if and when he took the time to recopy his poems in a faultless calligraphy—wrote in a *state*, which was usually that of absolute debauchery. The Austrian poet, in writing to a friend, wrote that: "The day before yesterday, I drank ten (yes, that's right, ten) quarts of red wine. And then at four o'clock in the morning, I took a moon-bath and a bath of frost on my balcony. Later, for the final touch, I wrote a splendid poem that shuddered with frost." Simply to drink two and a half gallons of wine and then to take a moon-bath and bath of frost may not be sufficient to write a successful poem. However, we must admit that this is not without importance and that the experience necessarily enters into the "success" of "Trakl's" poem. For the moon and frost really do bathe the poem in moonbeams and an icy *aura*—both of which constitute the singularity of that poetic voice, recognized by the words "Georg Trakl." Moreover, the wine runs not only through the body of the poet who wrote such a "splendid poem," but also through the poem itself. Notwithstanding, we must not assume that we are necessarily engaged in metaphor. But if we are, then it is a *meta-phora*; here understood as an ecstatic transport or "metamorphosis" (*Verwandlung*).

Perhaps the wine is a god. Perhaps even The God? When I speak of a "state," I hardly mean the state of a purely subjective soul. In fact, Trakl wrote precisely when he was outside and beside himself—

dispossessed of Georg Trakl—and by this dispossession possessed. He never intended to produce a "text," no matter how worked over and poetic it may have been. Nor did Trakl aim at an effect. Yet, if we must speak of the soul, if we must say that it is a stranger or wanderer waiting for a place of its own, then it is because we are unable to grasp it; because it is it that holds the power. Hitherto, the mistake (inscribed by Plato in synchronicity with the stake), has been to believe that the soul is something that belongs to "me": that there is something that we can call *my* soul. But the soul—like wine—belongs to everybody and nobody. It renders itself only to those who abandon themselves to it and to those who take leave of themselves. Such was the lesson of the Mystics. In this fashion, to allow oneself to be carried away; and then, to allow oneself to be carried back in an ecstatic de-privation, is to become the Other: it is to become Alienation. And Trakl, though he spoke madness, was not mad; for he knew the Madman was dead—and that God *had* died: God that had ravished and enraptured and wrested himself from himself. Nor did the poet bestow upon the human being a new identity—disclosing one, as it were, of one's old clothes, simply to reveal a new species. Our species—which inhabits a very old universe without God—always and necessarily arrives too late for gods and too soon for Being (which remains without birth). And identity becomes engulfed within itself: a profound nothingness without bottom.

But Trakl still speaks, only from this wounding word and lamentation, and from this stillborn death—without cradle, without home. He speaks and says nothing other than the death of his own poem. Not so much that one day he stopped believing in the alchemy of the Word or in the inchanting magic of the poem. Rather, one day the gold of God was transformed, of itself, into lead (by what we might call an alchemical inversion). And the white wings of angels sunk deep into the city's shitty mire. Fall that was in repetition of Lucifer's Fall; for Lucifer, the bearer of light, was the first fallen angel, the first absolutely modern god. "To the Spirit lend your flame, O ardent and heavy heart!" or so speaks the poem addressed "To Lucifer." This burning flame is no other than that of the "prodigious dying." It illuminates, with sable snow, the poet's night and already—ours.

❁ ❁ ❁

In the first drafts of *A Season in Hell* we find two sentences that seem rather categorical. The first reads, "I hate, now, those mystical fits of enthusiasm and those peculiarities of style." And the second, "Now I am able to say that art is nothing more than nonsense." From these, it would seem that we are well within our right to interpret the final piece of *A Season in Hell* as a definitive farewell to "art." In objection, one might point out that many of those poems found in *Illuminations* were written after those of *A Season in Hell* and, therefore, that the poet repealed his "decision." Notwithstanding, this objection would be made in vain. For the *Season* was the one book that Rimbaud wished to publish *at any cost.* Oddly enough, it was precisely then that he had no money to pay the printer; and then that he immediately lost interest in the lot alloted to his book; and then that he left it to rot in a cellar, where it was discovered some forty years later. (According to legend, Rimbaud supposedly burnt the manuscript in the fireplace at La Roche. However, whether it was lost or burnt matters little.) We, at all cost, must understand that for Rimbaud's young mind—after having passed a hellish time in London with Verlaine—"publishing" no longer carried the same significance as when he first went to Paris to make a name for himself as a poet's poet among the Parnassians. The *Season* is not a poem, nor is it a poem in prose. Indeed, at the moment of its inception, it had nothing in common with that which offered itself as poetry. Rimbaud, in a letter addressed to Ernest Delahaye (this letter, dating from May 1873, Laïtou (Roche), Canton of Attigny, was written sometime between the poet's two trips to London with Verlaine but before their dramatic and final separation), articulated his project or occupation. At first, it took on an almost inoffensive and "innocent" aspect that was quite similar to that contained in a letter Hölderlin wrote to his mother, wherein he presented poetry as the "most innocent occupation of all"; and this even when he would later write: "*Now* I fear that it is finally slipping away from me—much in the same way as it did from old Tantalus, who received more from the gods than he could digest." Thus, Rimbaud worked "regularly." He was, in fact, a relentless worker: methodical and capable of giving himself wholly over—for days and nights—to *any* work *whatsoever*. Provided, of course, that he had made up his mind to do so. It was in this way the he would learn a language, a skill, and so on: indeed, in London, he would spend hours and hours at the library. Here, we find nothing of that conventional image of the fanatical, scatterbrained, and disheveled "artist" that posterity so loves to contemplate—as if one is able to become a poet without working laboriously, as if one need not become one of those "horrible workers" referred to in the Letter "from the Seer." At what, then, was Rimbaud working? First, he minimalized his project: "I'm just writing some small stories in prose entitled: Pagan Book or Black Book. Really, it is innocent and silly." Except that the innocence of these stories was anything but innocent and inoffensive. Also in his letter, Rimbaud revealed his abhorrance for the "French countryside" and its "rustic innocince."[6] There is, he wrote, "Not one book. Not one bar nearby. And not the slightest activity in the street." We know that the *Season* begins precisely with this leitmotif: "I am disgusted by every occupation. Masters and workers—all of them peasants; all ignoble. A hand upon one's pen is worth no more than one upon one's plow." And yet, in the end—in the "*Adieu*"—the poet sees himself "handed over to the soil"; sees himself a "Peasant!" Textually written with this exclamation point as if to reveal the disgust he felt for such a degrading and servile condition—which was essentially that of domesticity: as one who remains attached to the *domus*, to the house or "soil."

Soon afterward, and without any transition, Rimbaud would admit: "My lot depends upon this book, for which I still must invent at least a half-dozen atrocious stories. But how, being here, could I invent such atrocities? Even then, I have already finished three of them—though I won't send you any as the *cost is too great*." Perhaps this "cost" must be taken literally, for Rimbaud, as usual, was penniless and living "here, in a hole." (His mother remained as "inflexible" as ever.) But the cost was 'spiritual' as well: "Spiritual combat is as brutal as those battles fought hand to hand" ("*Adieu*"). The *Season*—this "Black" Book written by a fanatic from the underground (in a way, ghostwritten) from the darkest corner of the "harsh night" away from all "honorable" work—would cost Rimbaud "so much" that we wonder whether he did not swear by it with his own hand. For, that which his hand had to work, had to plow with an invisible plow, was, in effect, harder than the most arid soil in the most desolate countryside. It was nothing less than the . . . *now*. *Now* I am able to say that art is a foolish act; *now* I hate those mystical fits of enthusiasm—but at what price? At the price of the now: of the present recognized as the new hour—severe in its toll—of this harsh night and of this want of any present in which "we must be absolutely modern." It was at this price that the Season came to pass.

"It has finally come to pass. Today I know how to address beauty." Today—what day? Could it have been a precise date, sometime between the months of April and August 1873? Or was it, rather, the "virginal, vivacious, and beauteous today" about which a fellow poet sang? Now names the very moment of the caesura. A moment that is also that of the upholding and handling "of the very minute of the awakening that gave me this vision of purity." This minute remains unmeasurable by our hourglass. It cannot ascribe to any historical document that would afford it with a foundation of facts itself founded on a computation of exact time. On the other hand, this now constitutes the "very severe" hour of farewell. But there is farewell—and then, farewell. Even though we have no proof that Rimbaud never rescinded his farewell to poetry—a decision that was so definitive that he never felt the need to explain it—we must still *think* the character of such a farewell. In other words, we must think this farewell without those facts on which biography and criticism constantly cling in desperation; and without that "mysterious" date when Rimbaud (according to Mallarmé), performed his operation on poetry—which was "the equivalent of not being"; of committing spiritual suicide. Indeed, it would seem this farewell was required or dictated by the severity of the Season and by the urgency of the thing itself: that is, by the epoch such as the want of any Present would *dictate* it.

To seize the moment of the caesura—which is repeated throughout the *Season*—we must take a seasoned look at that place where it would inscribe itself: at those "atrocious stories" that cost him (whose fate was at stake) so much—even more than his life. Above all, we must look at the title itself, *A Season in Hell.* Does *Season* simply signify a particular time of the year? For here we might ask, what year? The year in which it was composed, 1873? How is it then that the final piece (the "*Adieu*" that gives the very texture and tone of the whole of "the" *Season*), evokes a sense of Autumn? And this, when the text was written and dated by Rimbaud himself sometime between April and August 1873? And how is it that almost all of the "atrocious" stories take place cloaked in darkest night? With the exception, of course, of those last stories, which elicit a sense of "morning" and "dawn"—but only by recalling them from afar.

But the word itself—*Season*—has something strange about it. Especially because Rimbaud often uses it in the plural: "O Seasons, O Châteaux!" ("*Délires II*") And even in the "*Adieu*" itself: "far from those people who die over the seasons." Is this simply the "poetic" pluralization according to a tradition that dates from as far back as Virgil and Hesiod? Notwithstanding, the following poem from *Illuminations* entitled "*Barbare*" begins thus: "Well after the days and seasons." And then, "reconciled to the old fanfare of heroism . . . far from the ancient assassins." I have already commented on Rimbaud's famous "*Matinée d'ivresse*": "The time of assassins has come." And, in so doing, have linked it, with a formal chain, to a famous formulation by Nietzsche: "God is dead." Here prudence is in order, if only on account of the very specific and presumed sense of the word *assassins* in Rimbaud. To be sure, the word itself descends from the Arabic *haschichins*. In his *Rimbaud*, Yves Bonnefoy notes: "What is so surprising about the fact that Rimbaud was familiar with the etymology proposed by Sylvestre de Sacy? All he had to do was read *Paradis Artificiels* ("The Poem of Haschich," chap. 2), which we know he did. Moreover, as soon as the hypothesis of this drug has been formulated, the entire poem becomes clear."[7] In effect, everything becomes clear, but this clarity contains something that is much too obvious—indeed, blinding. Obviously, Rimbaud had never read Nietzsche, but he did read Beaudelaire. This is indisputably exact. However, inasmuch as we are involved with a poetry that is so absolutely *new*, can we still proceed with the same old critical machinery that catalogues "literary influences"? If somehow the word that speaks the time of assassins contains something poetic, it is precisely because it erases (or leaves unsaid) the possible etymology of the word—which the average reader cannot immediately decipher and which one does not even consider as the very "key" that opens up and illuminates the entire poem. Only the poet has the key to "this savage dis-play." At the same time, he never uses it—if only because he has no need of it. I hardly wish to offend Yves Bonnefoy—himself a poet—by raising up against him the word of another poet; namely, René Char: "The observations and the commentaries [we make] about a poem are sometimes singular, profound, brilliant or verisimilar, but they are unable to avoid the reduction to a single signification or project a phenomenon which has no other reason than *to be*." The poetic is never a brute fact. It is not like a rose that "blooms because it blooms," even though it tries to imitate the rose's want of any "reason." As Hölderlin once remarked in a *poem*, there is always a need for interpreters: poetry demands it; at least as long as it itself is born under the mantic sign of interpretation. Formerly, was not the poet the spokesman of the gods? Speaking the divine word that spoke by "signs" and not with words: it was this sort of intermediary that Hölderlin called a *demi-god*, and which we might call an *interpreter*. Except, now that the gods have become phantoms—only traces of traces—we wonder what has become of the poetic *vocation*? Ought it inhabit that place which has been vacated? Or, on the contrary, ought it *leave* that place vacated that it might disclose it as such? It is between these two alternatives—from one pole to the other, and sometimes simultaneously—that the de-cisive movement of the *Season* dangerously alternates. The first possibility mentioned would nevertheless be returned to its excessiveness: a Clairvoyance (and this, *for example*, by the effects of hashish) quite incapable of keeping the place and of holding it within the confines of a now. Hence, in a sense, the assassins are the *haschichins*, but always the *ancient* assassins. Inasmuch as they dare inhabit the vacated place, they precipitate the fall—and assassinate God. For Baudelaire, as well as for Rimbaud, hashish was a *religion* and not a "drug." Even in the radical a-theism that constitutes our absolutely modern way of Being, everything is determined from a fundamentally religious view point.

Confession: I am not so sure these "explanations" clarify, definitively, the meaning of the word *assassins*. To tell the truth, they most certainly do not. For, at the very heart of such clarity, there remains—like the gray ash of the hearth—an obscurity that can never be revealed except by destroying the poetic fire. In the *Season*, if we listen carefully, we can hear the faint echo of the "time of assassins." But this echo is still clarifying inasmuch as it is an echo of God; of His absence and of the way that accedes to His vacant place of which the Season calls into question—or seasons. For, is not a season that which returns cyclically? The eternal return of that which, in order to be the same, is nevertheless never the same? A return that would inscribe itself in the text and that inscribes itself with that much more intensity as it nears its final crisis: the de-cision or moment of the caesura? Indeed, now the Season has come to pass and, yet, never ceases to return. Like a thundercloud that turns ever and ever about without ever exploding or that explodes only in the end—but at an end that refers only to a beginning. Does not the first piece not speak of that moment when the poet is on the very point of rendering his soul in one "last scream"?

What, then, is this time? Quite simply, it is the time of *season*. *Season* is a word that most likely comes from the Latin word *satio*, meaning "sowing time." There is a particular time of year—and of History—when seeds are sown and another when the harvest is harvested. But the season is something that takes place in Hell; its cyclicality is infernal. And yet, there is no season in Hell. Rather, and more exactly, it is the season of the nonseason; of the harvest of that which cannot be harvested: the *Abyss*. "Here" there is nothing that is in season; there is no "day or work." It is, for the earth, a time of rest; a return back to itself in all its profound profundity: becoming once again the Enclosed, the Occluded, the Impenetrable.

Thus, Hell would not only assign the psychic, social, and affective situation of Arthur Rimbaud at a particular season or epoch in his life (an epoch in which he would take leave of himself), but also it would name (without speaking it) that which is seasonal for everyone and everything; the epoch as such; the one in which we might proclaim: "There is no Present." The one in which "the true life is absent," and so on. At the same time, during this time itself, the night of the season out of season remains near the dawning of another day. Near the crack of dawn, when the sun rises within this end or within the confines of the world; and with it rises and raises the possibility that something else may soon arise, *finally*, in the profound night of Hell. Finally, in the farewell to Hell, Morning comes: "Nevertheless, *today*, I believe I have ended the recitation of my hell. It truly was hell; the Ancient one whose gates the Son of Man opened" ("*Matin*"). The poet's hell—*my* hell—must not be confused with the Hell of Christianity. According to the *New Testament*, the "Son of Man"—Christ—opened up the gates of the "ancient" hell through his ressurection. That is, he opened up the Greek hell: that dark kingdom intersected by the river of Oblivion and forever separated from the only existing world—the earthly. Separated because here it is a question of Hades: the invisible (*a-eidos*) and the want of any present—if, in fact, *eidos* names the existing presence. Yet, how is it that the poet could remain in such a Hell, when he knew himself to be the "slave of his own baptism"? This is one of those mysteries brought about by the strange situation of a being for whom contradiction had become the essence or diction itself. For, if this "hell is unable to attack the pagans"—by this we must understand the Christian Hell, the Gehenna—then from whence arises our present pain? The first of these "atrocious stories" undertakes to unravel the mystery of *origins*—but finds nothing more than the initial barbarism. "I have never belonged to this people. I have never been a Christian; I am descended from that race that sang in its pain. I do not understand the laws; I do not have the moral sense; I am a brute . . ." A brute, a "black." A peasant or *paganus*: pagan. Black Book or Pagan Book? If Rimbaud experienced a particular attraction for the dark continent—where, in fact, he spent the latter part of his existence as an adventurer and merchant—then it is quite possible that Africa appeared before his eyes, wearied as they were of Europe, that "continent ridden with madness," as the very place "bereft of your light"; that is, the supernatural light of divine Grace and the "natural" light of reason. At the same time, Rimbaud saw that, in reality, there were only blacks. Even if they were white. Especially whites who thought themselves sacred and saved—they too were black. But they were fake blacks: the merchant and the magistrate, the general and the emperor—all of these figures were the product of a calculating, evaluating, commanding and reigning reason. For the "inferior" race—with which the poet is the first to ally himself—has invaded the entire world. This race *is* everybody. And thus, any attempt to escape its hold on us would be in vain: "The inferior race has covered everything—the 'people' as one says, the nation, science and reason." The people "as one says" said here with condescension—just as *one* says "the people," as if this *one* was not of "the people." This "one" that always excludes itself from the common lot; perhaps, because it is unable to share or even because there is nothing to share for "*want of any whole*."

"Peasant!" In the end the word returns. The exclamation of it expresses all the disappointment of a poet reduced to that which he abhorred the most. Yet, it was precisely this abhorrance of the "fatherland"—not only as a nation, but also as that which puts forth from its own soil—that constituted the night of hell. Having been "handed over to the land," "with an obligation to seek and embrace a rough reality," the poet was only able to experience the harshness of the fall. In effect, he experienced it to the extent of his past fascination and enthusiasm for the Clairvoyance. Nevertheless, in this fall, not everything has been said; or ended. On the contrary, a song and even an existence has opened up. Such that the poem "*Génie*"—a poem of farewell as well—would speak in the name of the "world": "O world! And the sweet song of new misfortunes!" New misfortunes as opposed to those old and ancient misfortunes that were brought by the Clairvoyance; by those "poetic hand-me-downs" in which Good Fortune became a "fatality," a "remorse," a "worm." The Clairvoyance or Alchemy of the Word was an attempt—non compos mentis—to establish a Present simply with the magic of poetry. Yet, does this poetry still bequeath a rhythm to action? No matter!—"Action is not life"—and poetry shall be well "in advance." But this dream is the "Impossible" itself. Such is the sense of the farewell—of the sudden change—that is played out thoughout the Season as its caesura. The severity of the new hour that follows is hardly a pure and simple abandonment or poltroonish renunciation. The truth—the true life that is "absent"—is always the principal question of the day, and now more than ever. Yet, this turnabout is brought about and realized *as* resistance to the "pernicious" instincts of return. As an almost heroic acceptance of the want of any Present: want that is recognized as central and unfulfillable. To be handed over to the land is no way to be handed over to nothing. It is both a disaster (a "rendering misfortune") and a recovery or, rather, a liberation (for "free must be this misfortune")."*No canticle: preserve the step we've won! Harsh night!*"

For the Greeks, poetry was the canticle: singing to the glory of the Present. Poetry gave action its rhythm; that is, carried it into the unique presence of the word and then rescued it—action—from oblivion, from hell (Hades). Thus, the Present is not without the presence of this word that speaks it; or at least, the Present cannot be brought about or fulfilled if it has not been handed over or ex-posed. The very name of *poiesis* suffices to ensure its coming into Being. Yet, how can there be a song precisely when there is nothing more to sing?

Or perhaps, *now*, poetry ought to restrict itself to itself; that is, to an *action restricted* to the solitude of the pure word. But then, how could such a restriction accomodate the openhandedness of poetry and its power to hand over a present? Moreover, does not a pure word (with which nothing is really said except itself) sink, merely, into the high-sounding inanity of something paultry? How is poetry able to remain without submitting the common-lot to its own rhythm? How can poetry take part and therefore, in this way, *give*?

Well before everybody else, Rimbaud measured the hole that modern poetry had dug; and he recognized that this hole had pledged poetry to a certain vanity. The vanity of having created—or having believed to have created—with a "pure" language (indeed, one separated from the common world), a world apart: radiant, full—*present*. Mallarmé, for his part, hardly knew how to resist the "undeniable desire of our age" that wished to separate—with an eye toward the different attribution—the double state of both Being and the word: here vulgar, there essential. The poetic word, in seeking to purify itself of every vulgar excretion—of the"inferior race"—would also *exclude itself* from the common lot. Consequently, it sinks into an extreme vulgarity for "want of the whole of mankind" and the want of any poetic *presence*. Poetry, in purifying itself, digs a certain hole between an action without rhythm and a word without import. And then, poetry itself would suffer the consequences: by rendering itself absolute, it ends in the idiocracy that awaits every language shut up within itself; it becomes nearly autistic.

Certainly then, this farewell is a farewell to poetry as well. But also to those "poetic hand-me-downs" that encumber so many so-called modern poems: "those mystical fits of enthusiasms and peculiarities of style" that hope, in vain, to acquire supernatural (perhaps even "surreal") powers that they might bring into Being that which is not. But all this, it would seem, is nothing more than a sort of smoke screen; for want of being able to open our eyes to that which is. To that which is wanting: a Present.

Rimbaud would never say to what land he had been handed over or to what rough reality he had resolved himself to embrace. Maybe none of this was nameable or identifiable. To be sure, he abstained from a game that, for him, had become "moldy"—rotten even—since the ruination of the Greeks. At the same time, he was the first to espy the absolutely modern land as that desolation that never ceases to expand and spread out. And yet, among the ruins of demonstrations and proofs, he fired a salvo; the modern season had sown the abyss—and he finally harvested it. But to know if, from there, a sudden change would or would not take place—from this There which is nowhere and where everyone has to be in one's own way—was no longer of any concern to him. He—he has gone: departed. Perhaps he has always already departed—nothing but a constant departing.

We would ask whether or not a certain allotment has not opened itself up here? Where the abyss does not swallow up, but rather would carry forth the step? Would this, then, be the one step won? Step won; never won?[8] And always to re-placed? Will we have the necessary patience—then, it can be only now.

❂ ❂ ❂

If an upright mind were to make a "balance sheet of the situation," modern poetry would appear—on the whole—in the hole. At the very least, the situation would seem "serious." How can this be so? And to what is it due? Perhaps from the fact that the poet's voice—which is always singular and unique—has been smothered by other "numerous unpoetic" voices (Hölderlin). Even though the poet is hardly satisfied with living apart from everyday "economic horrors," protected, as it were, within his cocoon of words, and even though, on the contrary, he mortally exposes himself to historical existence even to the point of inscribing it for the first time (and each time as such), we must see—before all historical determination—to what extent modern poetry has smothered and strangled itself. Yet does this strangulation arise from the want of finding those words that might speak this first and foremost anguish: that of the vacancy of any allotment? Or is it *on account* of the utter speechlessness of modern poetry—though it hardly remains utterly mute before the un-endurability of the *epoch*?

Let us take—if it is possible to take and if we must not already be taken by—the case of Rimbaud. Here, though, Rimbaud is in no way an example that one might follow whatever the wishes of those who love to follow! Rather, let us take Rimbaud that we might learn in what "state" that poetry is which was the first to expressly want to be *absolutely modern*. Hence, we only are able to " follow its appearances—its inspirations—its body—its days."

Rimbaud? The very case of a failure on every level. The "work" he left behind is so little (but brilliant), that we hesitate to even speak of a corpus or work per se. It is hardly any secret that it was necessary to gather no small amount of ingenious devices and long-winded and inept commentaries to fabricate one volume for the *Pléiade's* collection. But most of all, he is the one case of a poet who—at an age when the rest of us still babble—had literally burned *everything*.

Let us ask, now, a few questions. This failure, does it come from Rimbaud—this man who played with fire? Or does it emanate from *us*—we readers, critics, and amateurs who are unable to measure the excessiveness found in such a destiny? If there is a failure, then it must, primarily be ours. Failure that stems from our radical unhandiness and mishandling and our obstinancy to establish a "balance sheet of the situation" instead of seeking to adapt ourselves to the dexterity and slight-of-hand of the poem. If there is a failure—and there is—then it is also on account of never having seized the chance or the sense: this failure of the work is not a simple fault or default. There is nothing negative about it—for a work is not a work unless it fails; unless it burns. Thus, it would testify (make a deposition) in favor of (and beckon to) that against which it breaks apart: the Opening itself, which can never be mastered. The work would de-pose (or testify) in the absolute sense of a self-deposition; of an original dispossession of all "identity." In the same way, the poet, in order to remain who he is—an inhabitant of the poetic calling—must renounce his self, even as an author; for nobody is the author of the Origin. Determinably the poet must be an other—*I is an other*—indeed, the Other: the de-parting Stranger.

One poem, "*Génie*," speaks this deposition as the first "illumination"—though it does so without ever articulating or displaying it. According to René Char, Rimbaud "describes himself as in no other poem." Upon a first reading, it is very much in this way that we read it: as a poet who ingeniously describes himself as the quintessential genius—who writes in *A Season in Hell*: "I! I who used to call myself seer or angel, exempt from all morality. . . . " Indeed, Rimbaud describes himself as the genius *in person*; as the creative subject who relates his "colossal life" with extravagant images and in an unheard-of language. Triumph of an exacerbated and absolute subjectivity . . .

Notwithstanding, is it only the "I" that is in question here?—that is, the poet, genius, "seer or angel" who "believed himself endowed with supernatural powers," and who has created "every festive occasion, every triumph, every tragic occurence?" Is it a question that begins with that of the divination of the self? The text "itself" never says I. From a strictly grammatical point of view, only two personal pronouns take the position of subject: *we* and *he*. Still, it is impossible to identify either of them clearly: for we know not who either *he* is (the Genius?) or who *we* (which does not name a single person) are. In other words, neither of the two can be reduced to an "I."

Surely, from a grammatical perspective (which implies both a logical and metaphysical one), *we*—inasmuch as *we* constitutes the first person plural—always includes an *I*. Yet in this case, the Genius—inasmuch as *he* contitutes the third person singular—cannot include the first person singular. Char would add that Rimbaud, after having described himself "as in no other poem . . . " would conclude by "granting *us* leave." "Like Nietzsche and Lautréamont, both of whom demanded everything from us, Rimbaud asks us to dismiss him." Even if Char has taken note of the most essential word of the entire poem ("to dismiss")—a word that gives its texture to not only this text but also that of the "Farewell"—he still speaks of Rimbaud in the third person. As if Rimbaud was the Genius and not a *part* of us—part of "we" precisely in-so-far as he is an "I." Which is to say, in-deed, "he" grants us leave, but it is not Rimbaud (the person) who grants himself leave—which would not only be absurd, but impossible. The Genius grants *us* leave, and thus, to the poet *as well.*

But *who, therefore, are we*? Do we even know? Surely we can always answer in the following way: that we . . . are we (and that he is he). This is a hell of a tautology! And it is all the more hellish when we interrogate it and discover there an abyss: we *our*-selves the same as we our-*selves*?[9] Have we a circle here? Yet, identity exists only in the a-part. We are not *ourselves*—as we are old or black, for being one self is hardly a simple attribute like weight or race or age. Quite simply, it is not an attribute attributable to a subject. And yet, it is the very essence of the subject, the very essence that determines the subject as such (equal to itself) and, consequently, the essence of which he "himself" is not the master. When we say "we ourselves," we already open a gulf . . . by which the Other—He—is fatally engulfed.

Between Him and us there is a relationship—perhaps even the Relationship. However, it is a relationship that cannot be *represented* phenomonologically from the "other" term: it is neither Him nor us, but a proximity—and therefore, an a-part—in which we are "predicamented"—"it is predicamental, he being . . . "—predicamental to be (that which we, ourselves, are). For no subject exists prior to the relationship; rather, the relationship renders possible the existence of a subject *such* as ourselves.

The difficulty in thinking this relationship comes from that which is anterior to all identity. Relationship that may be expressed as a presence *to* . . . , or as a staying or dwelling close to, and thus also, far from. According to Heraclitus (fragment 119): *ethos anthropô daimon.* Relationship (and hence the very existence of man), is articulated as an *ethos* that, in turn, articulates not only dwelling—but the character proper, the singularity and "genius." In a sense, this fragment from Heraclitus articulates a tautology—even the Tautology. "The genius proper is, for man (we ourselves), the Genius." Of course, the transcription is inadmissible since Genius—in the sense of *daimon* (the demon of Socrates, for example)—names, genuinely, the Other, the divine Being. But this only on condition that it—the Other—is not identified as such and such divinity, but as a divine being that is anterior to every god. We know that Heidegger translated the fragment as follows: "For man, the accustomed dwelling-place is that region open to the presence of god (the unaccustomed)." The tension of this fragment rests entirely upon the opposition between the habitual (*geheure*) "dwelling place" and the presence of the in-habitual (*Ungeheure*, or "monstrous"). This tension designates the "proper" of the human being or at least that which is most "monstrous"—if, that is, we remember those lines from the *Antigone* to which Heidegger returns again and again. Man lives properly only inasmuch as he ek-sists: inasmuch as he is uprooted in the radical sense of being turned away from every home and expropriated from all property. Such inhabiting "is" the inhabitual itself: the dwelling near to the Unknown.

In a way less violent, it is this the poem "*Génie*" would tell us. It never stops saying who he is, this Genius: insofar as he "has made the *open house*"—the open dwelling place—he is the affection and the present. And yet, the Genius is never identified: "he" remains unknown—and un-named. Or named only by his own unknown name—or proper name whose proper is that of disappropriation: "Genius," *daimon*. Why, then, does he remain without a name? Is it merely because the poet wishes to keep the name hidden, and so sustain some sort of "mystery"? A mystery produced only as a poetic exercise? Or rather, is it because the poet does not know the name—because *there is no name*? According to Hölderlin, "we are in want of sacred names . . . " But this want is one that cannot be satisfied; no, in fact, it complies with the very "nature" of the thing—or no-thing. "Is God unknown? / Is he manifest like the sky? I'd sooner / Believe the latter."[10] However, "unknown" and "manifest like the sky" are in no way antithetical; rather, they are the very way in which the unknown appears and dwells near to us.

The Unknown belongs not only to the not-yet-known (that shall be known with time . . . and the progress of "knowledge"). Nor is it simply the exterior limit of knowledge: "there," for example, where it ought to stop and make way for another attitude—namely, that of faith, according to Kant. "Not only" because the Unknown is the very dwelling place of existence—which is existence only insofar as it proceeds toward its own limit and only insofar as it *is* (inhabits) this limit and, thus, is always in transgression. To poetically inhabit this limit consists in sustaining and bearing the un-inhabitable, the unknown. Such bearing (*Haltung*) constitutes the one attitude that is properly human. The only one that is able to ob-serve, directly, the Unbearable (death), but also, the only one able to pre-serve the "pure god"—and thus his unbearable presence—without immediately dying.

More generally, poetic is the relationship to Being that pre-serves it as unknown and still bearable. This hardly signifies that elsewhere (within the realm of positive knowledge for example), Being is better known. No. Being is everywhere equally unknown. But this itself is hardly acknowledged. "To not know" is always presented as a simple ignorance: as if bearing the unknown were not the highest possible knowledge from which an existence draws sustenance.

The poem is not an eulogy to mystery, insofar as *mystery* is here equated with ignorance. Instead the poem dwells within this unique Mystery: that dwelling is possible only within this place where there is no "within." And this impossible possibility defines the very place of existence: being out of place. Once again we read Heidegger reading Hölderlin: "Even more obscure than obscurity is the most radiant clarity." That the Secret hides in broad daylight (and in the common dwelling place), is, itself, the secret. It is not a-part from the common-dwelling-place—dwelling not in the inhabitual or bizarre—but rather, is the very a-part of this dwelling place within which all inhabiting, under the unbearable, opens itself *to itself*. For nothing is able to bear up beneath: neither subject nor god. Upon its arrival to presence—Presence itself as a remaining near by or to—no name can be assigned. Instead, in a way, it would resign and depose. It is for this reason that we must still bring about that which is most unbearable: the dismissal to itself. It is this that the final farewell of the poem would disclose: "May we, this winter night—from cape to cape, from the blustering pole to the castle, from the whole to the beach, from look to look, our forces and emotions being exhausted—hail him, see him and send him on his way, and under the tides and from above the snow deserts, follow his appearances—his inspirations—his body, his day."

The "winter night" is that night of the world in which the world stops, stays, and dwells: the common dwelling-place, the night now come of season. That which the poem asks is that which is highest and hardest: "May we know how to hail him, to see him"—to hail, that is, to call. Such is the salutation: a call to come, but also to dismiss. To dismiss, but not in the sense of a pure and simple dismissal—as one might dismiss a class or chauffeur. For, to grant leave is also to liberate; to give someone *liberty*. To grant leave, to dismiss can be only *if* the mission itself has been received. And this mission or delivery, the present itself as well as the future, should be dismissed because it exceeds all possibility of reception, other than the deliverance of liberty. The gods die only when they stay among us, therefore we have to send them away—back to themselves—to free them from this human bond. In this double movement—that of the dismissal of the gods and the renunciation of the self as the one and only measure of presence—an *a-part* would de-sign itself. That is, a place would open up in which all dwelling-in-common (though without any "domain" or assigned territory) is possible, a place that sheds light. It is to inhabit, though not to occupy, a space: the more the place is free or vacant, the more it is inhabited, haunted. The Genius is nothing more than this haunting of the open place: this house rendered free.

In this way, the poem would dismiss us. Yet, in liberating us, it would also invite us to follow its appearances, its inspirations, its body, its day—and its dwelling place. The poem itself has become the unique dwelling place of the allotment. Allotment wherein we hear the call: "O Him and Us!": the very dwelling place of Being-in-the-world. "O world! and the sweet song of new misfortunes!" Thus the poet too would dismiss "himself." He is he who must liberate himself, depart from himself, and hence, accede to dwelling poetically. The Genius—hailed and dismissed—would then become [the] dwelling place—both loving time and time beloved. For "he is love, the reinvented and perfect measure, the marvelous and unforeseen reason."

The poet, the Genius is love inasmuch as he is like a lodestar (*aimant*). It is "he who loves us for his infinite life." Surely we can hear in Rimbaud's poem a faint echo of Christian theology. Though in the following sentence, the poet—who always fought against the theology of Redemption—leaves little ambiguity as to his religious sentiments: "He will not go away; he will not redescend from heaven; he will not bring about the redemption of the plight of women or of the high spirits of men or of Sin." Nevertheless, the love of God has something troubling about it inasmuch as it is without interest. In a way, it is the very gratuitousness of a gift given "for nothing." It is what theologians used to call *Grace*: "Grace" by which we must understand something other than Providence. Rather, we should hear the faint accent of the Greek *charis* (for example, Sophocles's "Benevolence [*charis*] calls benevolence"). Or we should hear that which Hölderlin called *pure friendship*, whereby disinterestedness is the very figure of the Sacred—or the "living" relationship. However, this should not be understood in terms of a disinterested love—if such a love were to exist, it would merely mask a profound indifference, a deep disinterest. On the contrary, there is something selfish in the Genius' love—"Selfish affection and passion for him"—something, at least, that re-calls a passionate love. He (the Genius) is the very Interest itself of an *inter-esse*: a double genitive, "we have all experienced the terror of his concession and ours"; an allotment or double con-cession that calls to the discession (with the "self") and which would thus provoke the "terror."

At this level of intensity (of *Innigkeit* according to Hölderlin), can we still speak of the love of God? Can we, even if we refrain from representing Him in any way, shape, or form? Would this not rather be the love of "the" Poetry—as that poetry which allows us to dwell upon this earth: to dwell and, thus, to exist? The love of Poetry as the only God—not one that we know, but one that dwells within us, unknown and, not-with-standing, apparent like the sky?

May it as that be, poetry is not a god. And if it were possible for poetry to come and haunt us—and thereby transfigure us—it would do so only through thunder and lightening, and never, ever, in the form of some final redemption. Why? Because poetry itself is nothing more than its coming; one that would carry us a-part from ourselves and even into the opening that it itself is: that is, the free dwelling place and the *free* use of the proper.

Yet, if Poetry (I am well aware that this term is improper, but we still are in want of names!) ought to be able to come and rule freely, then we must also know how to dismiss it. For this *intercourse* with the Unheard-of is best translated by simple words—words that resemble other words . . . The poetic word endures the common destiny that every human word endures: it too must appear only as a common word. Perhaps somewhat rarer, somewhat less common, but always centered within the same framework as that of the commonplace in discourse.

Hölderlin once wrote, "Why a word? or so I think. For he detests discourse, He who/would spare the light-of-life, the nutrient of the heart" ("To the Madonna"). He—the poetic Genius—detests discourse, and yet must, at the same time, pass through it. His heart is not there. No, it is entirely in the song that is existence (Rilke) and in the essential "music" that sounds throughout the entire poem by Rimbaud. "I am, even, a musician, who has found something similar to the key of love." It is a music that, itself, is not limited to anything sonorous but that names, rather, a "rhythm" or unheard-of "harmony" or even that which begins the beginning of the poem "*Solde*": "The re-assembled Voices; the fraternal wakening of all the choral and all the orchestral energies and their immediate applications"!

Nevertheless, this music of being itself—or of that relationship to Being which expresses itself as rhythm or *harmonia* or the infinite preservation of its own conservation (conversation perhaps)—may be found in this poem "for sale." "The applications of calculation and the up-bounding of unheard-of harmonies are for sale! The unexpected discoveries and the unsuspected terms—immediate possession." To be sure, the poet is an "inventor." He is the one who *discovers* "discoveries" that come to him immediately—like a bolt of lightening. The poet, perhaps, is the original discoverer, a word that, itself uncovers the poet *as* dis-coverer: *discooperire*, to uncover, the reversal and *not* the removing of the cover.

Now we note that music, voice, rhythms, and even the poem itself is—" for sale." What could this possibly signify? What is going on here? Could it be that which Kierkegaard observed with respect to philosophy? "What philosophers say of reality is often as deceptive as that which we see written on a signboard in an old curiosity shoppe: 'Ask For Our Ironing Special.' And so, we bring in our wrinkled laundry. But we've been had. For only the signboard is 'for sale.' " So it is with the poem, a poem that literally promises marvels and mountains ("The wealth abounds at every step!"), but that can only deceive. In this way, it is similar to the signboard: we can buy it (on the pretext of the printed text), but we cannot bring in our laundry to have it pressed.

The poem "*Solde*" speaks this inevitable loss. It is the dispossession responding to the "immediate possession" advertized by the "signboard." (We know that the word *illumination* which entitles Rimbaud's almost posthumous collection does not designate a suddenly illuminated "light" or an "ingenious" illumination, but rather, the signboard or *enluminure*, as we can read in the "Alchemy of the Word."[11] "I adored those idiotic paintings found above doorways; the sceneries, the canvas covered with jugglers, the signboards and popular illuminations"). The buyer is, in a way, swindled; or better yet, *possessed*. Just when one thought to possess everything, the sale falls flat like a sail without wind.

"For sale that which we shall never sell." In effect, do we not simply sell some wind? Some hot air? A "sale" is not only the selling at a discount, it is the giant liquidation sale when, as we often read, EVERYTHING MUST GO, and EVERYTHING MUST DISAPPEAR. To disappear, the poem must "do it." But in a sense that is different from the simple reduction of everything to the status of merchandise or commodity. To be sure, the poem can be sold only at a discount. But then, how could a poem have any value at all? It cannot be exchanged for anything and thus, would be exchanged for nothing: for a mere trifle. The sale is the difference between supply and demand, such that it becomes a question of bookkeeping and accounting for in the world of business. Inevitably, the poem would inscribe a sale caused by demand that is all the more important inasmuch as it pretends to assure us of an infinite supply. In other words, poetry pays us in words . . . "That which we shall never sell—the bodies, the voices, the unquestionable and enormous wealth—everything is for sale. And the sellers haven't reached the end of the sale! The travelers needn't render accounts so soon."

An infinite sale—an inexhaustible supply. Later, when Rimbaud became a businessman, he never sold his poems—most of which he forgot rather than disclaimed. For everything must disappear . . . In fact, Mallarmé put forward a far more engaging "supposition—more interesting—than that of a manuscript contradicted and disclaimed by a perspicacious look" (that is, by an unedited poem, written "over there"). How would Rimbaud have taken his growing glory as a poet? Would he have disclaimed or "gathered up" his poems? Mallarmé's response contains a certain irony: "Nevertheless—as regards this lofty career which was without compromise that of an anarchist in spirit—we ought to presume that the interested party might have welcomed, with a proud carelessness, the outcome ending in celebrity—as concerning, certainly, someone who had been him but who he was, in no way, any longer: unless, of course, the impersonal ghost [writer] hadn't pushed his care-freedom to claim, in claiming the rights of authorship, the money yielded thereof."

Inasmuch as the poem has no author, how could one benefit from the rights of authorship? At the same time, Rimbaud's obsession for gold was not foreign to the poetic "fire"—if, of course, fire is a figure of Being. According to Heraclitus, "All things may be exchanged for fire, and fire for all things; just as gold may be exchanged for goods and goods for gold" (fragment 90). We must remember that for Rimbaud, the poet is the "thief of fire"—both the fire of Being and of the Word. (Here we hear the Alchemy of the Word—of Being.) This fire is not some "thing" (not a being), and yet, it may be exchanged for all things. Just as gold is not a good, it may very well constitute the Good par excellence. In a way, it constitutes the very motor of the market—of this becoming—whereby everything and nothing are interchanged to form a world.

But if fire is exchanged, can we then say that it may be sold? And can one who brokers such fire ever collect a commission? Engaged by a business or enterprise that necessarily surpasses the original proposal, the poet must, in a way, resign his post. Everything must disappear, beginning with the poet: "Here is the mysterious date," Mallarmé wrote, "when Arthur purged himself of poetry" and dis-appeared "far,

far away." "Oblivion comprehends the desert space and that of the sea." Poetic excess can be measured only by its own excessiveness: here words no longer have a value. Indeed, they are without price. This ambiguity is the very sign of the in-finite allotment: the infinitely big and the infinitely small would combine in this inestimable jewel that Mallarmé would call "nothingness or the principal piece."

We may also speak of a liberation from every value that is transcendental "in itself." In other words, farewell (*adieu*) is bid to God (*Dieu*) (Rimbaud would have written "To hell with God" on the walls of Charleville). Yet, in this farewell—similar to the one bid to a Season in Hell that is necessarily dismissed—the fire, which does and does not want to be called *God*, would return, freely, for one last farewell. God without god, or . . . Genius: "The new signification, now come to our language, and articulated in but a few syllables: *Arthur Rimbaud*."[12]

Notes

1. Arthur Rimbaud, *Complete Works*, p. 294. This was a letter that Rimbaud wrote from Marseille on November 9, 1891, to the director of the Messageries maritimes (the transport line). The rather bizarre beginning of the letter runs as follows:

UN LOT: UNE DENT SEULE
UN LOT: DEUX DENTS
UN LOT: TROIS DENTS
UN LOT: QUATRE DENTS
UN LOT: DEUX DENTS

No one seems to know what this could signify. It could be that by *tooth* (*dent*), he meant "leg"—inasmuch as his leg had been recently amputated and replaced with a wooden one which cost him 5.50 francs. In a letter written by his sister Isabelle—who cared for him in his last moments—she claimed that he was confusing her with his "boy" Djami; and that he would imagine them again in Harar, but always in the process of leaving for somewhere else. ("*Vite, vite, on nous attend, fermons les valises et partons.*" "Quick, quick, they are waiting for us; close our suitcases and lets go," p. 706, in *Oeuvres Complètes*).

2. It is interesting to note this change in identity when Rimbaud, having become a businessman, no longer went by the name Arthur but by his middle name Jean. In a letter written by Frédéric Rimbaud (Arthur's oldest brother—considered the idiot of the family—who signed simply "busdriver from Attigny"), he wrote the following: "My brother had to remain in Harrar, or Horor, and had, I think, to take care of business."

3. Martin Heidegger, "Language," in *PLT*, p. 195.

4. Rimbaud, letter to Paul Demeny, May 15, 1871, in *OC*, p. 250.

5. For a more thorough examination of Trakl's relationship to his sister Gretl, see my *Tombeau de Trakl.*

6. This "strange" orthography of *innocence* is simply Rimbaud's employment of the dialect spoken—and written—near Charlesville.

7. Yves Bonnefoy, *Rimbaud par lui-même*, p. 157.

8. The French reads "*Pas gagné, jamais gagné . . .* " An ambiguity surrounds this *pas* which cannot effectively be translated into English. *Pas*—in French—signifies both "not" as well as "step," such that one could read the sentence as either "a step that is won" or simply "not won."—Trans.

9. The self-relation has always been thought of as an "inner mediation" (Hegel) by means of self-reflection (return to self): it posits the Self as itself *and* as the other—an Other alienated but already reappropriated by

the Relation (which Hegel called the *absolute relation*). Thus we have an Other *sublimated* in terms of dialectics.

10. Hölderlin, quoted by Heidegger in "poetically man dwells . . . " in *PLT*, p. 219.

11. *Enluminure*, is rightly translated as "illumination," since Rimbaud used this word in the English sense.

12. Mallarmé, *Oeuvres complìetes*, p. 509.

4

Should Trakl Be Burned?

Foreword

This chapter was not included in the original French version of the book. It is the text of a lecture given in the frame and on the margins of a colloquium entitled *The Social Bond* in April 1990 at the University of Washington (Seattle). I read my contribution, "Should Trakl Be Burned?—Of Poetic Uncommunicability," in the present translation by Douglas Brick. Two months later, I was invited by Michel Deguy to repeat, in French this time, the lecture at the Collège International de Philosophie in Paris. The text of this somehow "different" lecture (if only in the language) was first published in the review *Po&sie*, 55, pp. 130–149 [Paris: 1991]. Then, I decided to rewrite both lectures in another perspective, and with another title, "Au Nom de l'Autre" ["In the Name of the Other"] for my book *Tombeau de Trakl.*

In a way, although it is a translation, the present text is the "original" one. But, in another sense, there is no original, even in the vernacular, "own" but never proper, language, or, put in other words, every language is at the same time a translation and an original, because the "origin" (the language *itself*) has to be trans-lated, doubled, even before it can appear *as* such. The simple mention of this "as" is the sign of what Derrida has called *différance.*

What does Trakl have to do with the "social bond"? At first glimpse, quite nothing. He was the least sociable person and did not care for social questions. And yet, he had the fortune to be born into a dazzling world. We have a very hard time, at present, in this other "end of the century," imagining the splendor of what was called the *Empire du Milieu*, especially in Vienna, capital of the arts and of "spirit," before the torment of the Great War put an end to a world and perhaps also to European civilization as such.

It was a dazzling world, but rotting from the inside and eaten by what Freud euphemistically called "discontent." An old world that lived on decomposition by vampirizing everything. Untamed capitalism, in its Austro-Hungarian autocratic version, which, although giving itself music and airs, in swirling waltzes, was a mad, bloody hunter, not realizing that it was itself the wounded prey it was about to finish off. The catastrophe inscribed in what is called the *Joyous Apocalypse* was just days away, and there was no need to be a prophet (or poet) to feel it wandering aimlessly like some hoodlum in the narrow streets of the city that Trakl, in a letter, calls *Dreckstadt*, "Muck City." "With or without a war," Karl Borromäus Heinrich wrote to Trakl in 1913 (and thus before the beginning of the end), "such bad days are coming that men will have to turn their eyes toward a poet."

The poet came, someone will say, but he came too late—or too early, because (as another spirit who came too late or too early said) to this very day he remains unheard.

When he arrived from his "beautiful city" of Salzburg in 1908 in that cosmopolitan city bubbling with life, to take up his pharmacological studies at the University of Vienna, Trakl was horrified. Writing to one of his older sisters, he said that he saw for the first time "life in its own clarity, without subjectivity, naked, just as it is." And that vision of reality appeared to him as a terrifying "nightmare." A hell. In addition, it was a hell into which he was cast "completely alone," as he confided to his childhood friend Buschbeck, who, nonetheless, was spending time without counting it, but also without much success, to introduce the young unknown poet into the literary circles of the avant-garde. German expressionism undoubtedly claimed Trakl as one of their own, and names such as Oscar Kokoschka, Egon Schiele, Else Lasker-Schüler, Karl Kraus, and so forth associated with Trakl, and yet there was always a gap: Trakl was alone, he was the Solitary One, as was the Stranger of his poems.

One might of course say that *solitary* does not mean "alone," at least not in the sense of "detached, isolated, without bonds." For that one would have to be Heidegger and speak another language, not only German, but a yet more original language, and fly back to the etymology of the German word for *solitary*, *Ein-sam*, in which *sam*, allegedly, comes from the Old-High German *sama*, which repeats the Greek *hama*, "together." Thanks to this return to the language of origins (Greco-German), we can now understand, wrote Heidegger,[1] that the lack of social bonds that rules in the solitude of the *Einsam* simultaneously constitutes that bond and, in fact, the bond that is the most binding with the community.

I shall leave the question open as to whether this conversion or reappropriation of solitude in the supreme bond "with the community" recalls another conversion, that of Negativity in Hegelian dialectics; nor shall I enter into the systematic avoidance of the word *society* (*Gesellschaft*) by Heidegger, who replaced it with *community* (*Gemeinschaft*), which does not have at all the same resonance or even the same implications or connotations. (In short, let us say that the first was repressed as the representative of liberal democratic ideology: the social contract that presupposes the position of an individual and autonomous subject, whereas the second is valorized as the nonrepresentational presence of Being-there in its transcendental unity, from *Sein und Zeit*'s *Mitdasein* to the *Volks* community, which, more specifically, is accomplished through the community of knowledge that is copresent to itself in the unity of the German uni-versity.)

On the other hand, what is brought to question in the present speech, in this communication with the a priori disconcerting title, "Should Trakl Be Burned?" really is the *bond*—I am not sure whether it is social or whether it is in a form more radical than what Mallarmé, in his "*Grands faits divers*,"[2] called "Society, that most empty of words, the heritage of philosophers" and of which he thought, "to speak about it is equivalent to speaking of nothing or of being silent as a kind of amusement."

This bond, which may or may not be more original, which is worn out and threadbare, is called *communication*, communication in the most extreme and paradoxical form of its impossibility, the absolute impossibility of communication—impossible in every sense, not just linguistic, but, above all, as that "essential" communication of beings between themselves. Logically, it should be a priori impossible to communicate anything at all of this "uncommunicability" so that this communication, "Should Trakl Be Burned?"—incompatible with all communication—should have been burned before it could even be presented . . .

❁ ❁ ❁

With that, we finally come to the question of the question, a second introduction, and this time an introduction of the title, which presents itself as a question: "Should Trakl Be Burned?" But is this a question? One that can be posed in all innocence? In any case? In any state of the question? What is the state of the question? What is its state after the treatment inflicted on it by Derrida in his book *Of Spirit*, subtitled, *Heidegger and the Question*? Who should be burned: Trakl—or Heidegger? Heidegger commenting on . . . no, "situating," speaking the unspoken site of Trakl, in his text, "*Die Sprache im Gedicht*, subtitled (once again the subtitle appears to say more than the title), *Eine Erörterung von Georg Trakls Gedicht*,[3] an untranslatable formula, insofar as it contains two of the most important words of (Heidegger's) language: *Ort* (place, site) and *Gedicht* (this word was translated in French by Jean Beaufret as "*Dict*", some sort of edict; usually, a *Gedicht* is a poetic work; in Heidegger's use, it is not simply a poem, but the whole (*ge-*) of the *Dichten*, the poetic saying).

"I shall speak of ghost [*revenant*], of flame and of ashes. And what, for Heidegger, *avoiding* means."[4] So begins *Of Spirit*. So, too, shall I begin, again: speaking of what returns to the question from one commentary to another. "Questioning," Heidegger writes at the end of a text that is a question ("*Die Frage nach der Technik*"), is the piety (*Frömmigkeit*) of thought. Piety in the sense of the point, thus of thought questing its place—if, as Heidegger writes, on the fringe of his *Erörterung*, the place, *Ort*, signifies "at the origin," at its place of origin—or its language of origin—the "point of the lance," that toward which everything converges, toward which it launches itself, sends itself—what we may call the One of sense, and, here, of the *Gedicht*. Questioning is only a prelude, just like thought itself, the prelude itself. The same is true for the sense: it must announce itself, precede itself, in hermeneutic precedence (pre-sense—in French *pré-sens*). It gives itself the sense in advance, like the One that gathers the question in the 'letting-itself-be-said' (*Sichsagenlassen*),[5] that is, the essential hearing (*hören*) that is a belonging-to (*gehören*) that sends itself. Here, the flame would not be a metaphor but the very place in which the question folds itself to the fold of hearing-speaking. The place of a metamorphosis, in which the question deposes itself, in which I already hear the unity of the flame that burns and shines, consumes and purifies, institutes and dismisses.

We have already heard the question burn in its own flame, so that the question "Should Trakl Be Burned?" already no longer resounds like a question—a question that is asked and to which an answer would put an end—but rather as a de-position, a de-position of itself. The question is out of the question, and that is the way I received it. To make you hear it anew, I must tell you the dream that gave it to me, bring back to life the dream in which the spirit of Trakl, or someone completely other, came to haunt me. In this dream, I was supposed to be giving a conference whose title (and therefore, subject) had already been given to me, imposed on me, or better yet, inspired in me, without my being able to know its author nor even if, behind the title and thus behind the apparent question, there was an author, someone who had already had the question in mind; it is very difficult for me to communicate this dream to you, probably because the whole conference seemed to be paralyzed by the question and because it was almost impossible for me to get beyond the title, "Should Trakl Be Burned?" which I saw shining above my head as if in letters of fire, so that finally, all I can remember are the last words, the only ones to actually be spoken, in a cutting, imperative, absolutely irrefutable voice: "BUT TO DIE SUDDENLY." Besides, this voice was probably not mine, and it woke me suddenly.

To die, sterben, is one of Trakl's fundamental words, one of Heidegger's too, although he prefers to speak of death, *die Tod*, which is not the same word nor the same "thing." In the poem "*Frühling der Seele*"—in which we find the verse "*Es ist die Seele ein Fremdes auf Erden*," which supplies the point of departure for Heidegger's whole commentary—there is also, exactly two verses earlier, the following: "*Gewaltiges Sterben und die singende Flamme im Herzen*" ("Mighty dying and the singing flame in the heart").[6] Can we be sure that death (*Tod*)—as the extreme retreat or House of Being—has gone beyond all dying? Is not dying merely a passage, an ordeal something like the ordeal of fire as God's judgment? I would not jump into the fire about it . . . Perhaps it is because of this mental, if not spiritual, reservation before the sort of dialectic that returns, nevertheless, in the Heideggerian eschato-logy (of the Turning), that the last words of the dream start with a cutting *but*; it would then be a matter of cutting oneself off suddenly from every eschato-teleo-logy of death . . . *But to die suddenly*, this in fact cuts the rug out from under one's feet, cuts speech short, even all discourse "of death," cuts one breath—and spirit—short.

Can spirit be guilty (or cut) [*coupable*]? An impossible question, at least for translation, and one that forces me to tell you another dream, an older one, directly inspired, so it seems, by a waking reading—Derrida's essay entitled "Heidegger's Hand" (and significantly subtitled, "Geschlecht II"), which has just appeared in the large collection *Psyché*.[7] I was explaining to a friend—a very dear friend who had recently died (but you know that dreams cause the dead to return just as alive as us)—that I had shaken Heidegger's hand, but that the hand, as if gifted with its own autonomy, did not wish to release me; the hand held me, and I could no longer release myself from its grasp. And yet, it was the hand of an old man who, in addition, was dead, as I knew quite well. At one moment I asked myself if Klaus Barbie had had such hands. But immediately my friend's companion—a black man, very much alive and undoubtedly American—burst out laughing, shouting in his laughter, saying, in American, if indeed it is American, something like, "Fuck you!" Immediately Heidegger's hand released its grip, and I heard him too (but without seeing his face) sniggering with laughter, like a kid, as if he had played a good trick.

In dreams dead people appear to be more alive than the living because they have been cleansed of that fault—the fault of being alive. So Heidegger appeared to me (as a ghost, *revenant*?) several years after his death—even though I had never met him while he was alive nor shaken hands with him. In yet another dream, the last one I shall tell you, he was still young, very young, almost exuberant, warm and friendly, and we were talking in a kitchen, one astonishingly similar to the little room in his *Hütte* at Todtnauberg, with the kettle, which had always fascinated me in the photos, sitting just behind, undoubtedly to allegorize the foyer, of which Heraclitus said, "Here too the Gods are present." Before he disappeared into the night, I wanted to offer him a copy of *La Disparue*, the story I had just written, which centered on the disappearance of the friend from the previous dream. It was the night before Christmas, and all the copies from Gallimard (the French publisher) had mysteriously disappeared from the bookstores, as if the work had been placed on the Index. To which Heidegger remarked, his face lighting up with a smile that was both childish and extraordinarily crafty, indeed, malicious and diabolic, "*Noël sur la terre*" (Christmas on Earth), in French, therefore quoting Rimbaud, as he well knew and which went without saying, "in the text," as he remarked with a bizarre combination of naivete and *amour propre*.

I have finished telling you my dreams, now it is necessary to begin the work of interpretation, that is, the work of mourning, which nonetheless I shall leave to others more qualified or more convinced of its necessity than I. For all that, it does not take much wisdom to see in the dream of the hand, the question (Heidegger and the affair) pointing the avenging index of the frail hand of an old man, trapped—as if by an aftershock—by the errors of his youth. As you know, this affair (Heidegger and Nazism) has created quite a stir in France, and it continues to fall upon us, like a ghost that we cannot pacify. Just the other day I read in *Le Monde* a letter that had been unearthed in Heidegger's private archives. In this letter, written in *1929*, he expressed his fears for the future of the German *spirit*, "Germany's spiritual life," and he said quite literally and in terms that are frankly no less than astonishing, that this spirit "is in danger of being totally overrun by the growing Jewification (*der wachsenden Verjüdung*) in both the larger and more restricted sense of the word"—therefore, in every sense of the word. Is Spirit going to be Jewified, denatured, altered, lose its propriety, its authenticity—or, on the contrary, will it be regenerated, finding its sources again in the authentic (*eigentliche*) force emanating from the "*terroir*," the "land."[8]

I shall not return to this affair (which always returns to us)—partly because I have already said what returns to me to say about it at the end of this book, partly, too, because Derrida's book *Of Spirit* already says it all—at least it says what, for Heidegger, *avoiding* means: to avoid returning to (or reexamining, *revenir sur*) the "error" (in quotes) *and* to avoid returning to (*revenir à*) the error (without quotes). This error, as Derrida remarks, is, at least in part, to speak of spirit without quotes, of the spiritual life of Germany as a possibility to which it would be necessary to return, having forgotten what he himself wrote two years before this letter (which, it is true, was a private one); that is, that spirit is not man's proper name and that to pronounce it, to write the word, it is best to put on gloves, that is, quotes.

It should be understood that what Heidegger is blamed for (especially since he can no longer respond, because death has shut him up so that now he can respond only by his *writings*) is not so much the error itself—an all too human thing, as everyone knows—but rather the fact of never having *returned* to that "error" (in quotes), even in a single word—and here I quote Philippe Lacoue-Labarthe, who said the word: "The most humble and most difficult word to pronounce, that word which the West, in its pathos of redemption, has never been able to pronounce, and which we still need to learn to say or else it is we who shall founder, is the word *pardon*."[9]

Because we have not heard this word, should Heidegger be burned?

But, if he did not say it, perhaps it is, nonetheless, written? What is the meaning of this return of the word *spirit* (*Geist*) twenty years after its affirmation without quotation marks, the self-affirmation of the German spirit via its thinking head, the university? Heidegger returns to spirit, but to a completely other spirit, a spirit that, far from affirming itself as the leader (*Führer*), is burning to disappear, to lose itself in the origin, above all, the origin of the word *Geist*: the spirit in flames, the flame, according to a mythological etymology, but also according to the spirit of that poet who disappeared in the flames of the first world torment, Georg Trakl . . .

So then, should Trakl too be burned . . . ? But because we have not heard him, because we shall never be able to hear him?

The question "Should somebody be burned?" returns to us from even farther back: it was Bataille who wrote: "Should Kafka be burned?" But, in fact, as you have no doubt recognized, that was exactly what Kafka wanted, at least what he wrote, not only in asking that all his texts be burned after his death (last wishes that his legatee, Max Brod, obviously, and luckily for us, ignored, but Kafka must have known this in advance: what he did not know, on the contrary, was that certain beings would arrive who were so deprived of spirit that they believed they could burn Kafka by burning his books in the public square), so, not only by this intimation, this wish that was impossible to fulfill, but because he was already burning to disappear, notably in writing *Amerika*, whose original title was, as perhaps you already know, *The Disappeared* (*Der Verschwundene*). This caused me to return to my second dream, which concerned another book, *La Disparue*, which itself had disappeared from circulation before even having properly appeared, an epiphanic disappearance or mis-appearance, which is analogous with (but only in dreams) that of Rimbaud's only book, of whom legend, in this regard more true than any "historical" truth, says that one autumn evening its author tossed it *into the fire*. *Une saison en enfer* (unearthed a quarter of a century later in the basement of the Belgian printer) could, spiritually, do nothing other than burn.

Noël sur la terre is a phrase that comes nearly at the end of the fragment entitled "*Matin*" (Morning), a fragment that comes directly from Christian spirituality, but that does so precisely to salute "the end of superstition"—as if nearly the same thing happened to Rimbaud as to Trakl: to signify his leave from Christianity by returning to its very origin, or to the spirit of its origins, by evoking a "Morning," a birth of the Savior, which, nonetheless, will not have taken place except at an inapproachable distance, always deferred, and "to come" (*à venir*), because, says the absolutely modern Rimbaud, we do not leave "the same desert on the same night."

It will be necessary to return to this Morning in regard to Heidegger's text on Trakl's spirit, its original place: a morning more original than everything, arising in the crossing of the desert or the "spiritual night," and of which Trakl's spirit (or ghost) would be the prophet or voice. It will be necessary to return there, but later. For the moment, I would like to just note that this comparison, the substitution of "Trakl" for "Kafka" in a ready-made formula is not as arbitrary as it might seem. They were both published by the same person (Kurt Wolff) and in the same collection, *Der jüngste Tag*, which literally means "the youngest day," in which we see once more that the German language already "thinks" eschatologically (or messianically, in the "pathos of redemption") because it names this last day, this day of the Last Judgment or of the end of History, because it names this day and this day alone *the youngest day, the earliest morning*, and so on.

❁ ❁ ❁

And so I pass immediately to the end—to Trakl's end? And I read you this last letter, sent[10] to Ludwig von Ficker on 27 October 1914, from the hospital at Kracow where he was placed (according to the doctors' report sent to his family after his death) "because of mental illness (*dementia praecox*)." He wrote: "Since your last visit to the hospital, I am twice as sad. I feel myself to be nearly beyond this world. In closing, I want to add that, in case I depart from life (*im Fall meines Ablebens*), it is my wish and will that my dear sister Grete receive into her own hands everything that I possess, both monetary and otherwise." In fact, he had just received some money, for the first time in his life, but too late for him to get his hands on it (or must we suppose that it would have burned his fingers?). This money came from the hands of a stranger, a Jew named Ludwig Wittgenstein, who had just given a gift to several Austrian poets (Trakl and Rilke included), a really extravagant amount, which would have allowed Trakl to live for at least four years without a care . . . But it was too late, as I have said, and too late also for the dear sister Grete, who blew out her brains three years after his second—and this time successful suicide attempt. The first occurred several days after Grodek, and this failed act just missed having him sent before a court-martial because, at the time, this sort of action, which was harmful to the morale of the troops, was not viewed with humor, so that, to escape the (last) judgment of arms, it was better to be taken for crazy . . . This he already was in the eyes of the authorities at the moment of entering the hospital, which undoubtedly explains why he was listed in the register of the deceased under another name (Frankl) and with ten years added to his age: madness makes one old before one's time!

Hence, to sum up the situation, Georg Trakl (but was it really him and not his double, his ghost?) committed suicide on the night of 2 November 1914 (Night of the Dead!) (1) to escape the judgment of a court martial (2) that would certainly have condemned him to death for trying to blow out his brains in time of war (3) if, in fact, the medico-military authority had not already judged him to be insane and therefore not responsible for his (failed) action, and (4) they did so on the basis of writings that played the role of incriminating evidence, of *symptoms*, which already betrayed his delirium in every way (and, in fact, as Trakl wrote, the Demented died and was buried).

Rest assured, however things did not stop there: another betrayal was to follow, that of his family, which was not burning to see the secret (of the madness) divulged and on this account hurried to burn every compromising trace; that is, the correspondence that had linked brother and sister, G. and G. (Georg and Grete), which, in fact, disappeared, body and soul, without a trace to let us know whether it had been lost or stolen. The only thing that could not be effaced, and that perhaps shines forth with an even brighter light, is precisely the fact that there had been such a correspondence, which was apparently so "burning" that it burned the fingers of those who knew of its existence and the nature of this "family secret," this "*Blutschuld*" (the title of a poem that, also, was excluded from the edition of Trakl's first poems).

At least this effacement has been communicated to us.

To communicate, *mitteilen* in German, to communicate the uncommunicable, that which burns in the hand, that would be the question. A question Trakl already answered, but in a quasi-apocryphal manner, because he did not actually write it himself, because this phrase was written, communicated by another hand, which wrote it in an *intimate* diary, the one kept by his friend Karl Röck. The reason we know of this intimate diary is that it was communicated, taken out of its intimacy. On June 27, 1912, Röck noted this sentence, allegedly pronounced by Trakl, and that perhaps constitutes his "Last Judgment": "It is absolutely impossible to communicate," or, in German, *Man kann sich überhaupt nicht mitteilen*. I have found this sentence reported in almost every one of Trakl's biographies, and it has inclined me, too, perhaps to write my own "Trakl's Tomb" (*Tombeau de Trakl*), long before this speech, which constitutes its impossible justification—because it is also the unjustifiable that made me write, the unjustifiable or essential incompatibility of every biography with what, for lack of any more proper name, we call *Trakl*.

It is just as impossible to write "about" Trakl *himself*, as it is, according to Trakl, to communicate (even with poems, he adds, or *especially* with poems?). In fact, poetic speech seems to escape from any concern for human communication, for exchange, or, as Mallarmé would say, "*universel reportage*." And yet, did not Heidegger write that "the communication of the existential possibilities of one's state-of-mind [*Befindlichkeit*] can become an aim in itself, and this amounts to a disclosing of existence" and that this could be the "sense" of poetic speech?[11] What does it mean to communicate? German expresses it in the form of a sharing—the sharing of sense and senses. A sharing that presupposes a gift, a present or presence. What is presupposed as given in communication is the sense for which speaking means to speak, the sense or "gift" of speech that allows it to be heard. To communicate supposes a common ground of agreement, even if it is only a common language. I cannot communicate anything to you if I speak to you in a foreign language. But is this not precisely what takes place in and as a poem? To understand the poem, do we not have to translate ourselves into its language—its own proper language, and in a sense, or to a certain degree, a language that is absolutely untranslatable and uncommunicable (in common language), even if it appears that the poem is given in a given language, that is, German, for Trakl?

But uncommunicability is not the specific property of the poem. It does not designate an "untranslatable" *part*, which would therefore resist universal communicability. In the end, there are not, for Trakl, two clearly separated kingdoms: a common place, made for communication, and a private place, essentially uncommunicable. No, it is absolutely impossible to communicate, literally "to share oneself." Elsewhere he writes that *everything* is "so inexpressible." Communication itself is forbidden. And this "communication" is not limited to mere speech—being capable of extension even to "essential" communication, that of beings between themselves. Or, let us say, of love. Lovers remain separated, all sharing is forbidden, and, in fact, a bed cannot be shared between brother and sister; copulation is not possible between the couple Georg-Grete, perhaps because they *share* (*partagent*) the fate that is a single heritage (*partage unique*): of being *separated* from every common place.

Something happened that cut off communications. In a letter to Ficker dated the end of November 1913, Trakl says:

> and, in addition, these last few days, such horrible things have happened to me that for the rest of my life I will be incapable of escaping from their shadow. Yes, my dear friend, my life has been inexpressibly broken, and the only thing that remains to me is a mute sorrow, to which even bitterness is refused. . . .
>
> Write me a few words, perhaps; I no longer know what saint to swear by. To feel the world break in two is a nameless sorrow. Oh Lord, what Judgment has erupted on me. Tell me that I must have the force to continue to live and to accomplish the True. Tell me that I am not crazy. A stony obscurity has erupted.

In this letter nothing is communicated to us: nothing but the very cutting off of communication. Trakl does not communicate the "horrible things" that have happened and that have cut, broken, and destroyed (*zerbrochen*) his life in an "inexpressible" manner. The only thing that remains is a mute sorrow; a "stony obscurity," which swept down on him, which broke and entered (*hereingebrochen*) like the Last Judgment, cutting the world in two (*entzweibricht*). Every judgment cuts—sometimes cutting off the judge's head—while respecting the letter of the Law, which the Greeks called *Nomos—Nemesis*: Heritage-Fate, Destiny. But in this case it is a matter of an unwritten and uncommunicable law.

Often, using (the supreme) metaphor, Trakl calls Judgment the storm. In a later letter, addressed to his friend Karl Borromäus Heinrich in the beginning of January 1914, Trakl writes: "As for myself, things are not going so well. Being lost between distraction (*Trübsinn* [troubled senses]) and drunkenness, I lack the strength and desire to change a situation that each day becomes more unhealthy (*unheilvoller*). The only thing that remains for me is the hope that a storm will erupt (*hereinbrechen* [the same verb as for the *Gericht*]) and purify or destroy me (*zerstören* [synonymous with *zerbrechen*])." The essential thing here would be to see that "salvation" merges into loss, in the coming of the storm or fire from heaven, a fire that would purify in destroying (purify *or* destroy: appearances notwithstanding, there is no choice, no division, the Judgment is precisely in the conjunction of purification and destruction, because to purify, *reinigen*, accomplishes the division between health [*Heil*] and sickness [*Unheil*]); it cuts to the quick—but is the spirit guilty (or cutable)? And if the Disease is above all Spirit, how are we to exclude it from the heritage (*partage*), and, above all, who will operate on the disease of the Spirit? What other Spirit?

In a certain way, then, we might say that Trakl himself has already answered the question—if it is a question—"Should Trakl Be Burned?" with the only wish (*Wunsch*), for lack of any other, that he had left: let the storm come. Let the fire come to purify or destroy me! There would be nothing left of his life—except ashes. It is a judgment (of God, of fire) that refutes all biography, a judgment that Heidegger takes up again, at another level, when he lays down the law and says (without ever literally saying it) that there will never be any question of Trakl himself, and especially, let us avoid talking about him, of talking about his life. Obviously, because to speak of a poet's life is the best way to avoid reading his poems, to read in the essential sense of being summoned by their dictate, of belonging (*gehören*) to them. A judgment has been pronounced (even if most often it is tacitly done), even before any "explanation" (*Erläuterung*) of poems, a judgment that has cut to the quick, by banishing to the hell of "subjectivity" the poet's *part maudite*, his life, as being inessential in regard to his "Poem," his *Gedicht* (which differs from *Gericht*, "the Judgment," only by one letter).

In the name of this edict, any inquiry into the personal situation of the poet *must* be taken as the most serious fault of all, a crime of *lèse Gedicht*, or at least a proof of blindness toward the Essential—the "Site" of the Poem. An edict that I have long taken as a golden rule; and is it not true that a knowledge of the poet's personality does not add two scraps of orange peel (to use an expression of Char's from a famous text on Rimbaud) to the reading of a poem? And besides, do we not find in one of Trakl's letters a prescription for impersonality: correcting a poem, Trakl writes that the new version is much better, "because [the poem] is now impersonal and exploding with movements and visions"?[12]

All of this is true, on the condition of understanding "personality" only as the skimpy old subject of "personality studies" and other psychological cases, the "*Tics! tics!*" already stigmatized by Lautréamont. But this "person" has been around for a long time: since Rimbaud, I is another: since Nietzsche and even since Heidegger, the "subject" (especially of poetry) has disappeared, has become a "(non)person" (in Paul Celan's sense of the word), but this disappearance itself is not nothing—in another sense, it is even the very "subject" of poetry. Biography, as a secondary literary genre—writing about the life of another and, what is more, of another who is other than himself or herself—in this restricted sense, would be absolutely incompatible with the writing of the poem, and even with its commentary, and we must applaud Heidegger for writing, on the threshold of his interpretation of the poem "*Winterabend*": "The poem was written by Georg Trakl. Who the author is remains unimportant here, as with every other extremely fortunate (*grossgeglückten*) poem. The extreme fortune consists precisely in this, that the poem can deny the poet's person and name."[13] We must underwrite this notion, at least as long as we do not consider the fashion in which the poem was first communicated to us: addressed to someone, to Karl Kraus, in a letter of which Heidegger is careful not to say a word, even though he then consider Hölderlin's letters to be *essential* to his poetry: here I refer to a passage from the Introduction of Heidegger's first course on Hölderlin in 1934:

> We do not disdain "the life and work," as they say, and the history of their creation, quite the contrary. In no poet is the *Dasein* , the distress of the creation and the destiny of the work, as intimately *one* as it is in Hölderlin. But for this

> very reason we do not have the right to expedite, in a brief summary, his life, work, and literary fortunes, in order then to consecrate ourselves to his "pure poetry." In its time and, for each time, in its place, we encounter in the most direct way, thanks to the prodigious treasure of his letters, the poet's *Dasein*, that *Dasein* without profession, without fire or place, without success or fame, that is to say, in that sum of misunderstandings that accumulate around a name [a hardly veiled allusion to Rilke's remark on Glory]; the "deranged spirit" at thirty-five years old, as they say: *dementia praecox catatonica*, as medical practice makes its astute diagnosis.[14]

It is possible that Trakl's letters do not constitute a "treasure" comparable to that of Hölderlin's, partly for the reasons I have already mentioned—the disappearance of the "treasure," the secret heart of those letters, that is, the correspondence between Georg and Grete—but we must recognize that they are all that remains to us for "reading" Trakl's destiny, or, if you like, his "Dasein," and thus his existence that, like Hölderlin's, was without fire or place—or without any fire other than the fire that burns it—which also is without that "glory" that would be the sum of misunderstandings around a name—but, in this regard, it is very tempting to return the *Erläuterung* to its sender: if the figure of Hölderlin has emerged little by little from purgatory or hell, let us say, from the "night," this is in part the result of a misunderstanding around a name, for which Heidegger himself, also in part, is responsible. And as for Trakl, the "situation" is even clearer: who now would remember that obscure poet whose word, so precociously interrupted when its author was twenty-seven years old, was contained in two thin volumes of *Gedichte*, if a certain Name (Heidegger) had not decided to write a "Situation of Georg Trakl"? Even though, and I quote; (deliberately misquoting): the "Situation" is not Trakl's, but his *Gedicht*'s, and, let us remember, the more successful a Poem is, the more it tolerates the *effacement* (the burning?) of the name of its author. Perhaps this is what Heidegger "does": effacing once again the poet's name, that is, re-writing the poem? And countersigning it: "Heidegger." I know that, on the fringe of his *Erläuterungen zu Hölderlins Dichtung*, Heidegger lays down the law, the deontological prescription for all interpretation: that the interpreter, at the end of the "exposition," remove oneself from "the pure presence (*reines Dastehen*) of the poem"[16]—is not this strategy itself merely a pious wish or, if you like, a beautiful trompe-l'oeil. For—and the whole (Heideggerian) hermeneutic is here to demonstrate it—there is no "pure presence" for a poem, unless this purity is understood as the sister of the flame. The poem is written with asympathetic ink, a writing that appears only at the moment when it burns. I refer to this (unwritten) law of Trakl's Poem—of that being which, as he writes in a letter, is burning to "disappear entirely under a veil and, going elsewhere, to become invisible"—using a word that, like *différance*, can only be read *Disparêtre* (in which can be read the disappearance of being and the being of disappearance).

But this *Disparêtre* is not nothing: in fact, it "is," in quotes, the whole movement, the whole "life" of the being that refuses itself to presence, that removes itself from the surface (of the Appearing), but that, in thus removing itself, does not re-fold itself in some hinterland, but rather returns into the Fold, the veil, and as that very Fold, but a veil that is always torn asunder—a veil of sorrow, a "petrified threshold." In the same way, Heidegger wrote, the nothing (*Nichts*) "is" the pronoun (or first name, *pro-nom*) of Being's veil, that is to say, its only name, for lack of a proper name. It is the effaced Name—and its Face: Being can only *disparêtre*. In a certain way, this is what the poem "*Winterabend*" says: the traveler who goes by obscure paths really does arrive at the doorway, he really does see the Bread and Wine radiating, but from the other side, inside the house, thus for the others for whom the table is set, never for him. He remains in front, on the threshold, just as Kafka's traveler will remain for his entire life in front of the doorway to the Law.

The traveler who goes by obscure paths, apart from the others, he whom the poem "*Herbstseele*" describes as being cut (*schied*) from "the Beloved, from the Others," how can we not see in this description the very figure of Trakl, of he who has left, who is separated from the common heritage—of the *Abgeschiedene*? We should read the few lines in the letter to that other Solitary one, Karl Kraus, that precede the poem "*Winterabend*," those lines that Heidegger avoids quoting in his commentary: "In these days of furious drunkenness and criminal melancholy, several verses have appeared that I beg you to accept as the expression of my respect for a man who, more than any other, gives an example to the world."

The days of furious drunkenness and criminal melancholy, of which Heidegger does not speak, admittedly do not explain the splendid poem, but they do nonetheless count for something: they enter into its composition, its chemical "formula," both spiritual and spirituous. No matter what a poem may be, it is not "born" from nothing; it does not grow like a flower. Even if the one who wrote it has been effaced. And the question—who wrote such poems?—is the most unavoidable of questions. It was the question that one of Trakl's first readers unavoidably asked himself, and not just any reader: Rilke, who in February 1915 wrote to Ficker that, after reading "*Sebastian im Traum*," which had "moved, gripped, astonished, and left him dreamy and perplexed," he asked himself this question, which I believe really is unavoidable, even though Heidegger, precisely, avoided asking it: "Who could he have been?" in German: "*Wer mag er gewesen ist?*" which, in that speculative language, says a great deal more. For, as everyone knows, *gewesen* does not name a simple past, but much rather the essential-being—or, collected in the essence, the *Wesen*, which is much more than the essence: the "living" being. A question that every biography avoids, but also every thoughtful "situation," which nonetheless (or precisely because of this fact) inclines everything to the side of essence.

To the question "Who could we really have been?" Kafka responded in a story entitled "The Metamorphosis" (one of Trakl's fundamental words also): once we were men—and now, simply vermin. In this response the whole destiny of the Jewish people (of the separated, excluded, *abgeschiedene* people) was already prewritten, and yet, remained properly unbelievable. Trakl, in another poem—quoted by Heidegger—responds in a manner hardly different: "God spoke a gentle flame in his heart: / O man!" The poem is called "Gaspar Hauser Song," and we know that Gaspar Hauser is Trakl's *proper* name (see letter 29, from Innsbruck: "and I shall always remain, to the end, a poor Gaspar Hauser"). He also is the one who has no name, the child of obscurity and caverns, who came forth into the world of "civilization" only to be murdered. "Man" is only a breath of God, an accursed inspiration, a pure "spirit." For man has forgotten, or perhaps never knew, the "gentle flame" and, if we inquire into his essence, he is nothing but a dead substance, made from a joining of cold metals.[16]

To the question "Who are we?" Heidegger had already responded—in a grammatically neutral form, as Derrida remarks in his "*Geschlecht I*" *(Psyché*, pp. 394–414): *das Dasein*, this word that we have already encountered in relation to Hölderlin. *Dasein* is the undivided [*das Ein*?[17]]—like that of the Republic, united and indivisible—or the inalienable, which never ceases to be mine. It is my own—and yet, common, because bequeathed to all, my own only when this "property" is about to be withdrawn from me, when death is very close. But only close; this "proximity of death," as Trakl also said, remains at an infinite distance, it is a burning proximity, that of the flame, in which all communication will be impossible, because no one can die in "my" place, because there is not even any "place" there, no place at that extreme point, where the "there" is no longer anything but flames. Being is there, *da*, when it is in-flame, outside itself. An unrealizable proximity, always remaining at a distance from itself, deferred and therefore only remaining (*de-meurante*), if we can come to understand *demeurer* in its effaced-originary sense, in which *demorari* means "to linger," "to delay." The place of being (*Da-sein*) remains (*de-meurt*). (Here I write this pseudo-French word *de-meurt*, which normally means "to remain," with a hyphen between *de* and *meurt*, and I also conjugate the verb as if it came from the root *mourir*, "to die.") That is to say, it remains (*demeure*) promised toward death, *zum Tode*, so that, in this promise it is sent to its "being" and to truth as promise, a word that is given and that must be kept (*Verspruch*).

By (or through) this promise, the *Dasein* (and "it" alone) has the experience of the land as a promised land, "a land placed-before" the peregrination of the soul, that strange and foreign thing. It becomes what it is: the Mortal, the proper name of man, the human being, the one who can experience death as death (as the promise of the There, as the place remaining-dying for the future, as "pre-sense," and so forth).

To which we might respond with the essential question posed by Derrida in a note from *Of Spirit*: "But does *Dasein* have experience of death *as such*, even by anticipation? What could that mean? What is being-for-death? What is death for a *Dasein* that is never defined *essentially* as a living thing? This is not a matter of opposing life to death, but of wondering what semantic content can be given to death in a discourse for which the relation to death, the experience of death, remains unrelated to the life of the living thing."[18] The same question may be applied to Trakl's strange world, peopled (or rather *haunted*) by dead people who are, nevertheless, alive, as Heidegger himself emphasizes in relation to one of Trakl's verses, "In his grave the white magician plays with his snakes": "*Der Gestorbene* lebt *in seinem Grab*," "The dead one *lives* [Heidegger's emphasis] in his grave."[19] (A provisional response might be this: we cannot experience death as death except while living and by anticipation, in the call of the promise, which remains-dies always ahead of us, in the space that Heidegger calls *Frühe*, the white-blank of the "magician" who plays with his serpents, which cannot harm him because he is already dead, desensitized.)

Nevertheless, we should be in no hurry to avoid the question, which if not essential is at least vital, the question of life or death, as they say: What does questioning mean, what does it even mean to be (to exist) outside of these vital interests? Which leads us to imagine the very existence of Trakl from that which is most proper to him, but which Heidegger, precisely, avoids each time, in a different and, I would say, more subtle fashion each time. To put it very crudely, I shall name three sites of the encounter with the Unavoidable: the body, the soul, and sex, or the divided oneness of the two; or, if you prefer to avoid these undoubtedly improper terms (it remains to be seen whether all words are not always already improper and whether this is not the luck of language), drugs, madness, and incest.

I shall proceed methodically, going from the most avoided to the least avoided (in the "Situation" of Trakl's *Gedicht*).

First, what has been completely passed over in silence, as if it had never been a question in the general economy of that existence, but that was nevertheless very flagrant: the role of drugs. It is true that this may be qualified as secondary, in the sense of its being added from the outside—as an element exterior and completely heterogeneous to the writing of poems. But here there is no need to spell it out nor to repeat what Derrida has written in "Plato's Pharmacy," for example, concerning the ambiguous and de-regulating role of the *pharmakon* in the economy of "presence"—both poison and remedy, both supplement and antidote. Trakl encounter drugs very early, apparently as early as 1905 judging by his first extant letter, in the form of chloroform, the "spirit" (essence or quintessence, like ether) that an-esthetizes and hence liberates an inestimable energy for "something other" than what is—for what Mallarmé named the *principal piece* of the literary machine: *nothing*. That this supplement became essential for writing or that it became, in fact, the principle piece of writing can be concretely read in the "fact" that Trakl himself became a pharmacist. Obviously, this was his only way to supply his material needs, to procure his "means of existence," but it was also the only way for him to continue to write poems, necessarily contaminated by that quintessential poison. This does not in the least mean that you can find any material trace of the drug in these writings, precisely the trace has been effaced, because to write "outside of oneself" is, above all, to efface any trace of "substance"; it accomplishes the secret wish of all alchemy: the disappearance of matter in the work in blackness—in writing itself. In a certain fashion, the effacement of all pharmacy is already inscribed in the poems, so that Heidegger is not wrong in avoiding speaking about it: he merely occults the poetic machination even more, above all by effacing all trace of writing as deregulation or anesthesia. We are then led to believe that the Figure of the *Abgeschiedene* floats in the ether of another world; which is not exactly false, but which would be, if we did not make it clear that this "other" world is neither a nether—nor a before-land, but rather that of anesthesia inscribing the poison in the very body of the writing and thus of the writer too; here I refer you to a letter[20] in which Trakl speaks of a strange feeling of "metamorphosis" (*Verwandlung*, Kafka's word) experienced "corporeally to the point of being unsupportable," of "visions (or faces) of obscurity, to the point of being certainly dead (*verstorben*)." The drug, and it alone, "explains" this "feeling" of total insensibility, of petrification or rigidity, to the point of a nearly schizophrenic doubling in which someone—already reduced to nothing or a pure "spirit"—sees himself physically, corporeally dead. In other words, the metamorphosis here in question—transforming the being into a body (corpus = cadaver)—might well be the effect of the poison, whether it is called writing or drugs, but at the same time it is the "remedy"—not for a "renaissance," but for an access to what Trakl calls the unborn or in-nate (*Ungeborene*): thus all the ambiguity of the *Abgeschiedenheit* shows itself, both dead (se-cession) and "life" foreign to life (ac-cession, "departure," *Abschied*).

But it takes precisely a foreign, heterogeneous element—like drugs—to intrude itself into the mechanism (or the organism) and deregulate everything, to accomplish the scission. This quasi magical operator must at the same time efface itself, efface every trace of its presence.

The second "point" that is avoided (this time, simply avoided, or rather, sidestepped) by Heidegger has already been touched upon, or rather more than touched upon, when we spoke of the foreign, perturbing, de-ranging element, that is, the literally *alienating* element in the metamorphic or poetic "operation." To be clear, what about Trakl's "madness"? It is easy to understand Heidegger's dislike of this sort of question, whose only definitive response lies in outside parameters—those of psychiatry or psychoanalysis. So the best means to avoid the question would be to declare it null and void. Not a simple negation—saying that Trakl was not crazy, at least what we ordinarily mean when we say crazy (as the cabinet maker Zimmer said of that other "madman," Hölderlin), but simply a reversal: WHAT IS CALLED CRAZY? The madness of "dementia" (which is the concern in a poem like "Psalm") is not "ordinary" madness—as if there could be such a thing, where someone would lose their spirit or their sense—it is something other, because it is another sense, another spirit. Quite precisely, it is the spirit or the sense of the Other, of the Stranger.

The strategy that Heidegger employs to neutralize the (ordinary) sense of words, to metamorphose them, is quite admirable. He does so, as Derrida re-marks, each time by returning to the *lost* sense of words, lost in ordinary language, in its usage that is also a using-up, a degeneration. This happens several times in a row, and for precisely those crucial, difficult to avoid words. First, the German word *fremd*, "foreign," is referred to an original word in High German, *fram*. This allows Heidegger to say that the Foreigner is not he who has lost his way and is wandering about, deprived of "sense" (of direction, of destination) but he who is searching for the "proper" place, the site (*Ort*) where he can finally "find his home." Second, the word *Wahnsinnige*, ordinarily meaning "crazy," "aberrant " is broken down into two elements: *wahn*, referred to its *etymon*, *wana* = *ohne* (without), and *sinnige*, in which it is easy to recognize *Sinn*, "sense." So, quite logically, the word should really mean "without sense." But no, that would be too simple, or rather, it would be the same as the "ordinary" meaning of madness that Heidegger is trying to avoid, the one that takes charge in the "astute and wise" diagnosis of the doctors, which permitted them to tag Trakl, as well as Hölderlin, with the defamatory label *dementia praecox catatonica*. Therefore, it is not the noun, *Sinn*, that Heidegger contemplates, but the verb, *sinnen*, "to contemplate," which is further referred to *sinnan*, and from there to the Indo-European root, *set*, which means "path." Thus the *Wahnsinnige* is he who (like the *Fremd*) is traveling "toward elsewhere," and hence has not lost his sense or his spirit, but merely *one* sense—the ordinary sense—and who is searching for another sense (and above all, another sense of words and language, of sense and spirit).

So this other sense is decrypted in the very body of language, where it has been conserved, but like a dead person in the grave. This is like saying that, if language is the House of Being, it is the funeral crypt, like the urn that contains the ashes. For example, the proper sense of *spirit*, *Geist*, buried under a layer of ruins (the ordinary senses, including that of "sense"), which we have to unearth by going back to the original root, *gheis*, "the flame." Must we emphasize that *gheis* is not a word of any language and that it was never "living"? Thus, in one sense, it is like that mysterious "being," Elis, in the poem, who has been Dead for a very long time—forever even—but miraculously preserved and bodily intact, ready to come forth as a glorious body? "Mysteriously," but also quite simply, for, at bottom, this Dead person never died, at least in the ordinary sense of the word, because he was never born: just like "spirit," just like the proper "sense," just like the Origin—and finally, like that Being that is not, that *Etre-disparêtre*.

Let us then measure the madness of sense itself, that madness expressed as well in Trakl as in Heidegger, although in the latter it is less perceptible hidden beneath the mask of the apparent depth of German etymology. There is no need to add that this etymological madness, in a mimetic, almost hallucinatory fashion, adds to the Poem, quite precisely, the return of that "ghost" (or *revenant*), the Spirit, in the spectral and hallucinatory form of an original sense, lost or dead under the oridinary sense, in decomposition just like the "form" of the *verwesene* species. The quest for a *Wesen*, for a "living-essential-being," more proper and more original, beyond (behind? in the past? or ahead? past-*gewesen* or future-anterior?) the *Verwesung* might be even more crazy than what the psychiatrists call *dementia praecoz*, it might be the De-mentia (the de-posed, other spirit) of the praecox, of that enigmatic "primity" (*Frühe*) that Heidegger decrypts in the name of the Occident, the very myth of the lost origin (but to-come also), which has constituted the Occident in its very spirit, in its hauntedness, and finally, which makes it, as Rimbaud said, "fly into madness," the madness *to lock-up* (in a grave, obviously).

In other words, so as not to leave you in what may appear to be a vast delirium, what about this demand for a proper sense, this quest for a sense "of being" (the more original temporality, that in which time falls into Spirit), which never stopped animating, inspiring, burning Heidegger's "paths of thought"? If, to put it even more bluntly, there was not another sense—except hallucination, spectral doubling of the sense—except the lost, dead, and buried sense that is always found in front of us? Then we must hear with a completely other ear the verse: "Evening changes image and sense" and hear, in this evening of sense, which since Morning calls itself properly "Occident," that the metamorphosis is not the magic turning of the Evening into some radiant Morning, but rather that of the Evening into itself, into what it has always already been without ever being it: the country of lost sense, that continent in which Rimbaud says, "madness roams." Madness is the sense of sense and vice versa: there is no place *of* the Poem, no place of the place, nor sense of the sense. Or again, it is always too late for the question of sense (of history), too late or too early—both return to the Same—and that is precisely why the Turning will never take place, except in a fantasized, mimed fashion—that is the only fashion for it to take place.

At the same time, we can also hear in a completely other sense the verse that starts the whole Heideggerian "situation": "Something strange is the soul on the earth."[21] It is quite true that the Platonico-Christian representation of the soul (as something supraterrestrial, insensible, etc.) must be put aside (like the ordinary, corrupt sense, which presents itself to us even before any understanding of the word) and that the soul is not endowed in advance with an already known and familiar sense or essence. But is the inversion of the ordinary sense sufficient to reintegrate the soul with its fatherland, its proper place (the "land" it is going toward, to search out a foundation, the institution of a "home," a *demeure*, a poetic one as is proper, if, as one [Heidegger] presupposes, one dwells properly on the land only "poetically," *dixit* Hölderlin)? Or rather, is not this reappropriation of the proper sense of the soul, like the other (who gives heaven as the "fatherland" of the soul), a fashion of effacing the alterity, the inappropriable foreignness of what Trakl calls *the soul*? If, in other words, the soul is what, by "nature," has no nature, has no sense or proper place: the foreignness, which has a sense only phantomatically? What of the soul, of Psyche, of Spirit?

Whoever says *soul* says its indissociable complement: the body. Perhaps this division goes no farther back than Plantonism; it is nonetheless, in a certain fashion, insurmountable, like metaphysics itself. Heidegger was quite careful not to quote a letter in which Trakl seems to entirely support this metaphysical division: "I can already see the day when my soul will no longer wish to nor be capable of remaining in this accursed body infested with melancholy, the day when it will leave this grotesque form made of shit and decay, which is nothing but an all too faithful reflection of this Godless and accursed century."[22]

It might be said that this day had already arrived for Trakl. What is the *Abgeschiedenheit*, if not the already accomplished separation, even in life, in which the body is abandoned to decomposition (*Verwesung*), in which the soul has become the errant one, without body, without fire or place, and precisely insofar as it is the Animating one, the Inflaming one? The ideal specter lives, like the white Magician, in his grave, that is, in his body, but insensibly, anesthetized, reduced to ashes. The soul haunts, and thus "inhabits" (they are the same words), as the hallucinatory, in-existant place of cut off "sense."

The separation of body and soul—such that the body, sworn to *Verwesung*, becomes the grave, the crypt of the petrified sense, following a tradition that goes back to Plato and even before, deposed in the Greek language by the closeness, to within one letter, of *soma* and *sêma*, both "sign" and mausoleum—this leads us unavoidably to the third locus "avoided" by Heidegger in his "Situation," although this time the avoiding is accomplished in a very complex strategy: in an untranslatable play of words, but this time in French, *comment taire par un commentaire* (or, roughly translated, how to hush-up through commentary) . . .

It is a commentary that, nonetheless, notes all the marks, literal and textual: the punctuation marks as well as the unique accentuation—unique in the entire text of Trakl's *Poetry*—of that unique word, which itself expresses the Unique: "*Ein* Geschlecht." Accentuation badly translates the German word: "The *Ein*," Heidegger says, "ist *betont*, is stressed [tonalized, as we might say]. As far as I can see, it is the only word so stressed [*gesperrt*, printed in spaced characters, which is the German method of "emphasis," where we use italics] in Trakl's work. This emphatic (*betonte*) "*Ein* Geschlecht" contains the key note (*das Grundton*) by which the *Gedicht* (Poem) of this poet hushes-up the Secret (*das Geheimnis schweigt*)."[23]

The commentary remarks the marks that the Poem uses, not to say (to reveal, to communicate) its secret, but to hush-up (*schweigen*) this secret: *Ein* Geschlecht. How it arranges itself so that we see only the fire: the spaced, cut-apart letters, the very letters of the One—*Ein*, one. One what? One *Geschlecht*, a properly untranslatable or idiomatic word, not only as can be directly read in the ordinary, spoken German, as a result of its irreducible polysemy, which goes from the human species to sex, by way of the *souche* (a French term almost as untranslatable as *Geschlecht*, but the two terms intersect in their relation to lineage, stock, race . . .) or generation (the term selected by Heidegger's English translator). But, in this context, *Geschlecht* is rendered even less translatable because it has already been re-trans-lated into the original idiom, THE language of the *one* origin, "High" or Old German—exactly as with the words *fremd* and *Wahnsinnige* (or, as Derrida emphasizes, it is the very word *sense* that appears to be untranslatable and has no sense outside of the original idiom)—or again, as with the fundamental words, *Ort* (place) and *Geist* (spirit).

Polysemy differs entirely from dissemination, for, in the last analysis, *polysemy* (Trakl's "good" polysemy) refers to a unique origin, to a univocity, or more precisely, to the uni(voci)ty (where the "voice" of uni-*voci*-ty is parenthesized, emphasizing both the "unity" and the "voice" contained in univocity) of a unique-tone, a *Grundton* or *Einklang*, which, at bottom, is the silent voice of the *Gedicht*, of the *Ort*: that "place of origin"[24] is nowhere other nor anything other than the poems, but it is not confounded with them, because it remains "unspoken" (*ungesprochene*), hushed, precisely as the secret place (of the secret): *Geheimnis*, the intimacy of the *Heim*, another untranslatable word upon which Heidegger plays such harmonics as *Heimat*, *heimische*, *unheimliche*, and so on.

Just as the *Gedicht* is not "elsewhere" and yet is not the same thing as the poems, the place of origin is not elsewhere, and yet is not the same thing—let us say, not the same "Occident" . . . It is the place of origin, the place of the place, the sense of the sense, but, as such, it cannot take place—it "*de-meurt*" (remains-dies) in that "anteriority" of the *Frühe* that, nonetheless, has already gone beyond the end.

We might say that the place of origin is a *Vor-wesen* that can never be other than *Gewesen* in as much as it has gathered together in advance all *Wesen* in the unity of the fact (the before-the-fact, the *coup* of the *avant-coup*, the cutting before the cut, the striking of the first strike); therefore it has already, in advance, appeased the difference or, rather, the dissention, which strikes like a second blow (*second coup*), an *après-coup* (an after-the-fact, an after-shock), which cuts the *Geschlecht* into *Geschlechter*, into opposite—and opposed—sexes. This second blow or cut repeats the first, but we might well ask ourselves if it does not do so in a mimetic fashion, for it is equally possible to reverse the "primity," the priority of one blow in relation to the other: does not every "salvation," every reconciliation in the unity of an original simplicity presuppose the original fall? The *Vorwesen* would then be merely the double of the *Verwesung*, of the "decomposition" or, more exactly, already the envoy of the fall. I refer you here to what Derrida writes in guise of a *chute* (a fall, cadence, or resolution) for his text "*La main de Heidegger*":

> What happens to the *Geschlecht* as its decomposition (*Verwesung*), its corruption, is a *second blow* which comes to strike the sexual difference and transform it into dissention, into war, into savage opposition. The original sexual difference is gentle, peaceful. When it is struck with "malediction" (*Fluch* [one of Trakl's words, taken up and interpreted by Heidegger]), the duality or duplicity of the two becomes unbridled, even bestial opposition. This schema, which I am here reducing to its simplest expression, is claimed by Heidegger, despite all the appearances and all the signs of which he is quite conscious, to be non-Platonician and non-Christian. It arises neither from metaphysical theology nor from ecclesiastic theology. But the (pre-Platonic, pre-metaphysical, pre-Christian) originarity to which Heidegger recalls us wand within which he situates Trakl's own proper place *has no other content and, indeed, no other language* than that of Platonism and Christianity.[26]

In other words, could we not just as well say that the place of origin is none other than the scission, the division, and that it has no other "race" (species, genre, sex) than the *de-generated* (*verwesene*) race? It is true that in French, or in any Romance language, "sex" already speaks the *coup de la coupure*, the blow of disseverment, of section . . . Conversely, there is no saved or re-generated "species" other than, precisely, that which has escaped from the striking-imprint of sexuality: in other words, the *ungeborene*, un-generated genre or species . . . This is precisely why Heidegger, at the very body of the poem, effaces all trace of sexuality. He neutralizes the (human) being just as he had already done in naming it with a neuter, *das Dasein*, but Trakl, too, does this often, notably in calling the soul (traditionally of feminine gender, *psychè*, *anima*, etc.) *something strange*, *ein Fremdes* . . .

Let us admit that we are in the very middle of that theology in which those discussions, which seem so Byzantine, so trivial to us, return, those discussions about the sex of angels (or "spirits"). Does not the angel correspond point-for-point to the original being, before the fall? The *in-né* (un-born, in-nate) being? And yet it remains ambiguous: after all, is not Lucifer (an eminent figure in Trakl's Poem) the first Angel—the fallen angel . . . ? In what measure is Trakl's poetry not also inspired by a whole "mystic" (*geistlich*) tradition of the original Man, the Adamic man, unengendered by the sexual union of man and woman? Why, in the only interview that has been communicated to us, does Trakl claim that he is totally Christian, and even "Protestant," which, for his "free-thinking" interlocutors, must have sounded like a properly unbelievable paradox? Derrida is right to emphasize the fact that Heidegger's efforts to tear Trakl away from the "spirit" of Christianity—and even from original Christianity, returning to its sources—can be nothing other than laborious and forced. Else Läsker-Schuler, a Jewish poetess whom Trakl had met in Berlin in 1914, at a moment when the "dear sister" Grete had almost died from a miscarriage, said—in guise of a funeral epithet?—"*Er war wohl Martin Luther*" ("He [Trakl] was quite a Martin Luther")—which, in a certain fashion, could also be said of Martin Heidegger . . .

❂ ❂ ❂

In the same interview, people usually avoid quoting the *chute* of the text, which immediately follows the violent affirmation: "Nietzsche was crazy"—physically crazy, says Trakl, from the same shameful malady as Maupassant; to be more specific, the sexual malady par excellence—and, after a moment of embarrassed silence, Trakl returns from Nietzsche to Christ: "It is incredible to see to what a point He resolves with a single word the most profound questions of humanity. Is it possible to decide the question of the community of man and woman any more radically than by this commandment: 'And they shall be one flesh'?"[26] Admittedly the word is not *Geschlecht*, but *Fleisch*—however, the word *Ein* (one flesh), as written by Dr. Limbach who recorded the conversation, is furnished with a capital *E*, which thus relates it immediately to the only accentuated, *betont* word in Trakl's poems: *Ein*

Geschlecht. This "co-mandment," a mandate to unity, a *Gebot*, closer to a prayer than to an order, but with something of the *Gericht*, of the *first* edict—is it not, in fact, the *Grundton* of the *Gedicht*?

Nevertheless, such an (e)dict cannot be spoken, formulated. It must remain hushed, secret. Why? Because intimacy is always *interdite* (prohibited or "spoken-between"), because it falls within the promulgated law against incest. Incest is at the origin, and that is why the *Fluch*, the malediction, weighs upon the *Geschlecht*. The fault is original, and it cannot be "redeemed" by any poem (no poem is a redemption, Trakl said to Ficker, on the steps of the train that would lead him to his death, to the war, on the paths that *all* lead to decomposition). This fault is nothing other than being born, "Great is the fault of the born."[27] If there is salvation, it is as if anterior, anterior to the origin itself or, as Derrida writes, heterogeneous to the origin. But then what is this anterior, this *blanc*? Is it the white-blank of virgin wax before the inscription of the trace? But *before* in what sense? And, to appear as white-blank, is it not necessary that the trace already be deposed? Deposed, imprinted and effaced; whitened, like ashes, and we shall never see anything in it but the fire.

Notes

1. Heidegger, *Unterwegs zur Sprache*, *Gesamtausgabe* 12 (Frankfurt: Vittorio Klostermann, 1985) p. 256; English translation, *On the Way to Language* (hereafter *OWL*), pp. 135–136.

2. Mallarmé, *OC*, p. 419.

3. Heidegger, "Language in the Poem: A Discussion on Georg Trakl's Poetic Work." *OWL*.

4. *Of Spirit*. p. 1.

5. This word, *Sichsagenlassen*, is translated in *OWL* (p. 76) as "to let ourselves be told something" and in *Of Spirit* (p. 134, note to p. 94) as "letting-oneself-say"; the French (Derrida *De l'esprit: Heidegger et la question* [Paris: Galilée, 1987], p. 153) "*se-laisser-dire*" comes perhaps closest to the original, (Heidegger "*Das Wesen der Sprache*," *Unterwegs zur Sprache*, p. 170): "*Insofern jedoch das Denken allem zuvor ein Hören ist, ein Sichsagenlassen und kein Fragen* . . . "; I take it as a passive (as in "*Das lässt sich leicht sagen*," "that's easy to say," literally, "that lets itself be said easily"), hence the present translation, "letting-itself-be-said"—Trans.

6. *OWL*, p. 197.

7. Derrida, "La main de Heidegger," *Psyché* (Paris: Galilée, 1987), pp. 415–451.

8. The article in *Le Monde* does not give the German word, but the French *terroir* ("land," "country," the *Volks* place) has interesting, if not terrifying, connotations, that merit its being left undisturbed in this article—Trans.

9. Philippe Lacoue-Labarthe, *La poésie comme expérience*, p. 58.

10. Although it was not the last one received. I would have to go into the whole history of these postcards: censured, lost, returned, never sent, etc.

11. Heidegger, *Being and Time*, p. 205.

12. Letter to Buschbeck, end of Autumn 1911.

13. Heidegger, "Language," *PLT*, p. 195; trans. modified—Trans.

14. Heidegger, *Hölderlins Hymnen "Germanien" und "Der Rhein,"* *Gesamtausgabe* 39 pp. 6–7.

15. Heidegger, "Remembrance of the Poet," *Existence and Being*, p. 235.

16. *OWL*, p. 168.

17. *Dasein* could be read as *das Ein*, "the One." Unity as the most proper feature of Being-there would mean that *autology* is the truth of the so-called ontological difference. The *Dasein* is the proper-*proche* of *Sein* and vice versa.

18. *Of Spirit*, p. 120 (note to p. 57).

19. *OWL*, p. 173.

20. To Karl B. Heinrich, 19 February 1913.

21. *OWL*, p. 161.

22. To Ludwig von Ficker, Salzburg, June 26, 1913.

23. *OWL*, p. 195, trans. modified.

24. *Psyché*, p. 447.

25. *Psyché*, p. 451.

26. The biblical quotation is from Genesis 2:24, requoted by Jesus in Mathew 19:5.

27. *OWL*, p. 189, trans. modified.

5

Solitude of the Word

It is a laughable, and even astonishing, error that people imagine and believe themselves—to speak in the service of things. Yet, the proper of language—to know that it is utterly and evenly taken up with itself—is unknown to everybody. It is, indeed, why language is such a marvelous and perpetually impregnated mystery. That someone speaks simply in order to speak—then, only, does he speak the most magnificient and original truths.

This fragment from Novalis—taken from a text entitled *Monologue*—begins the last text of Heidegger in *Unterwegs zur Sprache* (*On the Way to Language*). To be sure, Heidegger only cites a single sentence from *Monologue*—the very one that names the proper of language. A brief remark precedes the citation, "That title [*Monologue*] points to the mystery of language: language speaks solely with itself alone." Even if Heidegger did not share Novalis's romantic notions ("the horizon of absolute idealism beginning with subjectivity"), he did, however, adopt the primary thrust of his intuition: "Language *is* monologue. Assertion that must be understood in a double sense: language *alone* (*allein*) is that which, properly speaking, speaks. And language speaks solitarily (*einsam*)."[1]

The distinction between being-alone and solitude may seem to be the very distinction contained in Byzantine rhetoric; that is, the ruse of an impoverished thought that hides its lacunae and blind spots with ready-made jargon. Heidegger would tell us that "solitary" does not signify "alone," or at least not in the sense of a negative isolation. That there is a want in solitude can hardly be contested. Yet, this want—want where one is separate from others, from the common lot—constitutes a certain relationship: the "most exacting relationship" with the community from which the solitary is separated. Is it possible that we have here a small memento of dialectics? What, in effect, is it that distinguishes Heidegger from absolute idealism? Without a doubt, it is the very thought of the "negative" or negativity. In fact, Heidegger already spelled it out in *Being and Time*: the ontological essence of *Nicht* (notness) is as obscure as the general sense of Being. Ontology found, before itself, the *Nicht* and subsequently put it to (good) use. "But is it so obvious that every 'not' signifies something negative in the sense of a lack? Is its positivity exhausted by the fact that it constitutes 'passing over' something? Why does all dialectic take refuge in negation, though it cannot provide dialectical grounds for this sort of thing *itself* or even just establish it *as a problem*?"[2] It was to these kinds of questions that Heidegger's conference *What Is Metaphysics* responded two years later. Here he was to assert that nothingness (*Nichts*) precedes and makes possible every "not" and, a fortiori, every negation. Not only is nothingness not nothing—without being *a* thing, because it cannot *be* in an absolute sense—but it would determine the relationship with the world in a most remarkable and decisive way. In the anxiety that reveals nothingness, there is no longer anything that holds—or anything on which to hold. There is this nothing itself, signed by the caesura (or by the extreme solitude that reigns in the relationship to death). This solitude—which, in *Being and Time*, was the lot of an authentic and decided existence as opposed to the dissolution into quicksand of the common lot (of the "We")—is later taken away from *Dasein*. Such solitude is no longer *Dasein's* first and foremost privilege, but returns to *Sprache*, to language. Which speaks, *alone*, and solitarily.

Here we find a double exclusion. On the one hand, *Dasein* sees its gift taken away: no more is it the privileged being endowed with *logos*. On the other hand, as speaking is no longer the privilege of the subject —for it takes place simply for itself—it would seem that no world whatsoever is able to hold sway over this *place*. Nothing will have taken place save the place; and consequently, neither humans nor things have any right to the word. Quite simply, it is no longer one's business: language speaks all alone—we need only hear and understand. (It is precisely upon this that everything turns: What does it mean to hear? And to understand? Heidegger, playing within the nuance of German, remarked that, to be under-stood, one must take part in the play of words. No longer must one be alone or isolated; rather, one must enter into the monological solitude of language. However, this monologue cannot be compared to the "interior monologue" of one who speaks only to oneself. On the contrary, it is a monologue that explodes all interiority.)

At first glimpse, the Monologue of language is a matter that can matter little to us. Inhuman and sterile, it would unfold elsewhere: in a place that is uninhabited and unsettled. (I should remark that this place is not even over our heads). We can only say that it occurs elsewhere—but only in itself. It is a language that shall never speak anything but itself: whether this be Being, the Same, or the One. It is no one's language and for no one. It is like a dead language insofar as it cannot be shared, communicated, or addressed to another. Thing in itself—or God—either way it amounts to the same—thing. Perhaps Paul Celan had in mind this unheard-of hypostasis of a "language of Being" when, in his *Conversation in the Mountains*, he remarked: "that this is a language for neither you nor me—for I ask, for whom is it meant, this earth, for I say it is not meant for you or for me—a language, to be sure, without I or Thou, merely He, merely It, do you understand, merely She and nothing more."[3]

"Properly speaking," this language speaks authentically (if, that is, we dare speak thus). Yet, it speaks of nothing; it speaks only to speak and, so, be itself: "to be language and nothing more." It is, and only is, like a rock. At least—at the very least—it does not say, if *saying*, here, signifies a showing or displaying of an other or if it signifies a signaling toward an elsewhere that *it* might be brought closer. It speaks, but only intransitively. It speaks from the compact position of an "is"—without any subject and without any determination. This language is massive, frozen, and forever petrified in the still silence of the inexistant "character" that Celan has derisively called *Hear me* and that, like a glacier in its slow and unyielding descent, speaks only in the cold cracklings of its crevasses. Language promised to disappearance; to the slow thaw of the snow.

Yet no one should be surprised by this. Languages come and go, but *the* language remains—like the glacier. And no one has a hand therein, nor, in any way, is at home therein. For language is the "house of Being," whose only inhabitant is itself. (It is thus that we must understand the metaphor: language is not the container, nor is Being its content. There is only a single process without a subject. The house, like the monad, contains nothing, being without a window or a door). . . . And what about ourselves? "The Same has lost us; the Same has forgotten us; the Same has . . ." silenced, if not killed (*tus, à défaut de tués*) our precious "self." All that remains is the Remaining Place: impersonal and sovereign in its stupefying solitude. A that that could be only that: itself, the impersonality of the *Es gibt* and of the *There is*. It speaks like it snows: "Language itself is: language and nothing more." Once upon a time, tautology was outlawed by the proper use of language. It was condemned and sentenced for having said nothing. And yet, now, for this very reason, it is exalted—because it alone speaks without saying anything other than itself; because it alone speaks at the height of a first and "authentic" *logos*. Indeed, this runs counter to the entire tradition of logic. For, in the land of tautology, only tautology—or language itself—can dwell. Unquestionably, there can be no question of anyone or anything but It. It is "*its* speaking and not ours." And if *we* are still able to speak, it is only on account of listening to it: as if we were only the instruments or organs or, even, the (unconscious) mediums of the word—as if we were in the same relationship with respect to language as the lips and tongue with respect to the uttered word. The lips do not speak. Nor is it that rose-colored organ, full of mucuous membrane and stopping at the glottis, that speaks. Similarily, it is not the human subject who, properly speaking, speaks: we only stir the lips of the Mother Tongue. We are the tongues of the language. (German has two words, *die Zunge* and *die Sprache*, as does English: one to name the "physical" organ and one to name language itself (metaphysical?). French, on the other hand, may name both by a single word, *langue*.) Heidegger hardly failed to take note of this: the fact that most Western "languages" are comprehended and named by the word for "tongue" (*glossa*, *lingua*, *langue*) implies the pre-eminence of a physical phenomenon—sonority. From the very moment we wish to represent, immediately, the phenomenon of language, we cannot help but take the sonorous being as model. Nevertheless, sonority is always thought of—metaphysically—as a simple medium for, for example, the *Spirit* or *pneuma*. To pre-cede the sound-sense or language-word dichotomy is to enter into the uni-verse of the Monologue: it is to enter into the One and Same language; and into that which Hölderlin described as "the flower of the mouth."

It is against this literally inhuman impersonality of the mono/tautological process that the singularily other voice of Celan would rise up. His is the voice of the Jew—the voice of the one who has been excluded from all naturalness. Celan raged against the Romantic-Symbolist tradition that had been expressed through Mallarmé and Gottfried Benn; particularly, the notion that the "pure work implies the poet's elocutionary disappearance and his ceding of all initiative to words." In "Conversation in the Mountains," he raged against the very idea of an absolute poem: "The modern poem is an absolute poem; it is a poem without faith and without hope; it is a poem addressed to nobody; it is a poem that consists simply of words that are brought together in order to fascinate."

Yet, we would ask, is not Celan's poem precisely one that is addressed "to no one"? Here I refer to his work entitled "No One's Rose" (*Die Niemandsrose*). In German, the construction is such that "no one" comes first. *Do-youhearme* (*Hörstdu*) is no one. Yet it is a no one that exists always in the ambiguity of the neuter and in that which Mandelstam called the *secret interlocutor*. The poem, which oscillates between these two ambiguities, seeks to free itself from the impersonal and sterile, that thus it might eventually arrive at the unknown addressee—to whom the poetic word is addressed. But, above all, this poem speaks simply in order to speak.

Speaking for the sake of speaking has usually exemplified an incorrect use of the word. Indeed, all chitchat and idle talk (*Gerede*), to which Heidegger dedicated an entire paragraph in *Being and Time* and to which he was not ill-disposed, constituted nevertheless, an inauthentic and improper pouring forth of the word. Yet Heidegger, at this time, hardly envisioned the "authentic" word as a speaking-for-the-sake-of-speaking or monologue. Still, today, we measure poorly the distance—indeed, the gulf—that exists between the analytic existential and the last "philosophy of language" contained in *Unterwegs zur Sprache* (which is in no way a philosophy). Even Heidegger himself hid this turning by handing himself over to a retroactive auto-interpretation that allowed him to re-integrate the intuitions of *Being and Time* (but not its fundamental categories, which were still stamped by "philosophy") in the "pathways of thinking" that occurred after the turning.

It would seem that, in *Being and Time*, the perspective on language is existential inasmuch as it is a perspective oriented for *Dasein* and from *Dasein;* and therefore, with an eye cast upon the human being (though this latter is not determined as a subject or consciousness). Language appears as an existential category or "property" of *Dasein* that is neither substantial nor purely instrumental. Nor does language constitute an absolute: for the word, insofar as it is communication and expression discourse (*Rede*), would itself constitute the substructure or "existential-ontological" foundation of language.[4] The different aspects of this existential reveal a definitively common character, or even a "communal" character—that is, if I dare distort the meaning of this word—as speaking always refers, in the last analysis, to a community or being-together (*Mitsein*). Traditionally, there is a speaker: a person who speaks and expresses himself or herself without the expression becoming a mere exteriorisation of "lived" contents. Furthermore, it is always *someone* who speaks and not language itself. The speaker speaks *to* another and, in this way, communicates. (We can always speak to ourselves, but this still remains communication—though a somewhat privative form of it. Similar to a *private* life, which is the negative modification of an existence in common.) Finally, and most importantly, we always speak *about* or *of* something, just as all consciousness is a consciousness *of* something. Every word is a word about or of something or, according to Novalis, "a function of something." And, with respect to such functionality, *Being and Time* proves to be in perfect agreement with the whole of occidental tradition—which has, in every way, been determined by the Greek beginning. Every *logos* is a *logos tinos* or *kata tinos*, "of" or "about" something. Usually, it is a common thing (*pragma*, *Sache*), common to "the common world" in which both the speaker and spokesperson take part. This common thing must have already been revealed to us—prior to the designation by words (which are always secondary)—in order for us to be able to speak about it. At this stage, to speak is simply to refer (usually implicitly) to a "totality-of-significations" that is and constitutes the common world—which (like the sign) is modeled on the model of utensility.[5] Sense is always already presupposed to the extent that it is not possible to speak simply to say nothing. Even the most nonsensical word contains, always already, some sense however hidden it may be. In effect, without some sort of meaning, we would be unable to point out that which could be characterized as non-sense. I would add, here, that the song of the nightingale is not nonsensical, because it does not belong to the realm of sense, or to that realm in Being given over to *Dasein*.

Thus, for the Heidegger of 1927, not only do we speak only according to things or others but we never speak alone—even when the other is not present in person. The "interior monologue" that Plato had already designated as a "dialogue without the voice of the psychè [speaking] with itself" is possible only based on the existential ground of an opening into the world or, in other words, upon the "voice of the friend" that dwells within each *Dasein*. To be sure, language, like *Dasein*, has no in itself or interiority. Language does not speak alone; rather, it takes place only as an addressed, communicative, expressive, and existential structure that denotes a way of Being always already open to the world. Thus the word remains ever under the thumb of signification. However, speaking for the sake of speaking—allowing ourselves to be taken a way by the rhythm of a word without referent or addressee—would constitute the common characteristic of every *Dasein* from the very moment it exists in and for the common world. The idle talk by which "we" are overwhelmed—like a river that washes away its embankments—rather than bearing witness to the solitude of the word, shows with that much more force, a nature nourished by the *common place*. Contrary to this, when the common world unconceals itself and the solitude of existence appears in all its severity—indeed, in its absolute mortality—the word would speak no more. Only then is *Dasein* "authentic." Only then does *Dasein* become silent and resolved—for *Dasein* remains open to its end.

It would seem the word is hardly decisive enough to constitute an existential of *Dasein*. On the one hand, it cannot and does not reveal any "revelation" of the world. Only a pure seeing is capable of this. In fact, the word has a tendency *to lose sight of* every enlightening intuition (i.e., sense.) On the other hand, without the word, we wonder whether it would be possible to keep essence in sight (*Wesensschau*)? Moreover, in our wonderment, we ask, How is a phenomeno-*logy* able to take place without some sort of presupposition that hasn't already presupposed a *logos*? Or a presupposition that has not already presupposed our ability to present the phenomenon in question?

Such questions forced Heidegger to radically revise the existential analytic and even—according to all appearances—to abandon it along the way. If the word were only a tool, used exclusively to communicate and signify a sense that had *already* been constituted before its expression, then, accordingly, it could be only a necessary and subordinate medium. Here, the subordination of the word is similar to the subordination of both the lips and tongue in the metaphysical scheme of language. At the very limit, we can dispose of either; for we can always transmit some "sense" or message by other, nonlinguistic, means. For example, data processing and computers provide our children with their "own" language. Words—in a world as saturated with images and numbers as ours—have become but "legends" or "captions."

Heidegger, continuing along this line of thought, thought that if language were merely a means of expression—as is every tool—then it could not possibly contain its own life. But then, how was it possible for a language to die? At the end of paragragh 34, he confessed his perplexity: "What kind of Being does language have, if there can be such a thing as a 'dead' language? What do the 'rise' and 'decline' of a language mean ontologically?"[6]

For quite some time these questions remained without answer. Yet, they would already point thinking in an entirely different direction; namely, the "Being" proper of language and its genius. Language had to live its "life" a-part; it had to be independent from us, its speakers—even when we believed it to be at our disposal, like a tool; and especially when it slipped or when we were unable to find *our* words. But it was precisely then that language was like an abyss that suddenly opened up before us. And precisely then that we remained fore-biddened; but still in a relationship of proximity—and nearly hand in hand—with an almost demonic power that, by hook or crook, escaped us. However, language, here, is not even like a tool that reveals itself unusable, broken, or ill-adapted; that is, improper. It can hardly fall from our hands: no, the hand itself is wanting, and with the hand, everything is lost. For this reason Heidegger would reverse the terms of the relationship. We think that we possess the word and that we have it well in hand, but it is the word that holds us, that handles us and sustains our life. Oftentimes, it is the last link that links us to existence, when its end comes.

What a strange companion is this word that hardly calls attention to itself and that travels incognito and would reign all the more intensely when, upon leaving us, discovers all its (dictatorial?) power. Leaves us though, without warning, at the intersection of a sentence; just as a passerby would pass us by, somewhere on the street, going his or her own way with indifference—almost to the point that it—language—is unaffected by *our* own failure. Indeed, the word seems to live off itself, to nourish itself with its own essence, and to breathe its own breath. No one is able to create a language ex nihilo. Every attempt to do so (for example, Esperanto and the neologisms that inundate every discourse—including the philosophical) is doomed to failure because it must utilize the very thing it pretends to invent: a language. We can always invent a word, but we are able to do so only from the standpoint of a language. And this creation is likely to last only as long as language so desires it. Yet, no one knows, exactly, what language wants—so mutinous it is to every slogan and watchword. Notwithstanding, perhaps the poets know something: from Rimbaud, who dreamed of "finding a language from the soul and for the soul," though succeeded only in writing silences; to Mallarmé, who himself was fascinated by the solitude of Herodiade (a "mad virgin") who flowered only for herself—a "desert"—and, with parting words, said: "You lie, O naked flower/that blooms from my lips."

Only and alone does language speak. And we, at every instant, speak—even in our dreams. Yet, it is not we who speak; for the metaphor of the Mother-tongue deceives inasmuch as we always need to imagine someone—an invisible subject (the soul)—who moves the lips of language, just as one might move the strings of a marionette. However, nothing is above or behind language; there is nothing but itself that, like the rose-colored tongue that moves within the human mouth, is already present. It is more than a constant repetition of the surf and more than some background noise or noise from the back of the throat—it is a tone or music or presence that is without any human re-presentation. It speaks without saying anything; addressing itself to no one: "*O einer, O keiner, O niemand, O du . . .* "[7] Perhaps in our never ending discourses, our conversations and chatter, in our interior monologues, our conferences and written works we continue to cover up this solitary and singular voice, but always with the voice itself. Similar to a translator who repeats—without comprehending—that which he has read and then believes himself to be the author of "his" discourse.

Monologue of language, it speaks all alone. We, too, speak all alone—and we do it constantly. We call it thinking. Yet, although thought remains silent and without need of the human voice or any articulated noise, it can never dispense with language. At times, too—though rarely—we speak aloud alone. It would seem this latter is a sign of mental alienation whereby the speaker comes under the influence of the other: of language itself. "All day long he speaks aloud alone; asking questions and giving the answers without changing his voice. . . . And then, when he is tired, he climbs up to his window and shouts words into the air."[8]

Words in the air. . . this must be taken literally, especially in light of what Zimmer said with respect to Hölderlin having become "crazy." ("Oh! Actually he wasn't crazy at all—not what you'd call crazy.") In the air, from the window where the "philosophical light" shined—the window open to the world, such that "one would think he thought to thus conquer the world," explained Zimmer. For even a monologue—as solitary and separated as that of a poet withdrawn into a tower in Tübingen—remains, still, addressed to the other and destined to be heard—even if this other is no one. Here, no real distinction can be sustained between monologue and dialogue; for the former already resounds in the mouth that sounds the words in the air—similar to a trumpet in a polyphony. Even if it is only a discordant or concerted exchange of voice, "asking questions and giving the answers" or "ranting like an actor." Every word—especially those "in the air"—would constitute a dialogue: an intended addressee or physical speaker or interlocutor need not be present. For the word, as word, opens up a dimension. Or better yet, it *is* the very dimension or *dia*. The dimension opens itself up within the architecture of the word, as well as with-in the indissoluble unity of the *double entente*. Speaking is already an understanding and a hearing of that which is said and of that which is in reference. Still, we must over-hear—absolutely. Certainly, that which is understood and heard most often are words, sentences, significations, designated things, and so on. Yet, the word itself is never heard: its sound remains silent. Without a doubt, it was this sound, sounding from the source, that Hölderlin sought—and thought to hear by shouting words "in the air." This latter expression must be understood as "within the very vibration of the word," though it can never be reduced, simply, to sonority. "From the moment we are dialogue and are able to hear and understand one from another . . . " However, we can be this dialogue only when we are able to absolutely over-hear, speaking.

It may very well be that Hölderlin sought to find, once again, the naked noise or insonorous vibration of the word. Or perhaps, on the contrary, he sought to free himself from this word, which fell upon him like lightening. Bettina von Arnim would lead us to believe it was the latter: "I think that Hölderlin was submerged by a divine power; that this power was language; and that it drowned his senses with a rapid and irresistible rush. . . . But to listen to him is to think of the wind's most admired disorder, for he was forever shouting out hymns that broke off like a wild, whirling wind. Just then, one would say that a profound science had seized him; then we abandon, utterly, the idea that he was insane. Rather, let us guess at what he says of poetry and language, and how close he was to en-lightening the divine secret."[9]

Seized as he was by the frenzy of a word liberated from every frictive force (from syntax, signification, and everything that had hitherto formed the architectonic structure of language from the time of Greek philosophy), the poet was able to rant and rave and shout and speak only the word that *inhabited* him, that haunted and possessed him. So seized, "he" spoke a language endowed with its own violence and its own measure and meter (its caesura)—and that traveled like the unseizable wind. With Hölderlin, we see that "speaking for the sake of speaking" takes on a tone entirely different from that of idle talk, which, in effect, speaks only to say nothing or to lose itself. "Speaking for the sake of speaking" speaks simply on account of its love of the word—and it alone. It is, so to speak, a doubling that is, itself, an intensification rather than an interiorization. Like a wind that grows greater by itself or like a snowball that falls down a slope and gathers into an avalanche, an avalanche of words, "like flowers."

But the word, having happened upon such liberty—must it still concern itself with "signification"? It speaks—and that is all. Yet, it itself is not the subject of the word; for the subject is engulfed by the flood and lost from sight even before it can claim subjectivity. It is such that language, unable to utter anything other than itself (the rumblings from its subterranean forge), would join, in its excessive profusion, the nudity of silence. An entire portion of modern literature (Joyce, Beckett, and Blanchot among others) inscribes itself in this movement that moves from both the proliferation and *outrageous* dissemination of "sense" to its extinction and exhaustion in what Heidegger called the *resonance of silence*. In truth, it is constituted by a single moment: excess and exhaustion. For, having attained this moment (which Hölderlin referred to as the *caesura* or *empty transport*), the word would break a-part. But then, it is precisely in this break that the word speaks: what, though, can it speak? The essential? Or only it-*self*? That which is never said, but which, nevertheless, speaks like a subject that has been crossed out; a subject that is broken-down, tattered and torn, engulfed and lost from the sight of every word. Out of this comes a voice from the source; a voice that is as solitary as it is shared and that belongs to no one though it haunts everybody. It haunts, but only as long as every-one allows oneself to be dispossessed and carried a-way, as if by the irresistible waters of a flood. Thus we can be only the spokesperson of the word—of that demonical power that *catches* us (in the sense "catching fire").

Hölderlin, in a late lightening-like fragment—of the sort that leaves one blind or totally bedazzled—wrote that the word was given to man as "the most dangerous of all his gifts . . . so that he could bear witness to the heritage that he is." Consequently, man is nothing more than the witness of a gift. He is one that witnesses the reception of the gift of the word. And he speaks, properly speaking, only in order to witness the reception of this gift; in other words, he speaks only for the sake of speaking. Like the gift of life, it is a gift that gives nothing other than its own power; gift that, giving "only" itself, gives everything.

This solitude has nothing—anything resembling isolation. In speaking for the sake of speaking—for the love of the word—we are not in any way removed from the world. The gift rendered by the word is precisely that gift that allows us to speak *it*. And, although it is a gift of nothing, it is also a total gift that renders without reservation; indeed, is a *sur-rendering*. Perhaps even the sur-rendering of a Dwelling Place. In a fragment signed by Hölderlin, we read the following: "Yet, the human being inhabits huts . . ." With this the Heideggerian image (which was actually borrowed from Nietzsche) is announced: the "House of Being." Speaking for the sake of speaking is to inhabit this singular dwelling place that dwells *a-part*, but which gives, in-part, the power to belong. It is what Holderlin referred to as the *infinite inclination*.

According to Peter Handke, the "instant of language" occurs every time the word succeeds in overhearing itself speak. All the same, this hardly takes place in the form of idle talk—though it always remains in the proximity of it. (Nothing is closer to idle talk than the "essential" word. In effect, the essential word becomes idle talk when *it sets itself up* as the subject of the word). The instant of language is not so much a listening to oneself speak, but an experiencing of the (properly unheard-of) experience of language as a simultaneous hearing and over-hearing. That which speaks is always *Doyouhearme*, but only according to an injunction that is other than the emptiness of idle talk. Rather, it is according to a call to belonging or to the *double entente*. (In German, one uses the word *hören* meaning "to understand" as well as "to hear." One can hear the word *hören* in the word *gehören*, itself signifying "to belong.") This instant is one in which one experiences the limits or confines of the world—according to a (lost) poem by Rimbaud. All the same, we read in the surviving rough draft of *A Season in Hell*: "I certainly had other things to do than live."

The proximity of language to death is petrifying. Trakl experienced it; experienced, above all, the unheard-of power of silence *as* word. "The solitary wind of God always sounds / Against the black walls" ("Elis"). This hardly constitutes a metaphor for the word in its solitude. *It is* the word itself—the solitary wind of God sounding, always, against the cold walls for as long as an other (a Stranger) has not heard or followed it. Yet, where does such a call lead? To "decline," to death. To the confines of the world. Such confines, simultaneously, open up a possibility that is impossible inasmuch as it re-fuses itself in the a-part (*écart*) while surrendering itself in its refusal. This opens up pure possiblity, or the rule of the word itself in an ecstatic solitude that is outside of sense. "But to listen [to him] was to think of the most admired disorder of the wind. . . . For he was forever shouting out hymns that broke off like a whirling wind." It was this unique moment of pure rhythm that Hölderlin referred to as a caesura: in which everything would whirl about and turn. In which a certain generosity, without restriction, would open up, would render itself—*sur-render* itself. It would open up as well a present now become the space or interior music of the world; opening of the dimension.

Whirling wind, yes; but one that blows in suspension: what Celan called *Atemwende*. A death, yes; but one without dying: a death whose sense has, in a sense, been lost in the loss of sense and is approached only in the poem, that is, the "*Abschied*"—signifying a departure that de-parts from everything. *Abschied* is to go without any possibility of return—a going that never goes to the source. An *evanescence*, or better yet, an *evan-essence* (*disparêtre*). For, where could such evan-essence return? Especially when the very place toward which it advances has never been attained; and especially when (no) body yet inhabits it? Place that never attains itself, that never arrives at itself, that ever draws infinitely back: dwelling place, place a-part and forever postponed. In a way, drifting toward the headwaters of language, therefore before the word, before sight and the sense of touch, utterly—out-of-sight—in the sense of a remote mourning and of a horizon spreading as far as the eye can see. Place that is out of hand—the latter is surrendered in its gesture of farewell.

Is this, then, a farewell to the world? The monk, inasmuch as he retreats into silence, "vanishes" from the world—but always *from the world.* The ensuing relationship is one of separation—which might very well constitute *the* relationship as well as *the* word. If the monk experiences God, it is in the "solitary wind"—for God dwells only a-part. Indeed, he has not removed himself *from* the world, withdrawing, as it were, to some super-celestial place. Rather, God dwells *as* the very name of this place a-part. Silence, forbearance, impoverishment, and surrender are just some of the possible ways in which one is transfixed by the a-part, but also, ways in which one may dwell, ecstatically, therein. At the same time, nothing forbids us from having the same experience by way of "contrarities." Song, for example, sings silence; Antoine is assaulted by the devil; and some religions gain access to the sacred by way of sexual orgy (as did Bataille).[10] As for absent-mindedness, this is simply another form of self-oblivion and therefore of ecstacy. To be sure, such examples and the contents they contain have no importance whatsoever; for this place—a-part—is not itself "accesible." Rather, it is the pathway that sends everything a way (*der Weg alles bewëgende* [Heidegger]): Pathway and departure.

Zarathustra is one who lives by inhabiting high haunts, "solitudes" and deserts. But one day, he decides to leave his cave and so begin his "decline" or "going under." Yet why? Is it simply in order to speak? Is it because Zarathustra cannot remain silent? What essential thing has he to say? The catastrophe that falls upon the word begins, always, in the illusion of a sense, of a "message" or mission that must be carried out. (Whether or not this message is "spiritual" matters little.)

The traveler "who used to call himself the shadow of Zarathustra" was the one who sang the solemn song: "The desert spreads! What misfortune for him who contains a desert!" This formula, used by Heidegger as a springboard to explain "European nihilism," could, on the contrary, constitute the only culmination of nihilism. So it is, if we listen to "the cries of virtue" that agitate every now and then the breast and withered heart of that "old shrew" called Europe. A Europe overwhelmed with solicitude and swelled with a nostalgia for a lost sense: above all, for that of the legendary Orient. But what misfortune, rather, for the one who curses the desert and solitude and the experience of want and destitution. "O cursed race!" wrote Trakl.

In the desert—in the free expanse that is both sweet and savage, solicitous and violent—there speaks another word. Where silence nears, as well as song. It used to be that the prophets ventured into the desert to speak—but today, we understand nothing of this. And yet, where, if not precisely in this place of "evan-essence," can the word, finally, be free? Perhaps *desert* designates the very word that takes place, simply for itself. Descendant of the Latin term *desero* (meaning to abandon, leave, depart—to desert), it speaks the departure, it speaks the separation or a-part. As well, it speaks a secession that is also an accession or initiation—to the very solitude that none but hermits and shepherds, fanatics of God and poets, the illiterate and the dispossessed may haunt. Of course, they never choose such residency. The precarious place in which they dwell, open to every wind, is nothing other than the earth—but the earth that is finally inhabited poetically. In such dwelling, there is always the danger that we may sink deep into madness or imbecility or aphasia; that is, "the madness to lockup" according to Rimbaud. Still, there is another danger, less obvious perhaps, but much more dangerous: that of never attaining the desert, of never being "brushed by the wing of imbecility" (Baudelaire). There is danger, also, in that we may be satisfied with nothing but the perfectly idiotic image of an imposter or sham seer. For with such, there is nothing to see. At least not in the sense of "seeing Venice" or some other "wonder of the world." And perhaps even, there is nothing to hear or understand, nothing but the broken breath of the word and the angelic silence that ventures forward from the desert.

When it came to silence, Heidegger did not always speak the same language. However, at a time when he still spoke of "expression," silence seemed nothing less than the password of speech—but always of human speech and communication. The silence comes from the one who silences (*Schweigen*), and not from the word itself, what in its burning heart, is calm (the term *calm*, *Stille* in German, descends from a Greek word signifying "burn"). On the contrary silencing or making silence takes place in conversation and can occur only in authentic speech. To be able to remain silent, one must have something to say to one's interlocutor. Consequently, we find that silence is an extremely expressive way to communicate, for it forbids idle talk. One who has nothing to say hardly knows how to remain silent. On the contrary, one speaks at random; one speaks out of an abundance of everything and nothing. In other words, one speaks simply "in order to speak"—or to say nothing. Authentic silence is not the characteristic of an uncommunicative character or even of someone who is mute (who can deny the "propensity to speak" of this latter?). Rather, authentic silence is a characteristic of someone who wants to say something essential and who would make oneself understood in a way other than by verbal proliferation (which, for Heidegger, was always secondary). Is silence, then, a want of words? No. Silence is the highest way of speaking—without saying a word.

Insofar as silence takes part in speech (even as expressive silence) and insofar as the indissociable dichotomy of speaking-hearing is still operative, the purely discursive schema of language already begins to weather away. For—and Heidegger already knew it—this dichotomy is not applicable to every type of word. Indeed, the poetic word takes exception. Moreover, it is not insignificant that the poetic word practically never appears in *Being and Time*; or rather, it appears in a way that leaves much to be desired: on the one hand, it appears as a preontological "document" (and what a document! The fable concerning *cura* or anxiety is a remarkable mark of literary impoverishment!). On the other hand, the poetic word appears in the much more significant incident of paragraph 34: "In 'poetical' discourse, the communication of the existential possibilities of ones' state-of-mind can become an aim in itself, and this amounts to a disclosing of existence."[11]

Only the dialogue with poetry (especially Hölderlin's) made the Turning possible and necessary. In the first place, it was a turning in the relationship between the human being and language, but also, it was a turning in the relationship between human being and Being. In effect, poetry does not respond to a single requisite of the discourse: for the poet is never the exclusive speaker of "his" poem. No, his effacement, and his quasi disappearance, is exacted in order that the "great" poem may emerge into the world. The addressee is hardly someone that has already been determined. (Undeniably, a poem may be dedicated to someone in particular; however, it still addresses itself to whomever hears it.) It is even possible that, as in the case of Celan, the poem is addressed to nobody: to the unknown or to the first first-comer. Finally, the poem never speaks simply as a "function of things." Like the painting (no matter how figurative) or the musical composition (no matter how vocal or theatrical), the poem no longer wishes to express a signification; for none of these "artistic mediums" can be reduced to the representation of a scene, nor can they stage the many states of the soul. The common world of *Mitsein* no longer has a prescriptive value for the poetic word inasmuch as the poetic word emanates only from itself. Far from dispersing itself in worldly significations, it tends to gather itself up in itself—or in its infinite *a-part.* Words are no longer tools, used exclusively to designate or to communicate things. They lift themselves up like living beings: they stand up and stand *all alone*; and by themselves they dictate their laws to the poet. This is particularly prevalent in Mallarmé, where the poetic word dissociates itself from the "elementary employment of discourse," precisely at the very point where it resounds like a foreign language: "The verse which, of several vocables, rewrites a total word—new and foreign to language—and, as it is spell-binding, achieves this isolation of the word."[12]

It is a solitary word, but sovereign even in its coldness: autarchical. This adjective describes rather well the language of Mallarmé. Yet, it also refers to something else: originally, the political autarchy of Ancient Greece never signified the cold and constrained withdrawal of a regime (or city) into itself and nothing but itself. No, it signified a government composed of citizens and governed by citizens. In other words, autarchy could be conceived as a "direct" democracy. We might even think of the philosophical determination of liberty as the autonomy of thought legislating its own (universal) laws and then adhering to them. Accordingly, it would be better to speak of *autarchy* as a structure distinct from both monarchy and anarchy. The *arche* or Principle legislates *itself*, principally, as the principle of identity; moreover, from this Principle the principle of equality emerges as well as every other republican idea.

The risk inherent in autarchy is an utter self-enclosure, an absolute sclerosis and asphyxiation. Today, the categorical withering away of modern democracies is a tragic example of this. "That the land not shut us up!" was Hölderlin's plea—and the subsequent motive for his exile in France, and even, perhaps, the cause of his collapse. Land or language—there is little difference. In the poem "*Der Gang aufs Land*," the poet associates the journey to his country with the discovery of the word as an open word . . . in the Opening. When "the word will have been found," and the heart whole heartily in bloom, then the Lightening will be open. The word goes forth into the opening; it traces out and flows forward; it is the word-river or word-flower. It is as natural and terrestrial as an animal endowed with its own respiration, rhythm, way, and its own native "air." Dream, perhaps, of an absolutely *physical* language. Living! Bounding forward and abounding; a language that is never fixed, but drunk upon itself and ecstatic. Such is the "flower of the mouth":

> . . . and you spoke, solitary.
> A wealth of golden words that you addressed,
> Happy! with the inexhaustible rivers that well up
> In every country.
>
> ("Germany")

Happy word, solitary indeed!—but always an *exposed* solitude that resides in the very heart of the world. Similar to the song that sounds from deep within the gardens of a city sunk in darkness. It is the word of the lover who stands beside the fountain or of the poet who dreams "about his friends." It is a word that gives oblivion and drunkenness, it is this always fragile legend and distant noise that remains so near to being lost.

The poet, according to Hölderlin, far from shutting himself up in his ivory tower, has need of others because, for the poet, the word—however happy it may be in its solitude—is too heavy to carry or keep. Notwithstanding, he stands "lonely before the God": the poet—whose only weapon is "simplicity"—must, without fear, hold himself erect and open:

> He has no need of any weapon; nor of any
> Ruse—as long as the want of any God avails him.
>
> ("Vocation of a Poet")

Heidegger notes that this want hardly comprehends itself in terms of a lack or absence. Such want *belongs* to the God: it is his proper mark. It is a want that wells from his wealth and excessive abundance and that founds the law of poetic allotment. And it is the poet who comes into collision with the want of any sacred name and with "images that are so simple and saintly" that they become unspeakable. Yet this inability of the word also constitutes its ressourcefulness and fortune. It is then that the word becomes pure song. And that which renders it even more eloquent—inasmuch as it exposes itself to the loss of sense and inasmuch as it renounces the ability to find it again—is that the word loses itself in itself and in its Orphic power. All the same, we do not experience such a power until it escapes itself, until the tide seems to tarry or suspend its flux, until the poet, far from singing, begins to "stutter." Or, as Celan has written, "*nur lallen und lallen.*"[13] In the break of the song, the word would open itself up into an abyss; breaking down into its primal silence.

❁ ❁ ❁

"Are you going to bury yourself up there?" He said "up there," though he dwelled much higher—in a hamlet high upon the pass. Yet, the said place was called *Marie-Haut*. Irénée's old car, which was quite dented, almost threw me over the bridge. He had turned around (he was coming down while I was going up "to bury myself"); he opened up the door; he spoke without stopping and looked with a look that was somewhat mad. (At times, one speaks more with one's eyes than with one's mouth). I thought the solitude had unsettled him—making him mad in consequence. But in all actuality, he must have thought the same about me—about this strange inhabitant of the city, come now to bury himself in a lost hole at the bottom of the Alps. He accompanied me to the top of the pass where the passable path came to an end; and then he disappeared. June's twilight shown through. The pathway, at times, was utterly obliterated. And when it was not, it followed the broken banks of the river, the depths of the abysses, and the desolate landscapes of black and frail shale. Oftentimes, the earth revealed itself, and I found it necessary to pass through by running, or rather, by a sort of complicated dance. Some images remain, still: they were the same from the same land. Stars and glaciers in the distance, a somber waterfall, and the river, rolling down its tree trunks, stones, and debris with incessant noise—was this the resonance of silence? Over the emptiness, there was but one bridge whose every other plank was missing. And finally, after what seemed to me like hours of walking (he had assured me with a good humored but hollowed out grimace that "I would arrive in half an hour"), I arrived before a prairie dotted with moonlight: and there I saw the bell-tower of the church of Templiers and the crumbled walls of the abandoned village. I saw a sort of refuge—a hovel constructed of dry stones stacked against the hill—that had once been an old school, but that had now been transformed into a sheepfold and that, naturally, stank of sheep. And everywhere, I saw sage and stinging nettles. Gold dust of time! I collapsed over the threshold, for finally I was there—there. But where?

Solitude may be defined as a "lonely and secluded place." Such was the way in which Lamartine used the word: "The rivers, rocks, and forests are such dear solitudes." This word descends from the Latin *solitudo*, whose significance is the state of a desert place. It is a place that would dissolve or destroy the question "Where am I?" First, there is the place; only then, within which there are things and beings that are either dead or alive, divine or of a natural nature. But, that which is there in the first *place* is the *There is* itself, in all its simplicity and autarchy. It is a place that approaches the pure identity with which Hegel identified—for good reason—nonidentity.

"The only thing his music wants," said Mozart concerning one of his colleagues, "is poverty." Was this the irony of the musician whom some envious composers reproached for having included "too many notes"? Yet, there is poverty—and then there is poverty. The former is an indigence caused by sclerosis and convention. The latter is the wonderment of the Simple. Although the two are distinct, they are not so easily separated. In the same way, we have difficulty in distinguishing between idle talk and the "absolute" word. For here, we need more than a sensitive ear: rather, we must be endowed with an aptitude for listening—over-hearing. "Thinking is on the descent to the poverty of its provisional essence. Thinking gathers language into simple saying. In this way language is the language of Being, as clouds are the clouds of the sky."[14] Such a language has not Being for object. Rather, Being belongs to language in the same way that the clouds belong to the sky; though, insofar as thought can be only *temporary*, the appurtenance is precarious—but also infinite. It is never fixed but free, finally, from metaphysical eternity.

"*Was geschah?*" "What has happened?" So queries the poem beginning the forth section of *No One's Rose*. In Hölderlin's poem "Germany," the secret speaker would respond that no one knows: "No one knows what one experiences there." Perhaps, we might respond that a language has been found; a language has happened that is simple and one, one and solitary. Language that is "more impoverished. Open. Native." Language that is sister of the stars and fraternal with the earth. Language of the There is.

This language shines splendorously forth from a spark that is both unbearable and sweet. However, in dwelling too near this language, we risk losing the use of the common word—of that word, without which, there is no communication, no exchange, no community. Even so, nothing is further from the common word than this "language which has become insignificant by virtue of its familiarity; this language of 'you know very well what I mean' common to the Communication Era."[15] In effect, what the Communication Era has actually achieved, has not in any way been the opening of a common ground; but only the cancellation of all distance. As a consequence, we have a frightful mixture of a certain banal and pretentious universalism and narcissistic delirium. "Express yourself!" "Speak!" may very well be the order of the day; but behind this supposed call to liberty and "direct" democracy, there reigns reality's dictatorship. Reality has entered into what Hegel denounced as *Selbstverständlichkeit* (the "you-know-very-well-what-I-mean"): the that that goes from itself.

No, you do not always know what I mean. And I—I do not always know either: *I no longer know how to speak*—spoke Rimbaud.

Nevertheless, he still speaks. But he speaks a word that refuses to slip silently—like a coin—from one hand to another. He speaks a word that has been bottled and thrown into the sea: "The pathways are rough. The hillocks are covered over with genista. The air is motionless. How the birds and springs are far away! This can only be the end of the world, going forward."[16]

The end of the world? The rocks of Barre-Tremble (name given to a vertiginous cliff above Marie-Haut), the megaliths of Britanny and the abandoned bunkers scattered along the Atlantic coast speak as much. Or at least as so many signs that will have neither concealed nor unconcealed, but that will have interrupted language. And out of this interruption—this caesura—these signs shall always carry some sort of stigma of the fore-biddance of absolute Saying that has now entered into evan-essence. Or perhaps we could speak of those abandoned tombs surrendered to the desert sands, those simple stones half-buried and apart from the river, from the living—and from idle words.

Must we then speak of a solitude that is mortal? I do not know. Perhaps dying is nothing more than that song sung at the edge of the inaccessible, at the very confines of the world. In any case, "action is not life, but a way to waste away some force or excitation." And that which would be above action—or "in advance" according to Rimbaud—will no longer refer to the same dualistic logic that designates as negative everything that escapes mastery. That which does approach, and which would lay aside all certainty—even that of being alive, of being master of one's body or master of one's word—is nothing. Or rather, it is the sarcophagus of Nothing.

To say, simply—from this simple saying that is free and solitary and that belongs to nobody—to say, the body firmly backed against the warm shoulder of the threshold—to say, at times, it would envelop me with its breath and lend me a helping hand in the walk "through the unthinkable" and, finally, would radiate as in former times—as a summer's night—through the larches of the landscape. And that this hour will come again; that it is ready to sound the day when the hourglass shall turn over again, strong now, by so many millions of geological years, ballasted in the heather, the evening wind, the strident swift.

Solitude, smile directed to the unknown, to the first-comer. Limbo of thought. Lost memory, and yet, the memory of the loss. It will have the flavor of a fresh widow, of a white dawn. And if someone tells me it does not exist—like silence that, in effect, does not exist—I shall respond: it is thus that there is solitude—and solitude alone.

Notes

1. Martin Heidegger, "The Way to Language," in *On the Way to Language*, p. 111.

2. Martin Heidegger, *Being and Time*, pp. 331–332.

3. Paul Celan, *Paul Celan: A Bilingual Edition*, p. 209.

4. "*Das existential-ontologische Fundament der Sprache ist die Rede*" ("the existential-ontological foundation of language is discourse or talk"), *Being and Time*, p. 203. I have commented on paragraph 34 of *Being and Time* in a text entitled "*Sans mot dire*," which has been published in the collective volume *Etre et Temps (Questions de méthode et voies de recherches)*, ed. J.-P. Cometti and D. Janicaud (Marseille: Sud, 1989).

5. *Being and Time*, p. 204.

6. *Being and Time*, p. 209.

7. "O one, o none, o no one, o you . . ." Paul Celan, "No One's Rose," *Poems of Paul Celan*, trans. by Michael Hamburger (New York: Persea Books, 1986), p. 153.

8. Gustav Kuhne's interview with Zimmer (the carpenter who took in Hölderlin when he left the asylum). In Hölderlin, *Oeuvres*, p. 1110.

9. Testimony of Bettina von Arnim (*Die Günderode*, 1840), in Hölderlin, *Oeuvres*, p. 1106.

10. Here, "Antoine" is in allusion to Flaubert's well-known text by the same name. Trans.

11. *Being and Time*, p. 205.

12. Mallarmé, "*Crise de Vers*," in *Oeuvres Complètes*, p. 368.

13. "Tubingen, Janner," in *Poems of Paul Celan*, p. 40. Commented on by Philippe Lacoue-Labarthe in *La poésie comme expérience*.

14. Heidegger, "Letter on Humanism" in *Basic Writings*, p. 242.

15. Peter Handke, *The Weight of the World*.

16. Rimbaud, "Enfance," *Oeuvres Complètes*, p. 124.

6

The Scaped Landscaped

Something strange is the soul on the earth.
Georg Trakl, "*Springtime of the Soul*"

This man is no stranger to the city; and still, he seems a vagabond. We see him wander through the streets and public squares with the carefree character of a tramp; and on a sultry day, when the sun is high and the hard earth burns to walk, we find him walking without sandals, his feet bare upon the ground. He meets a friend and deliberately takes him in hand, so that together they may speak: for this tramp loves to speak. Or rather, like a ventriloquist, he would make others speak, such that each begins to speak as if in a foreign language, but one that is strangely familiar. But he—he hears a voice within—one that speaks every time he would venture too far. This man rarely goes beyond the city walls, though when he does, it is simply to refresh his feet in a spring that flows somewhat apart. In no way is this devil of a man an ascetic: for he enjoys the company of other men and the sweetness of wine—just as he enjoys laying out upon a field of grass and listening to a friend tell a tale about that which he has heard among other men. Such sweet conversation would silence the song of the cicada—a creature that hails from the race of poets.

Yes, this man likes to go to springs and sources. He marvels at the beauty of such places; he marvels because such is his pastime, for he too is somewhat apart and still at the very center of that which is:

amazement. He has, so to speak, made a career out of it, which is precisely why both his friends and enemies are instilled with it—with such amazement. Indeed, perhaps we have overheard them say: "You, excellent friend, strike me as the oddest of men."[1] Why then should we be amazed at such a familiar place? But what a strange fellow that never leaves the city, "neither to travel beyond the borders nor even to venture outside the city walls." Stranger? Or simply strange?

The place radiates in its simple quietude: the cicadas, the plantane, the spring and the sultry summer day. Simple things—so simple and sacred that another madman would later say "that sometimes a certain propriety comes to describe them" (Hölderlin). And yet man is still the strangest thing there is:

> The strange is not wanting here and yet
> Nothing stranger than man would show itself.[2]

He does not see what is before his own feet; instead he looks up toward the stars; and then, walking forward, falls into a well—or perhaps into a quandry. Is there not something slightly amusing in this? To be sure, such a strange species of bird is rare. In fact, the first man to plane thus was called, ironically enough, a *philosopher.* And sometimes a *philomuse* or *philomath.* Without a doubt, he would like to know who he is; but above all, he would like to know what it is to know. Still, he does not know. Others think they know what it is—especially insofar as they know what "is" is. Still, he does not know: he is in a quandry, the passageway blocked. For some reason, it escapes him. Even that which lies before his feet seems to give way. For him, above all, there is no present: "No, a present does not exist." "It is true that he is unaware what his next-door neighbor is doing, hardly knows, indeed, whether the creature is a man at all; he spends all his pains on the question, what man is, and what powers and properties distinguish such a nature from any other."[3]

This man is not only strange; he is, in every sense of the Greek word, absolutely without a place (*atopotatos*). Perhaps this is so because he was the first to set out and seek a place and formula. Yet, wherever he may go, the place would forever escape him such that he is forever uprooted, an uprooting that is reflected back upon the most familiar landscape. Instead of drawing back into a thought-free obviousness that for most constitutes the least alienable ground—like the certainty of seeing the sun rise up in the morning—it appears, suddenly, like something never seen before. It is an obviousness of another kind: exorbitant. What is most amazing is that we thought we knew this landscape by heart, when in fact, we have never really seen it. Or at least, we have not seen it through such eyes. It is not extraordinary; it is not weird. No, it is always the simplest and nearest—and marked by a fatal separation, a mortal a-part. It is neither this nor that; neither the plane-tree nor the cicada. Rather, it is the one Wonder inasmuch as it is never seen and yet is always "in" sight: inasmuch as there is something rather than nothing—a presence. But this can come into sight only if the a-part would dig itself in between the things given by sight and by the gift of sight itself. This latter makes it possible to see whatever there may be. Presence—the magic word, so to speak, of the Ancient Greeks—can appear only if immediate things have already withdrawn somewhere. But where, we ask, can they have so withdrawn?

When the first philosopher named presence and attempted to say what it was, he spoke of a "sight" in the sense of seeing a landscape that was a "beautiful sight." Yet, this sight escaped most common mortals. No one could produce it—least of all the landscape painter (however true his paintbrush worked). At best, he could produce only pale imitations and phantoms of the various sights: he could give us only idols. The strangest thing about sight is that it itself remains invisible to the naked eye; it is visible only to the exorbitant eye—to the extra-eye or eye of the Cyclops that dwells at the very core of the human being. It is the eye of the *psyche* or soul that, "in truth, is a foreign thing upon this earth."

Still, Socrates would sink his feet deep into the spring—but already his thoughts are elsewhere. Elsewhere: in a place that he would call *supercelestial*, a place that no human eye could ever penetrate . . . inasmuch as it is not already there. Here, *is there* signifies: to belong in both *body and soul*. It is a place that not only escapes every common mortal, but also every poet—though this latter knows how to sing of such sources and their Nymphs: "If we need courage when speaking the True, then we'll need more when the essence of it, the unconcealment of the unconcealed, must come to the Word. For the truly present presence—without any color or shape and without therefore the ability to be re-presented or the ability to appear—is the unconcealed presence which can only be seen with the thinking eye, the very guide of the soul. And it is from the soul that true knowledge, that is, this disclosing sight, arises; for presence dwells, even now, beyond the world."[4] Metaphysics is the dwelling place of the thinker—at least the one toward which he tends and toward which he is drawn and withdrawn by Thought. It is an elsewhere—a beyond—toward which he must flee as fast as he can—even at the risk of returning "here," to the humble source—to the Cave once again. Positively, he returns only—with the power of the Sight that he has seen and the "true" knowledge (of thought)—to liberate those companions that still remain in chains.

As for the source and majestic plane-tree (the tree that provides him with the salubrious shadow in which he may unfold the entire network of the word and so have a dia-logue), there is nothing left either. Or almost nothing, for the decor is simple insofar as the scene is always elsewhere. What could a thinker learn from a tree? Silence? But Socrates loves to speak. He only feels at home—inasmuch as he has a home—when he is among other men. And even if these men are blind to the "true" light—to the true Day and Dwelling Place—they still remain in touch with true knowledge to the extent that they are able to learn, to learn the true sight. In Greek, *to know* signifies "to have seen." Yet, what is so strange is that this sight is not visible to the naked eye; and even stranger is that in order to make it appear, the thinker who made the invisible the essence of everything and claimed it as *the* true presence [*ousia*] had to have recourse to "images." At the outset, Socrates would dismiss every myth and "story." However, when he wishes to show the thing itself—for example, what it is "to learn" in the "parable" of the Cave—he has no other choice but to reinvent stories and make up myths.

Strangely enough, is not Socrates a "mythical" figure as well? Not legendary in the sense of a King Arthur—for here we do not wish to cast doubt upon his historical existence—rather, mythical in the proper sense of the word *muthos*. According to Heidegger, this word signified, in its origin, the same thing as *logos*. But today we can no longer perceive this sense insofar as we translate *logos* by "reason" or even "sense"; we cannot recover the original meaning of *muthos* because we are unable to perceive how much *logos*—at the origin—was a myth. Perhaps it was THE fundamental myth of the whole of Western History. Perhaps, even, it was the initial sending off of this history as the history of *logos* (of Being). Once again, according to Heidegger, myths are not destroyed by "reason" and its reasonable logic. Rather, when reason and logic rule, myths are already dead—indeed, they die in favor of one particular and almost monotheistic myth: that of an all powerful Rationality. Myths die because God himself would withdraw, though this resolves nothing; for, like Hölderlin, we ask: *Was ist Gott?*

For Socrates, God had already withdrawn himself. In effect, He spoke only as that mysterious voice within—the one that forbade: the Greek *mè*, the refusal; the voice that said: "Go no further! Do not transgress these limits!" (Could it be these limits are all that remain of God?) All the same, it was a voice that rendered Socrates even more enigmatic—though he would never admit it—to those with whom he spoke. Was he not a strange animal to the Athenians? An animal without a home, without a place, in the sense that we have come to understand these terms? At bottom, was not Socrates a monster, a being that had no place to be and no proper determination? An impossible and even utopian hybrid? It was in this way that Aristotle described, in his *Physics*, that every being—excluding the chimera—has a place to be. "Where, in effect, are the satyrs and the sphinx?" Yes, where are they if not in myths. For example, could the myth of Oedipus—in which we find the Sphinx (and its dethronement) and the original murder of the father—represent the myth of "reason" giving birth to itself? Yet, the Greeks had an even a greater expertise than we with respect to myths and chimeras—this people that seemed to have invented everything, beginning with rationality, was also the most chimerical and childish culture that ever was. And Socrates knew it. He always fought, but never against the myths themselves. Rather, he fought for the secession between *muthos* and *logos*. And this, so that he might assign a place to the latter whose limits could be first and foremost. It is precisely this that begins the beginning of the *Phaedrus*: "I don't bother about such things [myths], but accept the current beliefs about them, and direct my inquiries, as I have just said, rather to myself, to discover whether I really am a more complex creature and more puffed up with pride than Typhon, or a simpler, gentler being whom heaven has blessed with a quiet, un-Typhonic nature."[5]

On the one hand, the philosophical allotment would inscribe itself as a Typhon of sorts; and on the other, as an *a-typhos* animal, that is, one "without smoke." Yet, if Socrates called forth Typhon, it was simply to cast him back into the shadows from whence he came—and to show how the philosophic dwelling place was very near to being monstrous (*ungeheure*): enforeigning. It is similiar to a storm in which not only the sky, but everything—Being in its totality—finds itself obscured and overcast. Heidegger always brought this to the attention of those detractors of philosophy who simply considered it to be a hygenic exercise of a "sterile" rationality. For, in all actuality, philosophy begins where every pathway is barred, begins in *a-poros:* "It is precisely when difficulties from everywhere accumulate and gather; it is when everything falters; it is when precariousness appears that the time of philosophy is at hand."[6] For the being of such a storm, there is no longer any shelter in which to take refuge. But, if the "typhon" of Being rips away the reassuring certitudes of the daily dwelling place and of every old habit, it is not transported elsewhere; or rather, it is an elsewhere that is beyond this elsewhere—which simply constitutes another here and is further away, but still on the same map. No, it transports elsewhere in an absolute sense; for here, it is the here itself that appears in a strange light. The apparently simple dwelling place, the very one of everyday life, becomes obscure, smoky and abstract. While, on the contrary, that which seemed far away and nebulous becomes astonishingly clear and divine. Socrates, in questioning the very grounds of the dwelling place of his fellow citizens, would seem a hidious monster. Through such questioning he becomes a horrible plague that must be defeated—and who will, "logically," be defeated. In this reversal of roles and this peculiar exchange—one that prompted Hegel to say that philosophy was the "world inside-out"—it is fitting to find the trace of the initial allotment never really severed. Socrates presents himself to others—even to his friends—as someone who is radically foreign; as if he lived with his head elsewhere, in some chimera far away—even when he undertakes his march forward toward the true Day and when he considers his fellow friends to be prisoners in a smoke-filled cave.

Without a doubt, Socrates knows that the monster Typhon remains, always, hidden deep within the heart of everyone. Or at least, deep within Socrates himself—which explains the famous Delphic oracle: for he—he knows not who he is. It is not so much that he must seek within himself; nor must he necessarily become introspective and so cure himself psychologically (which would have been difficult at a time when the word, let alone the thing, did not exist). On the contrary, it is quite possible that the "interior" gives shelter only to arrogance, shadows and smoke. For this reason Socrates never tries to "return" to himself, but rather ventures, forever, through the city streets. Only in this latter place is he able to learn from others (from the statesman to the slave) just who he could be.

Strange that Socrates does not speak of the "typhus of Being." Could it be that a voice forbids him to do so? Could it be this voice of the *daimon* that stops him every time he ventures too far? Perhaps, at bottom, he has already severed the question—and dis-severed Typhon from the allotment? Dissevered and ripped out like a weed. From the sunny side—the only side that contains the full sense of the verb *to be*—and from the side of that which constitutes the humanity of man and even his divinity, nothing can be monstrous, savage, barbarous, arrogant, or smoky. No. Everything is peaceful, docile, beautiful, tempered, measured, and luminous—such that the philosopher wishes to know nothing of that portion which remains in Hell. It must remain forever excluded, annihilated—exterminated. Yet, this is not that which is most serious and severe; rather, it resides in the philosophical *arrogance* (oftentimes cloaked by good-natured airs) that appropriates for itself the right to decide, to sever, and to assess the good side and bad. This was an arrogance against which Nietzsche had every "reason" to protest; indeed, all the more so insofar as Plato—insofar as he was not satisfied with simply instituting an inevitable philosophical partition—*overdetermined* it with a hierarchy that was rarely explicit, that is, by the reductive identification of both good and evil *to a sense*. With Plato, the metaphysical partition not only opened itself up, but closed itself as well. On the one hand, we find the Good—or everything that emerges from the *nous* or "spirit." On the other—hand—we find the Bad, or everything that emerges from the *aisthesis* or senses. On this latter hand, the chain of identification—which found a very powerful proponent in Christianity—would remain unchanged, or at least nearly so, for 2,000 years. For, for 2,000 years, the sensible would be negated inasmuch as it was "chaotic," typhus, and beastly.

Insofar as such a separation has not taken place—the very one that allots the properly metaphysical allotment—the "physical" cannot be reduced to that portion which is "material" and base in things. No longer is the physical simply a denigrated portion or part of that which is (hitherto regarded as that which properly is not, *mè on*); rather, it is the way of being of Being itself, inasmuch as it is born of itself and blossoms in itself. If we look at the Greek statuaries wherein the athletic stature of the human being is exposed, we find him struggling to find his face, his limits, and his place of being; and we come to understand that no world has ever been as *present*. Furthermore, we find that in such a world of erupting presence (*ekphanestaton*), philosophy—with its *meta*-physical exigence—could appear to the "physical" eyes of the people as only a scandal. It appeared as a monstruous mystification or veritable act of terrorism against the very essence of *life*—an act that had to be punished by death: the death of Socrates. Only Nietzsche understood the absolute necessity of his death *from the Greek point of view.*

Nevertheless, ever since Plato "saved" Socrates, the human being has become ever more u-topian. Moreover, simply a simple reversal of Platonism cannot save us from the malediction of metaphysics; for, from the very moment that the place of "truth" is shifted to the only subject capable of presenting itself to itself, utopia spreads everywhere about—culminating in the fiction of modern space: space that is dedicated to the representation of objects and to the calculation of distances, though never to the appearance of things and to the relationships of proximity or distance. Universal space never constitutes a landscape—not even a desert.

❁ ❁ ❁

Whatever a land-scape may be, it rarely, if ever, allows itself to be easily represented. The entire history of Western painting demonstrates this—a demonstration of which Rilke had already taken note: "For let it be confessed: landscape is foreign to us, and we are fearfully alone amongst the trees which blossom and by streams which flow."[7] If the object itself is finished and formed, the landscape is infinite and without form; and if humankind has hands and a face, the landscape itself is deprived of both. In the paintings of Antiquity, only the human (or divine) body has importance. It was the athletic body of the Greeks that "one cultivated like the earth" and whose appearance alone epitomized the beauty of the world. As for landscape (especially one uninhabited and deserted), it was hardly worthwhile for the eye to remain fixed upon it—not even for an instant. With Christian art, even though the "glorious" body fell into disrepute, landscape still rarely received any specific treatment. However, when it did, it was an *idea* of a landscape. For example, a rock was sufficient to give the impression of a mountain; and what is more, painters, for many years to come, were taught to represent the mountain *according to* the rock. Nature was only a background, a sort of decorous frame that surrounded the only true subject dignified of being represented: the crucifixion, adoration or the Annunciation.

Landscape is infinite primarily because any given view can render only *one* view or "aspect"—depending, of course, upon the point of view. Yet, does not this "aspect" already characterize every view—which, as it were, allowed Plato to hold the view that every image produced by the painter was *the least proper* and least capable of rendering a full and complete presence (*ousia*)? To render nature, human beings, things, tides, and beasts totally present, it would be necessary to have a total mirror at one's disposal. In other words, one would need to become God. However, even a total mirror can produce only one aspect of the world, the world *as* aspect, whereby visibility is reduced insofar as it is only visibility.

Nevertheless, the fascination for totality inspired the first true landscapes: those that we call *Weltlandschaft* or *landscape of the world.* Not only has landscape ceased to simply be a background from which the central figures (subjects that orient their look towards a center) are detached, but more, it has become, in its own right, the totality of the view. The view that has opened up because it has been decentered; in fact, it has become the mysterious relation between the visible and invisible, figured under the form of the micro*cosm*. Bernard Lamblin, in his book *Painting and Time*, has clearly distinguished the two technical procedures by which the painting of a Patinir or of a Bruegel succeeds in elevating the landscape to the level of a world totality.

> First, the point of view from which nature is observed is very high. One has the impression that the painter has taken up a position somewhere atop a mountain from whence one sees the entire landscape unfold. Under one's eye it [the landscape] would tumble down and then climb, once again, after many peripeteia, towards a horizon far away. The line of the horizon is situated rather high on the surface of the canvas. . . . Next, the painter accumulates, without any concern for geographical verasimilitude, specimens representative of anything that the earth can offer as a curiosity. He hardly hesitates to juxtapose cultivated fields and empty deserts, savage forests and abrupt mountains, without forgetting clouds, rivers and oceans . . .[8]

This "cosmological Idea" arose at a time when the earth began to be perceived as a totality or terrestrial globe (for example, with Bruegel, we find certain views such as the "great angle" and the rounded outline). Furthermore, it arose at a time when, parallel to the scientific, philosophical, and geographical idea of representation, the European consciousness penetrated and explored the totality of the globe. This was the Age of Exploration and Great Discoveries.

Yet, to hold on to this "Idea"—which was similar to the mathematical will to master nature—would be too reductive. It is true that at the very moment when humankind seemed, finally, to withdraw from the forefront of the scene—for as Rilke wrote with respect to Italian Renaissance painting, "man stood before landscape and masked it"—Nature itself withdrew insofar as it became, simply, landscape. Notwithstanding, such withdrawing was not nothing. Rather, it was even the *drawing* proper that marked the painted work. Drawing that assembled the violent separation between the visible and invisible.

Let us consider the "Landscape of Winter" painted by Bruegel in 1565. In appearance (in effect, what else could there be to see but appearance?), it is a simple and familiar landscape, full of peaceful everydayness: a Flemish village under snow with a frozen river upon which dark, somber spots stand out. They are skaters whose faces are not revealed. In the distance, we see the white, flat countryside and a sky which is white as well and dotted by two dark marks: perhaps they are crows?

To describe painted landscape is an undertaking undertaken in vain. In a sense, there is nothing to see. There is no "action"—even if, as in Bruegel's painting, there are skaters. There is no signification, for there is no referent, neither mythical nor historical. As one critic has written: "It is a painting without subject: the village, like the scene, has no narrative function whatsoever. It is only a pretext that serves to deepen the painter's search for light. . . . There is, here, a haunting obsession with pure light (visible also as an interior light) that drives Bruegel to represent, in the same tonality, the profundity of the sky and that of the frozen river; as if the sky had descended into the water and dwelled therein—thus constituting a double mirror, wherein the creation is capable of contemplating itself. This clarity is a sort out of time. . . . It creates the fundamental irreality of the world; it is the color of the soul."[9]

Perhaps these are too metaphysical terms—for what, for example, is the "soul"? And why should the pure clarity be "out of time"? Is it not, rather, the very color *of time*, just as the landscape is the pure clarity of *the world*? The essential shows through: the world (the entirety of phenomena) is able to present itself only by tearing away from that which does not wish to appear and which the work would, nevertheless, show as such—as "invisible." This manifestivity, this transparency of the unapparent, is put into operation in the "Landscape of Winter;" secretly and yet within the unattainable proximity of that which never ceases to come forward—to come ever closer—to presence. This closeness is also a farness; just as the visible is, in its essence, invisible. To think this *aphanes harmonie* (unapparent alliance, as said Heraclitus), we need not venture far: instead, we must know how to see or, quite simply, to know. A knowing that is a seeing: a clairvoyance without the traditional "beyond," without hallucination, and even without any content.

Bruegel's landscape is the very color of the soul, but only if we think the soul as did Aristotle; in other words, as being in its beingness—as that being present in its "unconcealedness." It does not refer to some interior that has always been the exclusive property of an individual subject who has had the capacity to have various "states of soul." Instead, it refers to the interiority as such, the sense of which Hölderlin referred to as the "*Alles ist innig*" or "Everything is in inclination." Color—though not in the sense of a subjective coloration (which it would later be with the Impressionists). No, color simply as the simple tone of the world to which everything—Being as a unified totality in terms of a *cosmos*—is secretly harmonized. According to Apollinaire, it would be the color of time, or of the *Stimmung*, or perhaps, even (as

Heidegger would say), of the *Grundstimmung*. This latter is in harmony with the *Stimme des Seins* (the voice of Being). A silent *voice* that, in consequence, is that much more talkative (as is the stone for Trakl). The landscape addresses itself—has it out—ecstatically; for it is nothing more than an ecstatic projection of an Interiority that has never been enclosed. Neither here nor there, but there, where it is, there where there is a place. "There is a Light the wind has extinguished" (Trakl, "Psalm"). All of Trakl's "landscapes" gather around this one, unique: "*Es ist*" (There is). Indeed, to make the world visible without representing it is a poetic virtue. The landscape from the poem "*Landschaft*," "*Septemberabend; traurig tönen die dunklen Rufe der Hirten Durch das dämmernde Dorf. . . .*" remains absolutely undetermined. Unlike "The Landscape of Winter," it is unsituable; and yet, it is as intense as the former. The poetic place is not a place that can be situated in an exterior space. It never allows itself to be determined by independent and universally valid coordinates precisely because it is the Determination itself. It is the Site where Saying and Being are grounded in a common origin: the "myth" (*Sage*). Moreover, it must dwell in the legendary inasmuch as it gives rise to the Dwelling Place. The source cannot appear to itself. Whenever Trakl names the places of his Poem—notwithstanding the rarity of this occurence—he always leaves them undetermined, as if they were in suspense, suspended or floating. In effect, this is similar to Japanese landscapes in which a single feature suffices to say the essential: "mountain-water." The Poem, then, speaks the becoming-rock of the soul; and, at the same time, the becoming-soul of the rock: *Einklang*.

The last poems written by Hölderlin also speak the profound harmony of a "soul" transfigured in its terrestrial night. At the very least, they are nothing but landscapes, and yet, they are never simple landscapes. The last poem of the Stuttgart edition is entitled "*Die Aussicht*" or "The View Outside."[10] To understand it, we must return to a letter that the poet, upon his return to France, wrote to his friend Böhlendorf: "That all the sacred places are gathered around one place and the philosophical light around my window, such is my joy." This place that gathers around itself all the sacred places of the earth constitutes the myth of the Poem; it is the place of its saying, the place that burns with a "philosophical light"—one that is sweeter and more unapparent than the light of the sun and, also, more a-part—around the poet's window. In effect, it is his view outside, his *opening*. This place, far from being an enormous container, remains deserted and poor; it is a place that is essentially secret, invisible—or visible only to the *naked* eye. Naked, that is, open to the Open itself.

When far the dwelling life of man into the distance goes,
Where, in that far distance, the grapevine's season glows,
There too are summer's fields, emptied of their growing,
And forest looms, its image darkly showing.[11]

There is, nevertheless, a text that contrasts sharply with the general indifference philosophers have hitherto had for landscapes. It is a text written by Heidegger during his stay as rector of the University of Freiburg, and it appeared in a local newspaper one month after his resignation. Here, I shall not address the political question: I shall not determine whether or not this text bears painful witness to Heidegger's participation in Nazism. Rather, I shall point out one aspect, which to this day, has been little discussed. It is usually remarked that this text merely constitutes an eulogy of the peasant world—a remark that shall in no way be denied. But then what? For it can also be remarked that Bruegel's painting is such an eulogy! Still, Heidegger never went so far as to propose a "return to the earth"; whether this be modeled on the model of an old-fashioned "rootedness" (à la Pétain) or on the present day "ecological" model or even on the mystico-social plan (à la Simone Weil). Generally, we fail to read the end of the text that denounces the "fatal heresy" that has taken hold of city dwellers and that has pushed them to an excessive and even doubtful concern for the "world of the peasant and his existence" (*Dasein*). In fact, Heidegger stated that now—more than ever—we must "keep our *distance* from the peasant's mode of existence; abandon it *more* than ever to its own law. *We must not touch it*, that thus we do no violence to it. We must not expose—to the mendacious chitchat of literary men—that which constitutes the Being proper of a people and its closeness to the soil." Could there have been any less veiled critique of the *völkische* literature—literature that, at the time, reigned as a certain tendency of Nazi ideology?

Elsewhere—and later—Heidegger would say that the old "rootedness" (here I use quotation marks, for, whereas the English speaks of roots, the German evokes the solidity of the soil) is dead once and for all. Just as is the art of re-presentation. Of course, this hardly forbids us to seek another form or another way of being (which, in no way, is rustic).

We have translated the text by the title "Why Do We Remain in the Provinces?" And this would accentuate the anecdotal portion of the text (Heidegger's refusal to leave Freiburg and hence to teach in Berlin). However, the first part of the original title, "*Schöpferische Landschaft*," already constitutes the answer to the question. We remain in the provinces because there the landscape is "creator," because elsewhere we could not work as well. In a contemporary text on the origin of the work of art, it would be a question of *schöpfen*—though not as an ingenious or artisan-like creator, but as the simple gesture of drawing water from a well. Here, the source is the country itself, the well from which, each morning, a "strange" man—then Socrates, now Heidegger—would draw forth his "water." The water shoots forth from the earth; but the earth—from whence does it shoot forth? From nothing; it dwells within itself and is withdrawn from all enquiry that seeks an origin. But what can this word *earth* signify if, in effect, it does not designate materiality and the objectifiable form of the planet? Nothing; at least, we must forbear from all representation. We must leave the earth to rest within itself; we must leave be the rock, the water and even color—leave be everything that constitutes the landscape of a country. For color "radiates and only wishes to radiate." From the very moment we decompose color into a spectrum, it becomes distorted and disappears. Similarily, the earth shall never reveal itself under the harsh blows of a pickaxe or by the power of dynamite. It is earth only insofar as it is left to its essential occlusion. "And that itself is the Being of the Earth: that which, by nature, keeps itself occluded." (Heidegger, *Vom Ursprung des Kunstwerkes.*) Only by this essential occlusion can the earth bear the footsteps of humankind, and thus keep, for it, its earthly place.

In offering a Dwelling Place, the earth itself dwells—absolutely; and thus, it would elude all hurry and haste. It is this reserve—*pudeur*—that Heidegger would, in return, demand from the city dweller vis-à-vis those who (a species that he knew to be near extinction) dwelled, still, under the same law of the earth's silence. Tactfully (understood here in the archaic sense), he would write: "And we need this touch that knows how to touch without deforming." It is tact for that which refers neither to manipulation nor exploitation, but to a simpler human contact; contact whereby the hand rules as firsthand knowledge of the essence of everything and where knowing signifies "to have in hand." Though here it is not so much a question of dexterity as it is of docility; not so much a knowing-how-to-do as it is a knowing-how-to-comply-with . . . to win the hand and take the measure of everything that is according to its own law. It is a knowledge distanced from all ciphered calculation and from all "theoretical" estimation. It is a knowledge that has an accurate eye but that needs only to have seen in order . . . to know.

Strangely enough, Heidegger would begin by describing, in a rather objective and calculating way, the place in which he worked. He would give the precise mensurations of his *Skihütte* in Todtnauberg: "in all, six by seven meters." Moreover, he drew up an affadavit of the grounds that was hardly less sterile than that which a surveyor might draw up: such and such would constitute the landscape as "seen from my window." At the very least, we would expect it to be seen from other eyes, perhaps from the eyes of a visitor in passing or from those of an idle observer. But he would add, "Properly speaking, *I myself* never observe the landscape." That is, no more than a peasant would contemplate the landscape. (If he glances out the window, it is simply to see what the weather is doing.) This in no way means that either are blind or oblivious to the "charms" of the landscape; only that they have another way of being "there"—other than as simple observers of it. For these latter would transform, in advance, the countryside into a sight, before which they stop and stare like rubberneckers or amateurs who merely enjoy the view. In such a scenario, the place becomes a simple object; it becomes something that holds itself before us like a still life picture: it becomes dead. And those rare moments of aesthetic joy (grounded in "taste") shall hardly change the ontological status of the object—the object that, like a painting, may very well become an art object. Yet, an art object remains at an abyssmal distance from the thing itself, insofar as it merely offers us a view that is removed from its place. (Consequently, we must go to museums or galleries or private homes where it—the art object—is simply an object that takes the place of the "view.")

The thinker does not contemplate the landscape because he does not need to. He, like the peasant—though in a way that is somewhat different—*is there*, is there at his work and works the earth (the occlusion). For this reason he is able to enter into an immediate accord with the same world; and this world is better revealed by a peasant's shoes—painted by Van Gogh—if only because these latter are more intense and more intimate than any landscape represented as a mere "view." They show better its profundity and presence: "Through these shoes, the silent call of the earth would pass. . . ."

Or perhaps through Bruegel's "Harvest"? But then, at that time—that epoch—the peasant world was still alive and living in all its elemental force. Today, what has become of this world? Does its disappearance signify the disappearance of every "creative" landscape? No. At least not the disappearance of landscape as landscape. On the contrary. It was precisely the disappearance of this particular mode of being *there* that made possible the advent of the "simple landscape" or object-landscape, that view offered for aesthetico-romantic delight and for the relishment of that "space of leisure" which had resource to "natural energies." Is not such landscape far from the "poetic" dwelling so dear to Heidegger? How, then, can the thinker who dwells in his "*Hütte*" not be tied to the backward peasant who is condemned by "evolution" and mechanical progress?

According to Heidegger, the thinker has a way of being in the "country" that is somehow connected to that of the peasant. Furthermore, for Heidegger the country is not an object of contemplation or a setting, as it were, for "creative activities," but a place to be and to be in. Of course, this does not mean that he himself was a peasant. Even if he had attempted an infantile identification—such as was attempted resulting from the events of May 1968—he would not have become one. Rather, he would only have been an ineffective hybrid. Besides, one cannot *become* a peasant—for this in itself is already a bourgeois way of viewing things. (Let us not forget the misfortunes of Bouvard and Pécuchet!) Even if the work of thinking has something more to do with the hand than any other work, this does not mean that every intellectual must be sent into the field to be transfigured into a "vertible" worker of thought. The Maoist reeducation of the intellectual was one of the greatest monstruosities of a Marxism that had been misunderstood and even rendered useless for want of grasping that which was at stake in the modern essence of work. Heidegger repeated, often enough, that thinking was that much more *active* when it was *only* thinking—and then *truly* thinking—just as a peasant has nothing to gain, but everything to lose, in becoming an "intellectual," a "poet," or a "politician." (Unfortunately, Heidegger would succumb, for some time, to the philosophical temptation of politics inasmuch as he imagined that the latter had much to gain from the "Spirit.")

Nevertheless, the thinker is, in his own way, a peasant when he undertakes *his* work: that of thinking and thinking alone. Once again, for Heidegger, to think was "a work of the hand." It is by the hand and *not* by the objectifying eye that the thinker enters into the essence of that which is. The hand recognizes and knows without ever having to represent anything to itself. It has something of that supreme docility of which true mastery consists. A philosopher whom we hardly suspect of being nostalgic for feudality—Karl Marx—wrote in his "Remarks on the Prussian Law of Censorship": "Only the beggar is modest. . . . The modesty of genius shall not consist, as in the language of culture, in speaking without an accent or in banishing every dialect; but rather, in speaking with the accent of the thing and in the dialect of its essence. It shall consist in forgetting both modesty and immodesty and in extricating the thing." The thinker, by speaking with the accent of the thing and in the dialect of its essence, acquires an accent of his (or her) own. That is, he acquires the accent of his native soil: he speaks its dialect—which can be immediately recognized by the various tricks and turns the "language" takes such as it comes to him in hand.

Thus the peasant does not constitute the "model" to be modeled. The peasant offers only an analogy in the *way* and workmanship of the "thing," and in the way in which he (or she) is able to take the thing in hand, the way in which he (or she) handles his (or her) work. The analogy is an equality of relationship and not of state. That which is identical between the peasant and the thinker is not their social, economic, or cultural condition, but their relationship to the thing. Thing to be taken "in hand" and, in a sense, appre-handed—and thus handled.

The relationship is always more difficult to think than the state of fact. For a relationship is continually being done and undone; it would establish and fashion itself only to deteriorate and come a-part. Our text speaks (of) this relationship even as work. Such work opens up the countryside—even when, having it in hand, it remains involved with the taking-place of the place. For example, the logger knows—it is his work to know—what it means to be involved with a *Holzweg* (a forest footpath that leads nowhere—not elsewhere, but only there, where the thing is to be taken in hand). It is also the work of the thinker, though he would no more cut down trees, than he would trace furrows in a field. And yet, "With its saying, thinking lays inconspicuous furrows in language. They are still more inconspicuous than the furrows that the farmer, slow of step, draws through the field."[12] There is a *field* of thought to be broken up and ploughed with that same slow and firm step of the peasant. The question here is not one of simply metaphor; for if it were, we would remain within the confines of the bourgeois intellect that believes itself everywhere at home but that, in reality, does not know what "the thing" is and hardly recognizes that such a "thing" demands a certain accentuation, intensity, intimacy, inclination, and perseverance, and even stubbornness. Instead, this intellect is content to have others (humans or machines) work in its place. It is already elsewhere, satisfied with seeing the monetary benefits and capital gains.

The field—the field of thinking—is even more invisible than that field within which the peasant works. However, it requires the same docility and rigor and care for the Simple—which is nothing more than the way that is given rise to: different every time and yet, always, one way. Docility resides in a "view" that is anterior to the view; the view that, already, understands it and has a handle on it. It handles the handle of the dipper that draws forth the water from the well. This is the water that it needs—and with which it lives. The countryside is only "ungrateful" toward those who have no gratitude toward it. By nature, the countryside is that which gives—and always more than the hand is able to receive, even if this "more" is reduced to a thin trickle of water, trickling from a source that remains far away.

The countryside gives and, in this way, is a "creator." On the other hand, it is not insofar as it would keep a reserve of energy from which the city dweller (exhausted by a hectic and stressful life) would leisurely draw forth whatever he or she needs to "reactivate" a personal creativity. Such a bioenergetic vision is already, entirely, one of *techne*: for it considers Nature to be a stockpile of energy that is always at hand and ready for exploitation. In this vision of the "world," the destruction of the country-place is even more called for and redhibitory than in the simple contemplation of the landscape. (Notwithstanding, this latter vision would conserve a certain respect for this "before which we are awed"—and about which we speak romantically.) Today, there already exist "centers" of retreat deep in the middle of green forests where executives and managers may relax—retreat—and thus increase their productivity.

According to Heidegger, it is not in this sense that landscape is creator; rather, it is only when it gives rise to a work of the thing itself—be it of the "field." When it gives rise to a "work," it is not so much to that which has been worked, but to that which, of itself, works and opens up, operates, and labors. In effect, to experience the profundity of the opening-up virtue of landscape is to sink within it; it is not to plunge headlong therein in a problematical and always subjectively "empathetic" way. Rather, it is to enter into the very bottom of things until there is no bottom; it is to enter into harmony with that which, at bottom—and in a way that is even more invisible than the ploughshare—re-turns and penetrates, traces and opens-up, like the original writing of things. A land has its own way of writing and is in possession of a dominant tone: it speaks the dialect of its essence. It is this tonality of things—invisible and perhaps somewhat stale—that penetrates and touches. Right away (on the way and making way), to be in harmony with such a tone—in the twinkling of an eye—is to think in the very field proper to the land, in its maternal tongue. The landscape is also crossed-over by this tonality. It is variable like the weather: crossed and worked over by the variable opening of light and sound and odors and airs. For the place, before being reduced to a homogenous and undetermined space, gives rise to the *mood* [*Stimmung*]—even mode—of that which must be done—indeed, in due time of the season. It can hasten or slow the step; it is able to liberate or oppress. The time of the tempest would dispose the countryside to a particular "wavelength." Yet, we wonder, does not thought feel the effects of it? Thought too is a matter of time. A mountainous, mirky, and deeply dark land hardly gives rise to the same thoughts as a flat, smooth, and luminous land. Perhaps this is commonplace, but it cannot be repeated too often—especially now, when every place's particular genius seems extinguished. Inasmuch as thought ceases to believe in itself, as it does in an ubiquitous God or a Catholic Church, it shall find, once again, its "genius," that is, its accent. It is what Heraclitus called its *ethos*, its feature proper. "The gods are here as well!" he once exclaimed to those curious onlookers who came to see the great man at work—just as we might go to the zoo to see zebras or monkeys. And there he was, in his own place, going about his work: next to his fire cooking bread, as if he were near the thinker's workshop—but then, everywhere where there is a place, a genius dwells. Genius that has nothing ingenious about it, that is even the simplest and most familiar dwelling-place—and precisely for this reason, is *land-scaping* (*dépaysant:* disorientating).

Yet, at present, is there still such a place? The question itself seems improper and more than strange; and, in fact, it is. Though it is not as strange as this *atopie* that never ceases to spread out in place of places. The question does not ask whether or not there still is space; for, to be sure, there always shall be, even in the emptiness of infinite space. Rather, the question asks whether there is a present. And to this *formidable* question, Mallarmé has already responded: No, a present has no place.

❁ ❁ ❁

According to Hölderlin, there is still a place: for lands and landscapes, "diversely fashioned," do volunteer themselves. The poet sings and from his mouth "it was the voice of the most noble of rivers / The voice of the Born-Free, the Rhine. . . . An enigma is the purely flowing forth." It is possible that Hölderlin has played upon the assonance of *Rhein* (Rhine) and *rein* (pure). But today, such an assonance becomes a discordance—one that is even less pure than the polluted water of this river that serves as a sewer for every "European" multinational company. How can we see in the poem "The Rhine" anything but a beautiful utopia forever engulfed by tons of trash and dead fish? Or rather, might it not be to the contrary: that our modern landscape has become a utopia? Perhaps even a dangerous utopia?

Today it is quite common to hear that the poet mythicizes Nature. The poet gives to it a symbolic sense and humanizes it. Poetry does not conceive of Nature in terms of an exact and objective representation as do the "natural" sciences. In this sense (from the scientific point of view), the hymn entitled "The Rhine" is nothing more than a "supplement of the soul," a poetic vision, to be sure, but unreal and without value for one who wishes to know the geography of that particular part of the country.

Another poem, "*Heimkunft*" ("Return to the Land"), celebrates the poet's return to his native country, Swabia, by evoking the joyous crossing of Lake Constance. A creative mind might even re-create the traveler's itinerary: starting from Hauptwyl (in the canton of Thurgau near Constance, where Hölderlin had, until 1801, been a private tutor) and ending at Swabia. Upon this pathway, we would attain a more exact representation of the "places" of the poem. However, as Heidegger might add, we would think in a way that is entirely nonpoetic. How much longer? "How much longer shall we persist in our belief that there is, firstly a Nature in itself and then, secondly, a landscape for itself that, thanks to some 'poetical, personal experiences,' would take on a mythical coloration? How much longer shall we spare ourselves this experience: the experience of that which is as such?"[13]

This critique has a double edge to it. On the one hand, we wrongly represent a Nature "in itself"—and therefore independent of every poem—as if it were a raw material that exists objectively. On the other hand, we would posit the poem as something that is in addition, that thus it might confer upon this material in itself, a mythical "coloration." It is as if poetry were a coat of paint painted on a background already there—before all coloration. Yet, we must think all this in reverse: the Poem is primary. For by it and in it Nature comes into Being; that is, comes into the *word*. Nature is no more the "production" of the poem than it is of the so-called science of nature. And yet, this science is, in its own way, a poem. It causes Nature to be as a scientifically representable *object*. Likewise, poetry "causes" Nature "to be" as . . . a "poem of nature." Between the two—science and poetry—nothing clearly stands out that may be used to determine the way of this "causing to be" (the Be-cause) that is truest. Why? Because, each time, it takes place in a different mode of the Being-true—of the Being-unconcealed. It is this that Heidegger's conference The Question Concerning Technology would point out: the mode of "truth," of disclosing (*Entbergung*) is different each time; and for this reason, at the end of the text, he would appeal to art as "a realm that is, on the one hand, akin to the essence of technology and, on the other, fundamentally different from it."

But what is this way? The "example" of the Rhine reveals it to us in a most convincing way. We put it in place or, rather, we *install* it—in the form of a dam and electrical power plant on the river. This latter is called upon and summoned to produce its energy; and thus, it enters into the circuit of consumption (by which we must understand the unity of a summons, of a global order, and of a dispositioning: everything plays upon the verb *stellen*, to pose or posit in the sense of "pre-pose," "to place beforehand" in the circuit whereat we are able to dis-pose of it).

"The hydroelectric plant is not built into the Rhine River as was the old wooden bridge that joined bank with bank for hundreds of years. Rather, the river is dammed up [*verbaut*, which is a deformation of *bauen* or "to build"] into the power plant."[14] However, the essential here is not to rebel against the transformation of the "most noble river / Born free," into a reservoir that produces electrical energy and so subjugated to the "needs" of the industrial world. The essential is to hear—and to hear the following in the first place: each time it would take place in a way of Being different—indeed, with a different *word*. Yet, not everything is a question of words, especially there where it seems to be: the difference (minimal and, yet, unfathomable) between "The Rhine" as *Kraftwerk* (as an electrical power station, though literally as a work of force) and the (same?) "Rhine" as that hymn by Hölderlin, "*Kuntswerk*" ("as work of art"). A work of force (or of a "position in force") and a work of art—of de-position, of liberty. Or rather, it is the difference that exists between the liberation of energy and the liberation . . . of the place.

Do we see the landscape of this epoch in which "there is no Present"?—do we see the "*Lichtung* of Being in the way of technology"? Do we see, even more simply, the Difference between the ways and pathways which the Present render or refuse itself? Do we have the hand necessary to seize such a difference?

It would seem unlikely. It seems that we would remain always ever longer and obstinately inexpert to this experience however much we are more and more expert and "technically" qualified to establish the finest of analyses. We believe that we can go everywhere; and yet, we do not even attain to nothing. We hardly wish to recognize that we are blind; for to what view would we be blind? And from whose eyes? Those of the poet? But a poet too is effaced and rendered invisible. Still, we refuse—though for how much longer? for "Long is the Time . . . "—to see the loss of this view. And thus we refuse to transmute it into a clair-voyance that, in the present recess of any present—

lost as far as the eye can see—finally finds a poor place where it may dwell. Like Oedipus who, in the end, found his place at Colonus.

A first step would be to hear and understand the mute Word of the land, returned to its invisible dwelling place; or as Rilke wrote, to become "the bees of the invisible." For

> Earth, your will, is it not this: to rise up
> in us invisible?[15]

Notes

1. Plato, *Phaedrus*, 230.

2. Sophocles, first chorus of the *Antigone.*

3. Plato, *Theatetus*, 174 b.

4. Plato, *Phaedrus*, 247 c.

5. Plato, *Phaedrus*, 247, in *Plato: The Collected Dialogues*, ed. Edith Hamilton (Princeton: Princeton University Press, 1961), p. 478.

6. Heidegger, *De l'essence de la liberté humaine*, trans. E. Martineau [Paris: Gallimard, 1987] p. 142.

7. Rainer Maria Rilke, "Worpswede," in *Where Silence Reigns: Selected Prose*, trans. G. Craig Houston (New York: New Directions Publishing Corp., 1978), p. 7.

8. Bernard Lamblin, *Peinture et temps*, pp. 345–355.

9. Claude Mettra, *Bruegel.*

10. The reference is the German edition, *Gesammelte Werke*, ed. Friedrich Beissner, (Stuttgart, 1953).

11. Hölderlin, "*Die Aussicht*," quoted by Heidegger in " . . . Poetically Man Dwells . . . " in *PLT*, p. 229.

12. Quoted from Heidegger's "Letter on Humanism," in *Basic Writings*, p. 242.

13. Heidegger, *Erläuterungen zu Hölderlins Dichtung*, p. 11.

14. Martin Heidegger, "The Question Concerning Technology," in *Martin Heidegger: Basic Writings*, p. 297.

15. Ranier Maria Rilke, "Ninth Duino Elegy," quoted by Martin Heidegger in "What Are Poets For?" in *PLT*, p. 141.

7

The Horror of Emptiness

It may be that a city is not a rational object. Surely, the Surrealists were aware of this —which explains their predilection for this particular "object." In the sixth issue (dated May 15, 1933) of the periodical *Le Surréalisme au service de la Révolution* we find a series of investigations or "experimental researches" into the "irrational recognition of objects." These objects were, by definition, irregular, unusual, and strange; for example, the clairvoyant's crystal ball, a strip of pink velvet, "The Enigma of an Afternoon" (painting by Chirico), and . . . the city. The questionnaire "concerning certain possibilities of a city's embellishment" began in the following way: "Must we conserve, displace, modify, or suppress . . . ?"—questions asked with respect to thirty-one of the most typical monuments in Paris; from the Arc de Triomphe to the gare de l'Est (at the time, one hardly spoke of Orsay inasmuch as it did not yet exist).

As we might expect from Breton and his friends, the various answers did not manifest any great respect for convention or symbolic import. The iconoclastic intention is clear here, especially as regards the first monument on the list: the Arc de Triomphe. "To blow it up after it has been buried in a mountain of manure," "To bring it down, and then, turn it into the most beautiful piss-hole in France," "Replace it with a Morning-Glory, climbing up a halberd . . . "

To conclude, let us read the following text by Paul Eluard:

> The cities have suffered extensively from the horror of emptiness. Their inhabitants, in order to combat agoraphobia, have

> everywhere erected monuments and statues without any concern whatsoever for their blending in with the real and daily life of men. The monuments are either desert-like, useless, asinine, or dedicated to the most infamous superstitions and to the worst pieces of work. Apart from some very rare exceptions, their ugliness would afflict, disfigure, and render foolish anyone who dares contemplate them. The statues, almost always of derisive and nefarious individuals, are mounted upon pedestals that remove them from the possibility of any intervention in human affairs—the reciprocal being true as well. In short, they rot standing up.

"The cities have suffered extensively from the horror of emptiness": perhaps today we might think they have suffered from the opposite—from the massive destruction that occurred during the last World War. Entire cities, including Dresden, Hamburg, Saint-Malo, and Le Havre, were completely destroyed—or at least 90 percent so. In 1945, the mayor of Stuttgart uttered this strange proclamation: "The catastrophe of wartime destruction has given our generation the unique opportunity of a total renovation and innovation in urban matters." Is not the destruction of the ancient the most expedient way to reconstruct everything anew? (Consider, for example, Japan or the Federal Republic of Germany; for these countries—which had been practically erased from the map—such destruction provided an unheard-of opportunity to finally incorporate modern industry, indeed, these were countries that, unlike France, were able to "modernize" without being strangled by old, schlerotic structures.) "It is true that we never tear down all the houses in a city just to rebuild them in a different way and to make the streets more beautiful; but we do see that individual owners often have theirs torn down and rebuilt, and even that they may be forced to do so when the building is crumbling with age, or when the foundation is not firm and it is in danger of collapsing."[1]

Descartes—for whom architecture was a metaphor for the philosophical project of modern times (to find a *fundamentum inconcussum*)—was, perhaps, neither radical enough nor quite absolutely modern enough to envision, as necessary to the rational reconstruction, a period of total and systematic destruction of the ancient. Or perhaps he was more prudent—and thus less reassured of retaining any absolute certainty than his successors—as to what constituted the "rational" and to what did not. In fact, such an undertaking was so long and arduous that it would take more than three centuries for Le Corbusier to come . . . Whatever we might wish to say of his talents, he showed himself (along with so many other epigones!) a worthy heir of Descartes's fortune—at least, in the certitude that it was necessary to radically break with the ancient: "Similarly, those ancient towns which were originally nothing but hamlets, and in the course of time have become great cities, are ordinarily very badly arranged compared to one of the symmetrical metropolitan districts which a city planner has laid out on an open plain according to his own designs. It is true that when we consider their buildings one by one, there is often as much beauty in the first city as in the second, or even more; nevertheless, when we observe how they are arranged, here a large unit, there a small; and how the streets are crooked and uneven, one would rather suppose that chance and not the decisions of rational men had so arranged them."[2]

In this text, we find the germ of all modern architectural thought, what I call *totalitarian space*, and its corollary, the negation of time, experience, and places. Here the straight line, the order of the extent and calculation prevails a priori; but also, the will to power. We understand that for "those men who use their reason" (those engineers and technicians who are, nevertheless, architects), total destruction "gives the unique opportunity of a total renovation and innovation in urban planning."

The problem is that, on the whole (and it is only this that matters), the reconstruction of European cities after 1945—according to those principles judged "rational" and modern—was a catastrophe, even more catastrophic than their initial destruction. This at least is the point of view held by Léon Krier in his work that presents the architectural work of Albert Speer:

> *No, the German city was not destroyed by Allied bombs.* The destruction of German culture was not an accident of war. On the contrary, it was the act of a superhuman repudiation. In opting for industrial reconstruction, Germany has, in effect, disowned its history and individuality—to be sure, a heroic exploit. This country has exhausted all of its imagination, and the result of so many sacrifices has been nothing more than ugliness and futility. More than 90 percent of all Germans live and work in modernist buildings; and forty years after their defeat, they are still not at home in their own country. It is possible that Germany is the most advanced industrial nation in Europe; it is certain that she is the ugliest. . . . All this frenzied zeal has not produced a single *place* or *monument* about which a people could think with affection and that would cause such a people to dream.

There is, perhaps, a place or monument that escapes this categorical comndemnation; but, whether it makes one dream is uncertain. However, it is certain that the Germans do not reflect upon it with much affection insofar as it signifies a tangible sign that, "forty years after their defeat, they still are not at home in their own country." Here I speak of the Berlin Wall.[3] It was an involuntary monument without any aesthetic will; it was a nonplace, a line, a scar that never wholly healed and that festered indefinitely. "It is nothing but a wall, and yet . . . " It was not even a very high wall—barely 12 feet in height. (Now I am thinking of Hadrian's wall—the one that dissected Scotland.) It was a wall that demarcated the end of civilization—that marked out the boundaries of the civilized world—and thus surveyed the limits of the "other" world: that barbarous and unworldly one. Hadrian had even erected a temple to the god End. Today the wall is in ruins and straddled by power lines and several fast-paced freeways—such that a terra incognita no longer exists. Day by day the world becomes "smaller"—even to the point of becoming a single world: a "planetary village." At present, as regards the Berlin Wall, everything seems to be inverted insofar as such a wall no longer protects us from Barbarians. It is no longer a sanctuary, but a prison wall; and it is precisely the Barbarians (i.e., the *Evil Empire*) who have constructed it to protect themselves from the virus that, for them, constitutes the civilization of the Other (the point of view is relative; for the Barbarian is always the other).

Even more impressive than the wall itself was the empty space between the two walls—however, it was a space that was obstructed. If ever we were to climb one of the lookout towers that looked out over the obligatory pathway of the visitor (one was able to visit the wall just as one might visit a monument)—we found barbed wire, gunports, patrols, dogs, guards, machineguns, and so on. In short, we found all the repressive instruments of the prison camp. "If we had been earthworms or birds, what would you have invented?" Unfortunately, graffiti was able to be read from only one side of the wall—from the "good" side, from the West. On the other side, there was nothing; only a blind wall that was clean and proper and nonetheless dreary. On the Eastern side, one hardly dared to write upon the walls: for this would have sullied the collective proper-ty; but more, this would have shown there to be prohibition and forbiddence. Only in a world of rotten liberalism and irresponsible publicity are we able to write graffiti that is as absurd as: "It is forbidden to forbid."

It was possible to traverse the wall; just as in an earlier time, a line of demarcation separated the occupied zone from the so-called free zone (what those French living in London called the *preoccupied zone*). One had simply to show one's *Ausweis*. There was even—for those French "forces" of "occupation" (for Berlin was a city under occupation)—a rather curious diplomatic ceremony that is worthy of comment. As France did not recognize the authority of the East German government over Berlin, one hardly handed over one's papers: one simply presented them by sticking them against the carefully closed wall of glass, such that the schupo had to bend over to read the documents and verify the identity of the passenger.

By traversing the wall, we became immediately uprooted or expatriated in the literal sense: for beyond there lay another country or better yet another world. For those of us who had come from the West, the wall exposed the insufferable wound that had torn apart the center of a Central Europe that is, even now, dying—if not, dead. We needed only take a walk—that is, if we were capable of "taking a walk" free from any mental reservation—through the enormous rectilinear avenues of East Berlin to feel the pressing need (which is almost natural) to return "home"—to the West. East Berlin, with its dead, deserted districts without stores, without cafes, without terraces, without curious citizens, without advertisements, and without any images other than the repeated effigy of some bearded prophet, would begin to make us admire and like that which we had formerly abhorred: unadulterated capitalism, obnoxious advertisements, disordered disturbances, the frivolousness of fashion, and the insecurity of violence. Indeed, no one needed to worry about a drive-by shooting in East Berlin; and yet, we wondered, was there no other order than that of totalitarian order?

Order and harmony, the most beautiful monuments in Berlin are in the East, whereas West Berlin, like most Occidental cities, is anarchical. Certainly, every city offers a chaotic character (at least, every historic or ancient city according to Descartes), inasmuch as the various districts rarely fit together like Lincoln Logs or Legos. Rather, each has its own style and stamp, and even its own proper in-sect. In effect, the majority of all large historic cities are like organized patchworks: a superimposition of various styles and epochs as Freud already noted with respect to Rome. Yet, the strangeness of Berlin does not come from this Baroque-like profusion—this premature postmodernism as it were. No, it comes from the empty spaces. Here, I no longer refer to the wall, but to the many holes resulting from the multitude of bombs that fell. Quite simply, they have reconstructed nothing in its place. Perhaps, also, it is a matter of political will to have thus marked the memory: in this way a memorial church would ally a ruined belltower to a structure of steel and glass whose transparency designates, *visibly*, that which has disappeared. More often than not, the place remains empty; such that the city takes on the apparence of an ancient mosaic or wall fresco in which we see human members emerge, in which we discern portions of flesh and smiles and sandals, though never the whole. It is not even a puzzle; for the fragments are heterogenous. Furthermore, it is doubtful that by reconstituting them, we could achieve a unity of style or epoch; rather, this brings to mind that *geometry of nothingness* in which Stendhal, an afficionado of old cities, saw the essence of memory.

Yes, Berlin suffered severly from massive destruction; but might we not say that it suffered even more from massive reconstruction? Difficult to answer—more so because so few monuments remain from before, and perhaps even less of those that were erected by the National Socialist Party. Everything was destroyed but a few lampposts—and the Italian and Swedish embassies (or were they the Norwegian and Spanish?), which stood directly in the middle of the wasteland. Even their eventual demolition in 1980—by the proper authorities—was delayed for lack of proper funds. As for the rest, anything and everything that might remind one of a "past that will not pass away" (the Nazi plague was thus characterized by a certain German historian) has been suppressed—at least materially so—oftentimes with dynamite. At the very least, we can understand why the Soviets dismantled, stone by stone, Hitler's Chancellery—and Speer's tour de force—to erect an enormous, if not turgid, monument to those who died at Treptow. "However," according to Léon Krier, "it was not the victorious who, in 1967, blew up Speer's beautiful colonnade in Nuremburg." Nor did they destroy Tiergarten's round plaza in Berlin whereat they constructed—with no less pique to Krier—Mies van der Rohe's National Gallery. Quite simply, the Germans wanted to exorcise their past; yet for Krier, such "exorcism has not taken the shape of a judgment, but of a vengeance." Nevertheless, we cannot *judge* that which escapes reason; rather, this exorcism seems to suit the bewitchment that turned so many millions of Germans into a *possessed* race. "This ignorant anti-Nazism (as well as anti-Fascism), strongly resembles the anti-Semiticism of the National Socialists in that both are a destructive form of self-assertion." Let us note, however, that here, in this fine amalgam, it is only a question of stigmatizing the practices of the *ignares*.[4] Nevertheless, a suspicion seems to take form: those who destroyed the "beautiful colonnades" to exorcise a cursed past can only be Barbarians . . .

A priori, there is no reason whatsoever to hold Speer's architectural work in contempt—even if such work can be observed only on paper. Moreover, even if Hitler admired Speer's architecture, this in itself cannot totally discredit his structures. As Hans Hollein has humorously noted, "thank God Hitler wasn't too fond of Viennese scallopini," otherwise it would have been now removed from the menu of every restaurant.

From a formalistic point of view, a similar reasoning is valid. "Classical" architecture existed long before Speer—similarily, the existence of Viennese scallopini was hardly contingent on Hitler's appearance. But here the comparison would begin to contrast: more precisely, in the Führer's disdain for facts. "Viennese scallopini" are nothing more than a scholarly hypothesis, whereas Speer's architecture was a reality. For fifteen years all other architecture had been outlawed: even the Bauhaus closed down and would not open its doors again until after Germany's defeat and the repeal of Hitler's interdiction. Was it necessary, then, to wreak vengeance on masters of old by outlawing their works?

It would seem that Krier makes a more effective argument by changing the "givens" of the problem. "In total opposition to what we have wished to believe since 1945, Classical architecture cannot be used as a means to exert a totalitarian terror. The recent dictators of the world have been able to omit it with only too much ease." In effect, Pinochet has never had any need of a Speer. On the other hand, is it not precisely this that characterizes the Hitlerian "dictatorship": an aesthetic megalomania, even to the point of being able to think National Socialism as a National Aestheticism? Nor is it simply "Classical" architecture that is involved here (or rather, neo-Classical and its obsession with the Greek model that has infested so many monuments in modern metropolises, including most democratic nations). We must not forget the entire Germanic tradition that trembled before the spectacle of the National Socialist state conceived as a grandiose and *total work of art*. We can only imagine the abusive use of Wagner's music by the Nazis—which constituted no less of a real fact than the transformation of the Hindu cross into a swastika. Just as this particular symbol is even now equated with abomination; so too does the music of Wagner risk provoking in the listener an irrepressible quaking of the heart—even if he was not entirely responsible for such manipulation. ("Not entirely" I say, but still—somewhat. The Wagnerian conception of the total work of art—like the Germanic myths appropriated by his operas and that he vulgarized [not to speak of Wagner's own anti-Semiticism]—constituted so many elements favorable to such a manipulation. With Nietzsche, it was necessary to carry out outright mutilations and falsifications.)

Yet, if with Nietzsche and Wagner we can speak of propagandistic manipulation, then, we must admit that the case of Speer is totally devoid of all ambiguity—all identification being flagrant. We need only remind ourselves that Hitler had dreamed of becoming an architect—and twice failed the entrance examinations to the School of Fine Arts in Vienna. Speer would later give him the chance to bring this failed vocation to fruition—which Speer himself, as the Fuhrer's alter ego in matters of importance, never denied—and for good reason! But Krier, in an apparently rigorous argumentation (sophism always has a logical appearance—but only in appearance) limits himself to architecture "as such," "incapable of reigning terror by the force of its internal laws." True enough. No building, however "impressive" it may be, can reign such terror by itself—for the same reason that a machinegun or tank cannot do so—by itself. Speer did not construct any of the concentration camps that were to serve only as temporary barracks and were later to be suppressed along with those members of the "contaminated" race. Today, we visit the "Bridge of Sighs" and the dreary prison cells of the Doge's Palace in Venice—but it is Saint Mark's Basilica that we come to see.

Who, then, constructed Auschwitz and Dachau? Not Speer, or so Krier would respond. For, these were not *architectural* works, and not even "works of art" as were the German bunkers. Nonetheless, Speer built the Chancellery—and it was from this structure that the order to exterminate originated. Can we, then, totally dissociate the architect from the technician who executes the "plan"—especially in a State that proclaims itself totalitarian and *is* totalitarian? Inevitably, in a State that wants *everything* to be political and that desires everything be carried out according to the totalitarian principle, "pure" art is heresy. For this reason Krier's argument inevitably begins to fray and fall apart. On the one hand, he asserts that architecture, like art, is no more political than writing or painting. This is a correct assertion, but only from a traditional point of view—one that is never reached by the totalitarian ideology. On the other hand, architecture ought to be conceived as a "symbolic" art and not one of abstractions. Indeed, it must be conceived as an art of public institutions. However, what are public institutions if not the very places of the *polis*—and therefore the political? The Bourbon Palace (the common name given to the building containing the French House of Representatives—and which is a small leftover from the French monarchical tradition inscribed at the very heart of the Republican system) offers, on the outside, a neo-Classical facade; while, on the inside, we find a *hemicycle*—also inspired by Greek theater. Yet, properly speaking, all this hardly makes the building political. Where architecture and politics interpenetrate is precisely where the hemicyclical disposition imposes spatial notions that strongly connote left, right, and center.

As long as we consider, exclusively, the one facade, there shall hardly be any intrinsic difference between a so-called Republican architecture (even if it has often been inherited from the monarchy) and a "fascist" architecture. Although both utilize a neo-Classical style, Speer's is much more modern; yet, to reduce architecture to the facade is merely a wily way of evacuating the political aspect—and of blinding oneself. According to Krier, "Classical architecture was the policed domain—the civilized and respectable face put on an empire of lies." It is exactly like a screen or front. Perhaps we might think of the Mafia or organized crime that hides behind respectable businesses—housed in respectable buildings of glass and steel—and that launders its dirty money through respectable financial institutions. Or perhaps, we might even think of Versailles: but then, shall we destroy it on the pretext that it provided the *Roi Soleil* with a "respectable facade"? That which went on within the palace walls—the intrigues, the malignant acts, and the servility of Court courtisans—need not enter into the layout of the architectural plans—no more than the misery of a people confined to sordid shacks need be considered. The construction of Saint Petersburg cost the lives of thousands of serfs—and yet, who, as a consequence, deplores this building? Certainly not the Russian authorities who are only too willing to show off the magnificient marvels of their architectural patrimony.

It is such, continues Krier, that all architecture *worthy of this name* has, as its end, admiration and respect. Thus, "every institution that aspires to any lasting authority must—under penalty of severe depreciation of its prestige—be represented by a monumental architectural symbol (that is, both memorable and durable)."[5] From this perspective, there would only be that architecture concerned with the facade and prestige. Carried away by this logic of illusion (which still continues to wreak havoc on those in power), Krier no longer sees the difference between a comely Classical appearance and propaganda. The Classical facade reflects an internal grandeur that is always in proportion, harmonious, and relative; whereas the Nazi facade wants to be absolute. This latter pretends to produce, by itself, a grandeur, or rather, an *effect* of absolute grandeur. Henceforth, architecture becomes (for the same reason as cinema) an art of propaganda and publicity in the modern sense of the term. Far from representing a reality of the extrinsic order, it must effect, by virtue of its magicality, the effect of faith and belief. With belief, every reference to an external—and, therefore, measurable and critiquable—reality is abolished; and with it goes every criterion of truth. Everyone is aware of the stupefying effect that the spectacles at Nuremburg had upon a crowd that was already intoxicated with propaganda—but they also deeply affected foreign visitors. The English ambassador Henderson, who hardly had the reputation of being one to exaggerate, described the *Licht-Dom* in the following temporate terms: "The effect was both solemn and beautiful; I had the feeling of finding myself in a cathedral of light." Everything resided in effect(s)—just as certain films consist solely in "special effects." Finally, according to Krier, the finality of this architecture is nothing more than an effect of grandeur. Indeed, Krier himself concedes this when he states that Speer's monuments ought "to seduce, over-set, shelter and, finally, deceive the souls fascinated with the final intentions of the system." It is, accordingly, in such an aestheticism that any like architecture is eminently political; and, to this aesthetic will we must ascribe the almost magical power of National Socialism. To describe it—especially from the very moment it emerged—as a dictatorship and repressive regime that exercised total control over a passive and permissive multitude is to have understood nothing of the internal nature of the "Movement." Nazism hardly conquered the German people with force, merely—or violence, simply—but with an awful and alluring seduction. Nazism spoke the seductive language (however feigned its accents might have been) of grandeur, beauty, liberty, and loftiness. Every word rang with the efficacious sound of "land" and "blood" and of a "Sacred" Nature: it was a sound that awakened in the German people—people that had suffered from a morose *imbourgeoisement* followed by an even more morose misery—an instinct that had been long repressed. Call it archaic, unconscious, savage—call it what you will—but, until that time, only *art*, in its highest "spiritual" mission, claimed to incarnate and serve this deep instinct. Did not the Führer appear, as does the Angel of the first "Duino Elegy," to be endowed with a "stronger existence" (*starkeren Dasein*)? "For the Beautiful is nothing more / Than the Beginning of the Hideous."

As René Char writes:

> The poetic instrument invented by Rimbaud is, perhaps, the only answer of a teeming Occident, content with itself,

> both barbarous and without force; bereft of its instinct of conversation and desire of beauty, and even of the traditions and sacred practices of the Orient and ancient religions; bereft as well of the witchery of primitive peoples. Shall this instrument of which we are disposed be our last chance to recover the powers we have lost? Our last chance to equal the Egyptians, Cretans, the Dogons, and the Magdalanians? This longing to return is the worst perversion of Western culture—its most aberrant aberration. In wishing to return to the source, and of thus regenerating ourselves, we only aggravate our anchylosis; we only hasten our fall and punish, absurdly, our blood. Rimbaud experienced—and subsequently repelled—this temptation: "*We must be absolutely modern: And hold on to the one step won.*"[6]

Even though Nazism can hardly be considered on the same level, the Nazi dream was—because of its obsession with "purety" (strictly in terms of race) and its wish to return to a source (Aryan myths)—the worst perversion of Western *culture*. And such a retrograde culturalism composed that particular character (hideous, and therefore "beautiful") of National Socialism—or at least the form in which it was dreamed. With respect to its bureaucracy of terror, its imperialist technocracy and cult of the Chief—here it resembled most every other modern totalitarian regime, such as Stalinism. However, this in no way signifies that German culture *produced* Nazism—no more than the Enlightenment produced the Reign of Terror—though Nazism did destroy the former for quite some time. In fact, any unequivocal relationship of cause and effect can be pronounced only after the fact. Furthermore, it neglects the obscure link—which is neither logical nor illogical—that makes History. History *happens*. With Nazism, something happened to the Occident as a whole—something that made it impossible to want to *return*. In effect, that which happened was nothing more than the will attempting to effect such a return. As Rimbaud wrote in a text entitled "*L'Impossible*": in yielding "to those pernicious instincts, to an immemorial epoch" and, above all, to that desire—which obsessively and compulsively characterizes Western culture—to return (to Greece or to any other "Golden Age" with the intention of absolutely regenerating ourselves), we only, as Char has said, "aggravate our anchylosis; we only hasten our fall, and punish, absurdly, our blood." How better describe the destiny of the German people so taken by the *cultural* scourge of Nazism?

Nevertheless, we can never return to that time before, to that "other side" of what we are; and we are, whether we like it or not, modern. (It is precisely for this reason that we must be it, *absolutely*.) Nazism was modern as well; and its settled prejudice of a "violent salvation" was well within modernity. Certainly, it was a salvation executed with violence: though unnatural inasmuch as it wished to return to an original nature purified of all modernity. The will to return is, in its very depths, an absolutely modern instinct—just as is our need for "meaning," certitude, health and salvation. Yet, our abjection to *and* our fascination with emptiness remain its intimate jurisdiction. The will to return is modern insofar as it must begin by making a *tabula rasa* of the past; it must begin by creating an emptiness to thus impose its dreams of purity and eternity (a *millenary* Reich) and a petrifying face as mortific as that of the Medusa. No sooner said—than done—it would withdraw the very ground of that to which it claims to return. The will to return is merely the will for the will's sake—indeed, for nothingness. It unveils itself as the *apocalypse*—a word that literally signifies the "rising of the veil." The charred earth policy, which was Hitler's when he realized that his "dreams" (and our nightmare) was coming to an end, was the logical result of the will to return, and thus of the *tabula rasa*: and thus of any attempt at a New Order, and thus of beginning a new civilization at year zero.

Speer, who in 1942 was named Minister of War and Munitions, was opposed to the Führer's insanity: for Hitler wanted to burn everything behind his armies, wanted them to destroy everything in their retreat (we know what he had in mind for Paris). Yet strangely enough, Krier seems to reproach Speer for not having obeyed Hitler's orders; for this was the one chance to rid ourselves of all the ugliness found in industrialized civilization. In the same spirit, Krier approves of the Morgenthau plan that recommended that the ex-territory of the Reich be reverted to agriculture and livestock breeding. Under the impetus (of a "return") he pictures a politico-cultural fable where.

> in 1946, we see, troops of workers working, on the large expanse of the Reich's old land, to destroy the 9,000 bridges and highways built under Hitler; working to dynamite the "interchanges," the "on-ramps" and the brand new viaducts; working to replant the fields and forests precisely where, yesterday, gigantic industrial installations stood. In this expatriative fever, we shall not only transform the concentration camps into commemorative monuments, but we will destroy the "Herman Goering" steel works, the "Volkswagen"

> factories, the "Krupp" foundries and the assembly lines of the "Messerschmitt." . . . under the dumbfounded and confused eyes of the industrial world, the Germans shall throw into the heap not only the emblems and banners of the Reich, but also the thousands of metallic lady bugs with which the Führer was going to mobilize and subdue the German peoples and all of Europe.[7]

Instead of sending Speer to Spandau (we should remember that German socialism had its good side as well; most notably, "its love of landscape and architecture"), he is named Minister of Reconstruction . . . No doubt this fable would please the Green Germans whom one could acknowledge as the unacknowledged heirs of National Socialism. Notwithstanding, I understand this latter term in its original movement; in all its (mythical) purity and, thus, before its disfigurement and perversion by the Hitlerian "madness of technology."[8] It is true that the cold and austere monumentality of Speer's constructions would definitely please them less than the "authentic" landscapes of the German forest that has finally *regenerated* and been cured of acid rain and other chemical pollutants. But Krier goes to the very extreme of the paradox: for him, it is not the love of landscape and the finely hewn stone that is romantic, but the very illusion to which both Hitler and Speer succumbed, the belief that "the society of the masses and industrial socialism (autocratic or democratic) would correspond to the very essence of our time."[9] It is modernism that has lost Nazism; and this modernism itself constituted the "romantic" fault of Hitler. "Total mobilization" in no way corresponds to the "essence of our time"; and Jünger raved just one more time.

Yet who exactly is raving? Let us listen, rather, to Krier's fine hypothesis: if Hitler had held to the original program of "German socialism" (antiindustrialist and anticapitalist), and if he had not obeyed the demands of those industrialists from Ruhr and their bankers, and if he had not liquidated the "left" wing of the movement (the SA)—we would have remained true to the "German city" and would have returned to the "natural" bounderies of the artisan class corporation and small business!—and Speer would never have had to take the position of Minister of War and Munitions, thus leaving him to dedicate himself, in tranquility, to his great work: the *Gross Berlin*. Later, Krier writes: "In reading the decrees of Heinrich Himmler as regards the future colonization of the Baltic states, we can hardly guess that we have, before our eyes, the lucubrations of one of the most methodical killers in history. On the contrary, we believe that the matter is one that concerns the elegant synthesis of urbane theories—from Aristotle to Tessenow."[10] In short, if Himmler had only succeeded in urban planning, Speer in architecture, and Hitler in painting, then their names would remain forever engraved in the halls of history—as benefactors of humanity!

Yes, who is raving here? Krier? Speer? Hitler? Or History? Can we, as Krier queries, do the bidding of both Apollo and Titan at the same time? "The obvious megalomania in Speer's creations does not reside in the colossal dimensions of his architecture, but in the very nature of those industrial structures that the colossal dimensions intended to serve and articulate." (Indeed, everything is a question of scale: the Great Hall, were it to be placed in New York City, would be materially crushed next to the Empire State Building or any other skyscraper). In a poem, strangely entitled "Democracy," Rimbaud already warns us against "serving the most monstruous military or industrial exploitation." Yet, how is it possible to dissociate the aesthetic from the political and ethical realm? In our admiration for the Egyptian pyramids, we may forget the slavery of a people bound to serve a cruel Pharaoh—that thus we might admire all the more the unsurpassable grandeur of the monument. And Napoleon felt himself justified to do so in light of his historical role as *Imperator Mundi*: "From the heights of these pyramids, twenty centuries contemplate you." This alludes not only to the past, but to the future as well; even to a millenary Empire (and we are familiar with Napoleon's taste—like Speer's—for the Egyptian style). Contrary to this, Moses liberated his people from bondage, but never built anything; rather, he led them into the desert where no dream of stone or eternity ever haunted him. On the whole, the Jewish people hardly left a single architectural monument—especially after the restoration of the Temple was prohibited—unless, of course, we consider the Wailing Wall to be such a monument. This is the wall, perhaps, to which the Berlin Wall corresponded as a sort of reversal or expiation: called, the *wall of shame*.

Is not eternity—this "glacial wave" (Trakl) that has flooded Western metaphysics from its very outset—a "resentment against time?"[11] A death instinct that ends in petrification? Is it not this dream of stone that Nazi Germany exalted, even before it became its own executioner and grave digger? This, however, is not Krier's understanding: "The criminal element of Nazism does not reside so much in its retrograde culturalism, but in its industrialist-socialist-centralist-collectivist-modernist *Sturm und Drang*." This constitutes nothing more than a lot of amalgamated adjectives, spoken in a jargon that reminds us of the old Hitlerian propaganda: the "Judeo-Bolshevism," not to speak of the collusion between the Jews, Freemasons, Plutocrats, Communists, Starvers, and so on. What is more, all of these phenomena would have "survived the denazification; indeed, they would have found themselves morally purified and freed from obsolete cultural baggage." Thus, the criminal element of Nazism (an expression that suggests a noncriminal element—one that was unjustly "sacrificed") would not reside in its love of the blond beast and Classical architecture, but only in the "madness of technology" that abruptly snatched it from Modernism as from a mortally contagious disease. At the very least, we ought to applaud the Führer for having bannished and persecuted Modern Art—an art that had been characterized as "degenerate" for the same reason that the Jewish "race" had been so characterized. (Here I refer to the closing of the Bauhaus, the exile of Klee and many other artists and autos-da-fé). In return, we should not forgive him for having invited the wolf into the sheepfold—if I am permitted to employ such a pastoral image—that is, to have yielded to the demon of Modernism. For these practices that Hitler deemed "degenerate" in art were carried—by him—to an extreme paroxysm in the economy of a total war.

Demon of Modernism . . . Is this the simple expression of a paranoia that raves? Still, we must open our eyes; we must walk within the cities. By modern cities, I do not understand the historical centers that have been more or less restored nor by this do I understand the so-called prestigious projects accomplished by Modernity. No, let us try to simply pass through (if our hearts so speak to us), some ordinary "high-rises" where the average citizenry resides. Surely, such dwelling places are more modest, but therein live a considerable portion of the urban population. Every time I brought my daughter to the babysitter's home, I necessarily had to travel through the "spaces" (the nonplaces, the overpopulated deserts) of the high-rise apartments managed by ZAC (Zone d'Aménagement Concerté)—or that zone whose development is promoted by the government. Thus, by the Pont de Sèvres I passed, shadowed over by the gray, impressive towers constructed out of concrete. Concrete—cement—is the material consecrated to such structures. It creates the illusion of being more solid than stone or brick—although all the while deteriorating at a much faster rate. These tall towers, constructed some fifteen years ago, already seem to threaten us with their ruin—but perhaps at the time they seemed new? Around their foundations, which are piled one upon the other, whirl without tire, whirlwinds of dust and dirty papers; such that every other day my daughter, no matter how protected her face, would leave her "maternal helper" with a bad case of conjunctivitis.

It is not necessary to look long or far nor need we raise our voices: the disaster is everywhere before us—that is, if only our eyes could see. This solemn universe, this somber place—resembling, in a way, a concentration camp—could very well be characterized by its "concrete-refrain." Thus, the playgrounds situated in the middle of these housing projects are so structured—and situated—that they are open to the open air and centered on a great slab of concrete that constitutes the very ground of the various high-rises; but that, in reality, is already three stores above the city streets—these playgrounds, I say, had to be covered with a lattice-work (similar to those used in prisons) to protect those inhabitants below. For those who dwell above were much in the habit of throwing their garbage—from the empty beer can to the nonfunctional iron—down to the courtyard below. As Benjamin has already remarked, Modernity seems particularly prone to produce large amounts of garbage and refuse: from chemical pollutants to the city dump, and even—as some might remember—the "garbage barge" and, recently, the "garbage train." Even the inhabitant has become a form of refuse, a reject: an unrecyclable resource insofar as one cannot be returned to a former state. This inhabitant remains enclosed within a space to which he or she has become as absolutely indifferent as to the garbage can in the kitchen. This person is not even a stranger; for, no longer are there any native inhabitants. Nor need I mention the fact that these are immigrants who, in a sense, have been banished to these housing projects and there placed under "house arrest."

This description in no way constitutes an isolated incidence. In an article entitled "A Concrete Cruise Ship Floats Adrift: 2800 Apartments in Abeyance at Haut-du-Lièvre," a journalist describes the drift of high-rise-government-assisted housing toward a "social ghetto"—indeed, towards a veritable "medina." Further on in the article, he presents the renovation efforts undertaken by the HLM office at the beginning of the 1980s:[12] "First, the interiors of the apartments are renovated (including sanitary installations and soundproofing), then the common areas (graffiti is removed and antitheft lights installed), and finally, the exterior spaces are worked on. As of now, this renovation has not been able to transform Haut-du-Lièvre into a likable place for its inhabitants. Each week, more than ten tons of garbage is thrown *over the balconies*!"[13]

Modernism—in architecture and urban planning—amounts to nothing more than the application of rules as strict as those once applied to "Classical" architecture. We find a uniformity and standardization of spaces; all of which are measured solely in quantitative terms of the surface area. Consequently, space is conceived of as an abstract continuum: quantifiable and infinitely divisible but, above all, *homogenous* in such a way that *places* disappear. This neutrality has, as its consequence, a radical eradication of the inhabitant as such; for he or she has been dispossessed of all *ethos* or character proper; such that only an impersonality is left in its wake—the likes of which we would eradicate with our ridiculous and inane attempts to "personalize" the individual "units" with "personal" codes such as F3. Finally, the building itself is deprived of any unique style; and, it is this very absence of style that the Charter of Rome claimed as the "international style." Here we have rationalism pushed to its extreme; and so, as with every excess of reason, we have monstrosities. In effect, architectural modernism may very well be conceived as a variation on the theme of the "madness of technology." The resident, enclosed in a big building, hardly dwells there; rather, he or she dwells wherever—for the place is no longer important. This *wherever* goes hand in hand with the *whatever*; both of which lead to the concerted disappearance of places and things. Today, we have functional furniture that is composed of interchangeable components and may be assembled according to an instruction sheet (this latter doing practically without any language). Thus, the triumph of the *kit*!—following that of kitsch. The city, like the *kit*, is assembled by a series of urban components that, in themselves, compose a loose network that can be modified according to the will of the urban planners. That is, they may modify the housing projects by mixing them in with other quantified spaces: for example, with spaces of leisure, residential areas, offices or "commercial activities" (the word *commerce* no longer suffices by itself; we must underscore the fact that we are active, that we produce!), and with green spaces (on a billboard near the Seine, at the site of the old Citroën plant, we can even read that there will be 4,400 trees!).

Can we, in such vertiginous spaces, be strangers? Foreigners? Expatriated, even, when every space of belonging has been erased? Can we, as was Socrates amid his homeland's largest city, be *atopos*? Indeed, how can we be displaced when there is no proper place? When the place has been evacuated and emptied and treated as a simple parameter that must be taken into account according to the "plans" of the technicians? In much the same way, the "work" of art (that is, if we can still speak of work and art in the same breath) may be constructed wherever and however: as in an infinitely rearrangeable cultural space that is somewhat similar to the Lego set. The disappearance of the work of art coincides with the disappearance of places in the world. For the modern user, the organization of space signifies neither the ordering of things according to the world that sustains them nor according to "things" that give rise to the world; rather, modern use is such that things are placed (in terms of art, we might say "performed"), in advance, by disposing them to an indifferently divisible and homogenous framework. The world waxes utopian at that place where the thing becomes less than an object, where it becomes a question of a simple process, placement, or piece of machinery concerned only with the manipulation of *commands*. Such a thing may be placed *wherever*; for it functions according to *plan*. The place itself—far from *not* counting—can only count, can only enter into accountability, can only enter into the accounting of the plan that must take into account all the factors of production.

The vast network of mass media—which, itself, is a device of self-referential production—may serve as an example of such utopization. The thing becomes information, such that it gives way, in advance, to the informational scheme (of things). A command post connects the thing to the whole network—outside of which nothing has any meaning, and "where" nothing can have any meaning for itself. Here "meaning" means to respond correctly to the command (or demand) of information. The command precedes the "image," even though the presentation of the image (of a news report, for example) seems to immediately volunteer itself as the meaning that makes the reporter's explanations both redundant and, even, incomprehensible. The truth (if there is one *here*) is that there really is no mediatic image, but only a simulacrum of an image; such that between a necessarily "fallacious" commercial and a necessarily "authentic" news report, there no longer exists an unequivocal difference. In any case, this flow of images does not address itself to anyone—even though it seems to be concerned with everyone. It simply fills an emptiness; it merely produces substitutes for both places and things. In its own way, it places a universalized utopia in place of places by responding to a precommand.

Like Baudrillard, we might respond and say that this is nothing more than a common place of the civilization of the simulacrum, or of a civilization of a mimeticism without model; or of a self-*mimesis* that functions precisely by producing its own models—models that are always already imitated, as are Warhol's paintings painted in a series. That this be a common place can be only all the more worrisome: for we are incapable of saying *from whence* this common place comes to us. It loiters about everywhere and nowhere, such that this conjunction constitutes the very essence of the technological utopia. And this happens in the way that Being takes "place," at present: according to Heidegger, "inasmuch as the danger is Being itself, it is everywhere and nowhere."[14]

Yes, everywhere and nowhere. However, Heidegger *localizes* the Danger. In fact, in 1942, he tells us precisely from whence it comes: the United States of America.

> Today, we find that the Anglo-Saxon world of Americanism is determined to destroy Europe, and that means the Fatherland (*Heimat*)—which, in turn, means the Inception (*Anfang*) of the West. The Inception is indestructible. The entrance of America into this world war hardly signifies an entrance into History, but only, already, the last American act of a-historicity and self-destruction. In effect, this act is the renunciation of the Inception and the decisive decison for that which has no inception. The hidden spirit of Western beginning shall not even hold this process—by which that which is devoid of inception destroys itself—in contempt. Rather, it shall await its hour in the serenity wherein the Inception rests. To be sure, we still only think in half a manner—and that means absolutely not—the historicity of history when we measure History and its greatness only with respect to the length of that which has been, rather than *waiting* for that which first took place—the inception—as that which comes and still has yet to come. We, to be precise, hold on to the very inception of authentic historicity; that is, of acting in the essential from our being-able-to-wait-for the destination of the Proper. This "being-able-to-wait-for" hardly signifies an attitude of non-interference or of letting things go their own way without any engagement in thought on our part. Nor does it mean that we must shut our eyes before the gloom that surely comes before us. This "being-able-to-wait-for" is to keep oneself ready, already one step in advance, within the Indestructible, near to which devastation belongs as does the valley to the mountain. Yet, this shall never happen unless historial humanity, born of the Inception, becomes—thanks to the pain of sacrifice—ripe for the Inception as for its own proper being.[15]

It is an enormous text, the reading of which—toilsome as it may be—suffices to spark a suspicion: that this great thinker, ostensibly above the fray and scornful of current affairs, adhered, utterly, to the most repulsive ideas of the National Socialist ideology. An innocent reader—if such still exists—can only be but astonished and horrified by this profession of faith: that of the superiority—of essence, indeed of blood!—of the German people in light of American barbarism (which is both self-destructive and nihilistic). Be this as it may, when America entered the war in 1942—the same year in which Heidegger gave the preceding lecture and the year in which he offered his course on Hölderlin, "the poet of poetry"—this signified nothing essential, nothing "historial" insofar as America had already left History or insofar as it had never taken any part in it. The Americans . . . determined to destroy Europe? But what was Europe at that time if not, essentially, Germany? And what was Germany if not (via Greece) the very torch of Europe's History—its source and destiny? Accordingly, Germany was nothing less than the *Anfang* of the West—this latter being a key word of Heidegger's that may even be identified with Being. Now, the Americans—just because they are barbarians, vandals, and criminals—shall, in no way, be held in contempt by us, we others—we *Germans*, Peoples of Being. For the *Anfang*, the millenary *Reich* is indestructible.

Such is what a simple mind immediately understands; that is, on condition that one has sifted through all the jargon of authenticity and has translated, in one's own naive way, the incredible phraseology by which Heidegger paraded his primary "thoughts." We could even, instead of voicing a feeble protest, introduce some subtle distinctions; for example, we might distinguish between America as a nation (the United States) and America as an ideology or "world vision," and then (to buttress our apology) use Heidegger's *subsequent* statements (those uttered after Germany's defeat) when he kept his distance from those who "belittled" America by reducing it to the *American way of life*.[16] However, these subtle distinctions only cloud an issue that is relatively clear: Americanism is, in the eyes of Heidegger, a destructive principle that destroys the *essential*; consequently, it is criminal. Moreover, it is thus not by accident, but by choice: *entschlossen . . . zu vernichten* (where we read: "decided to destroy"). And we know how much the term *Entschlossenheit* is, in itself, invested with the power of decision as regards the essential—for it is, from its inception in *Being and Time*, the very motor of "authenticity" in the relationship to death. Americanism, was it then determined to destroy the essential: to annihilate Europe and the Fatherland? Of course, Heidegger would later assert—though once again, after Germany's defeat—that the word *Heimat* must be "thought in its essential sense, not patriotically or nationalistically but in terms of the history of Being." Likewise, the "German reality" (I would note that *das Deutsche* is neuter here), was not revealed to the world "so that the world might be reformed through the German essence."[17] Fine, but such "corrections"—corrected always already after the fact and after defeat—in no way mitigate our suspicions. We hardly see how the German people, already characterized in 1935 as the sole metaphysical people endowed with a great land, language, and history (of thinkers), could not have been the only Western people in whom (thanks also to Hölderlin's poetic word) was invested the world's salvation—from the "oblivion of Being."

Is this reading somewhat reductive? Perhaps. I well know that the oblivion of Being is really no one's fault but, rather, is a destiny that must be taken upon oneself and must be thought—and, I know, that nothing is capable of saving us—save a God.[18] I also know that Germany (or only Hitler?) failed in its mission precisely because it did not heed the "disarming" word of Hölderlin; nor did it heed the even more radical word of Heidegger himself who was there to point out the right path. (Such "spiritual" leaders were necessary even for the Führer-Leader himself . . .). It is no less significant that, after the defeat, Heidegger strove in every way possible to erase his verbal transports, going so far as to efface the very *word Germany*. Instead, he preferred to speak in terms that were more vague: of the "Occident" as the "Evening Land" (*Abend-Land*).

Yet all things considered, have we read well? Why did we remember only the stunning declarations about America? Why did we omit all the unfolding (to be sure, obscure), of the wait and the being-able-to-wait? Perhaps we should return upon our path, retrace our steps, and begin to think . . . about the beginning. The *Anfang* (if this be a beginning) should have taken place long ago; for it constitutes the beginning of the West. Nevertheless, according to Heidegger, we must wait for it; and even we must *be able* to wait for it as that which comes and has yet to come, as that which destines itself and thus constitutes the proper of History (in a way, this happens according to a semantic kinfolk of words: *Geschichte-Geschick*). Still, to wait for the beginning—even though it already began some 2,000 years ago? Is this then the "hidden spirit of the Beginning?"—which is, as we are to understand, indestructible? In effect, we can destroy only that which *is*—in one way or another—real or present. Yet the Beginning, containing as it does the having been and the will be, is neither something "real" nor a "being" as is a chair or table. We cannot wage war against a nonexistent "spirit," at least not from the point of view of "reality"—and, here, reality is that which counts.

Notwithstanding, this great war—whether or not this be in the form of a "spiritual battle . . . as brutal as a battlefield full of men"—

strangely reveals itself in a somber light: for if Heidegger had truly been a "good" Nazi, would he have not believed in total victory? Why then did he speak of a wait? Was it simply to wait—and see—the outcome of the war? Or, rather, was this wait something of a *withdrawal*; that is, of a retreat? Yet, a withdrawal in the form of a leap forward . . . into the Beginning and the Indestructible, "near to which devastation belongs as does the valley to the mountain." This is a twisted sentence, but one that leaves no doubt: danger—*devastation*—is at the very heart of the Saving Power. It "is" the Saving Power or Being according to the sentence cited previously.

A savage translation that slips into the political: Americanism, if in fact it is so utterly dangerous for Europe—more dangerous than anything else—it is because there is nothing outside of this Europe; it is because Americanism has originated from Europe and thus has already contaminated it in its very—German—core. At the very least (that is, if we know how to read between the Heideggerian word[s]), that which justifies his rigorous (perhaps ridiculous) "sortie" against America is that he sees, already, the infiltration of the American danger at the very core of National Socialism. It is sufficient to read a few pages more; for that which is said of the Colossal could very well characterize Nazi "aestheticism" *and* "Americanism": "The enormous itself is erected as its proper quality. Indeed, the preponderance of quantity is itself a quality; which is to say, a way of being that loses all measure. In effect, im-mensity is the very principle of what we call 'Americanism'—and Bolchevism is only a variety of Americanism. This latter is simply the most dangerous form of the loss of measure because it is cast in the same mold as the democratic bourgeoisie wherein it mixes with Christianity and the dross of an absolute a-historicism."[19]

In 1941, the film director Veit Harlan was sought by Goebbels to realize a "project of national interest" that would solidify the German people. Of course it was filmed with colossal means and colossal methods: 8.5 million marks, 6,000 horses, and 187,000 soldiers, most of whom were taken directly from combat divisions! *The Kolberg Affair*—a historic film that portrayed the "uprising" and awakening of the German nation against the French invader during the time of Fichte's *Discourse to the German Nation*—debuted in 1945, in a Berlin that had been pummeled to ruins: "In the cinematographic domain, Nazi madness reached a new height. Entire sections of the city of Kolberg were constructed as scenery around Berlin. Even a river was literally diverted from its course in order to produce an inundation, which is one of the "hints" of this film to which both Goebbels and Hitler attached as much importance as to a military victory."[20]

This film revealed the extent to which the Nazi bosses considered "art" as a means of propaganda (in truth, it was nothing less than the pursuit of war by other means). Yet, at the same time, this film showed war to be a total work of art. The Colossal—masterpiece of such aesthetics but also, according to Krier's own admissions, obvious in Speer's architecture[21]—was, in *The Kolberg Affair*, that much more beyond measure that its effect was reduced to almost nothing (any Colossus is an idol with feet of clay). For, at the time when the film was released, only in a few obscure movie houses, Berlin was burning. It became the film of the apocalypse; and yet, had the circumstances been different, we would have seen it as nothing more than the German version of a Hollywood blockbuster: a "Terminator" (of sorts) *made in Reich*.

> Industrial civilization is quite incapable of bringing forth cities, towns—or properly speaking, *places*. Its application is solely towards the construction of suburbs, outskirts, zones and the infrastructures of transportation, waste-removal, and concentration camps. And these always take the following forms: shelter of the masses, work of the masses, transportation and communication of the masses—and the extermination of the masses. To be sure, Auschwitz-Birkenau and Los Angeles are both offspring of the same parents. They are the quintessence of the social nonplace; of the inability to bestow on both human work and the common world, a dignified and agreeable form.[22]

The preceding passage clearly reveals the enemy responsible for our every ill: it is industrialism—which is nothing more than a variation on the madness of Technology. Thanks to this scapegoat, it is possible to cast a suspicious shadow on *everything* that presents the *same* characteristic "according to its essence." "Agriculture is now a motorized alimentary industry. *According to its essence*, it is the same thing as the manufacture of corpses in the gas chambers and concentration camps; it is the same thing as a blockade and the forcing of an entire land into starvation; it is the same thing as the manufacture of hydrogen bombs."[23] In a word, according to the essence of such "things," there is only one thing, one name, one "Being": Technology. From this point of view, it is always possible to view the concentration camps as an incredibly efficacious industrial enterprise—though no more so (or less so) than the agro-alimentary industry based on high performance fertilizer. Without some sort of hyperrational organization or technological method such as the use of gas, how could the Nazis have been able to successfully carry out their Colossal attempt to "cleanse" the world of 6 million Jews? In a certain sense, the "solution" to the Jewish "problem" contained something rather ingenious; and in a way, it was nearly as great a technological achievement as the first walk on the moon or the discovery of the atomic bomb—this latter having almost been discovered by the Germans ahead of the Americans. Let us imagine what the Western world would have been like if the Nazis, instead of wasting their time and energy on the solution to the Jewish "problem," had carried themselves in a way as "rational" as the American way . . .

Indeed, that which we forget, always already from the point of view of "essence," is the thing—irreducible in its singularity. Why is it that we speak of the "manufacture of corpses" *in general*, as if from the outset it was not a question of *Jews*? Certainly, here is a "detail"—one that necessarily escaped the very one who pretended to see nothing but the "essence"—that changed *everything*. Deep seeded anti-Semiticism constituted the *singularity* of National Socialism; it was its root, its ground, its lifeblood. And it was this that Heidegger, obsessed as he was with the essence of Technology, never saw or knew how to see. Or rather, he considered it inessential—an "accident" of History. But History itself consists only of accidents; it *is* itself the Accident par excellence. Consequently, philosophy finds itself in a quandry: for it cannot admit the Accident inasmuch as it is strictly concerned with essence and necessity. It mythifies Technology, treating it as if it were a sole entity—as if it were an individual endowed with responsibility. But this is simply an eloquent way to exculpate the "subjects" of history, treating them merely as programmed machines. True, *according to the essence*, the technicalization of the world leads to a becoming-mechanized of the human being; such that one is subsequently reduced to either a raw material or to a means of production that is obedient to the High Command that surpasses everyone. But such also was the story told by those who daily carried out the most heinous tortures: "We were only following orders as any good and loyal soldiers would do; why punish us, we were only the 'bureaucrats of Technology'?" (Heidegger). Yes, these men were not bloody executioners (no more so than other men), they only obeyed—more or less willingly—inhuman orders. But it is precisely *this* that we must reproach and this that we cannot forgive. The refusal to obey (what Thoreau had already termed *civil disobedience*) is not only the "right of every man"—whether or not it is guaranteed by the Constitution—but also, a condition of human existence as coexistence. It makes freedom possible, for the citizen defines the degree of one's *civic* spirit as well as one's commitment to the community. Still, Heidegger took no notice of such civicism, nor of a city seen in such terms. Only History has a voice worthy of being voiced; only History—that is, destiny. If Technology (as the final destiny of Being) determines the historiality of the modern person, then the question of an individual or collective "responsibility" can become only secondary. It becomes in-essential. In consequence, we necessarily surrender ethics to "humanism"—and who can vouch for the bloodless hands of humanism! Furthermore, we forsake civil society for "publicity"—though we must understand public space (*Offentlichkeit*) as a degeneration of the original opening (*Offenheit*). Finally—according to the pure thinker of Being—all this originates from the inauthenticity and dictatorship of the "They" (or "One").

Is, then, the common world doomed to a world of dirt and abomination? Can we still think that, according to the essential, there is no difference between Auschwitz and Los Angeles? Yet how is it that such a hyperindustrialized country as the United States has constructed no extermination camps?—a country that was once considered to be the sanctuary for all those—Jews and Germans alike—who were persecuted and preyed upon by the "Aryan law" of a people mystically tied to its Leader?

It may be that Los Angeles is a city that hardly suits our tastes—not a city in the European sense of the term—and most definitely, not that beautiful German city described by Karl Gruber: that small, bourgeois, and handcrafted city dismally destroyed by "Allied bombs." To be sure, Los Angeles is not a concentration camp. Of course, the "concentration" in urban modernity—the megalopolis—has a certain distant, though purely formal, relationship with the sinister camps—of concentration—that the French Republic instituted with success in 1938 and onward. Nonetheless, Los Angeles is not exactly the best example; for it is a "city" that is spread out over hundreds of square kilometers. Today, in this postindustrial era, even the notion of a "center" or downtown, with its architectural corollaries of an organic and hierarchically centered unity, has been shaken to pieces and fallen to the ground. This era itself corresponds to a mutation in the form of technological development. In lieu of massive mechanisms and technics that correspond to a heavy and centralized industrialization, electric-electronic technology tends to disseminate a lightweight network on a planetary scale. For example, as regards communications, we find fiber optics and transmission by satellite, whereby the actual organizations have virtually become invisible and immaterial: in a way, "rhizomes" that indifferently overstep borders and cultures. From this fact, any ponderous and centralizing power is entirely discredited in terms of efficiency—if only because its giganticism and rigidity render it unproductive and overweight. The postindustrial world is ruled by other laws that neither exhaust the will to power nor the will to technology. Rather, these latter are transformed by them into nonmonumental *forms*: as John Cage has noted, ephemeralization is the consequence of new, light technologies, based on data processing and microprocessors. We may all mourn the traditional forms of organization—the preindustrial or the heavy industrial manufacturing of the last two centuries—but this is nothing more than a nostalgic attachment to the past. Had Speer's monuments not been destroyed, they would have become utterly obsolete, like Mongolian palaces or excessive subprefectures, in a decentralized or "planetary"—signifying in its strict sense, a "wandering asteroid"—universe, where there is not *one* universal culture, but a continual and indefinitely recomposable crumbling of collectible elements concerned primarily with the need to circulate information(s). Though here I have no intention of setting forth a flashy postmodern creed: for the naive utopia of a "planetary village" à la Buckminster Fuller, is no more respectable in itself than that old regilded humanism that now sparkles as a liberally advanced society. It is quite possible that it is precisely by these underground voices of the "Immaterials" that the "madness of Technology" rules all the more enduringly (in fact, Heidegger thought for two milleniums!). As for Krier, he insists that from the moment we prefer the zonation and dissemination of networks to an organic and controlled growth, we thus sever and sunder any community of culture. But this is to mistake the effect for the cause. *The* culture—which is as empty as the "essence"—has been dead for quite some time (perhaps since Auschwitz?). And everywhere where we denounce the defeat of THE culture or thought, we dream, in all actuality, of a *return*—though no longer expansionist—to the domination of the late great Western monoculture. It is a culture that, moreover, is probably no more than one more illusion produced by the Western will to return.

Is there *a* single principle that we can call by the name of *Anfang*, *arche*, and so forth whose opposite term would be *an-archy*, *a-historicity*, and everything that Heidegger consolidates within the word *Americanism*? Is there even anything such as *an* Americanism that cannot be reduced to a "particular lifestyle"? This essence—whether or not it be an in-essence (*Unwesen*; monstrosity)—cheapens the singularities and accidents of history, while all the while imposing, in the name of an apodictic truth, cliches and commonplaces as old and moldy as that of the absence of an American historical sense that, as it were, is the very sign of American "barbarism." Needless to say, Nietzsche saw historicism differently, saw that Europe was perishing under its pretended "historical sense"—such that it had lost that positive sense of oblivion without succumbing to a total loss of memory. And if Europe sees the day—a day, we are told, that is near and that, nevertheless, seems to retreat day by day in proportion, even, to the *credo in unum Deum*—this will be only a variegated and incoherent patchwork of worn out ideas pulling in incongruous directions. What Europeans have never really understood is that it is possible to have more unity and cohesion in a synergy of heterogenous elements than in a homogenous reduction to the most common denominator. Synergy retains all "value"; it proceeds according to the nature of Nature, by the readaptation—and not the elimination—of that which is "decayed" into humus and fertile land.

Without a doubt, synergy constitutes the principal virtue of America. The true United *States* are a melting pot of heterogenous elements whereby antiracism is procured precisely through the regeneration of blood. It proceeds by inclusion rather than exclusion and by the acceptance rather than the extermination of the other. True enough, through the course of its history, America has not been totally true to this logic: we must not forget how the white man exterminated the Indian, even in the name of "Humanism" and other moral values. "Yes, we know that when you come, we shall die," sang an old Native American. And Chief Plenty-Coup gave the following words of farewell after council had been taken near the site of Little Big Horn:

> The ground on which we stand is sacred ground. It is the dust and blood of our ancestors. On these plains the Great White Father at Washington sent his soldiers armed with long knives and rifles to slay the Indian. Many of them sleep on yonder hill where Pahaska—White Chief of the Long Hair so bravely fought and fell. A few more passing suns will see us here no more, and our dust and bones will mingle with these same prairies. I see no longer the curling smoke rising from our lodge poles. I hear no longer the songs of the women as they prepare the meal. The antelope have gone; the buffalo wallows are empty. Only the wail of the coyote is heard. The white man's medicine is stronger than ours; his iron horse rushes over the buffalo trail. He talks to us through his "whispering spirit." We are like birds with a broken wing. Inside me my heart is cold. My eyes are veiled; I am old . . .[24]

In the time before, man was immortal. However, the scattered ash and bones of the Indian still remain upon the prairie plain—though this latter has become the ground of another hunt. Space remains—space; and America in its myth. Around 100 miles from Bogotá, we find a colonial city that has been almost perfectly preserved. It is called Villa da Leiva and sits in the very heart of the Andes. It is a city that contains no "modern" building other than the bus station. It is a small community with hardly more than 1,000 inhabitants, almost all of whom are peasants who work the day long in the surrounding fields. There are few skilled workers. It is a city without suburbs—a vestige of another time—such that once past the last house, there is nothing but countryside. The majestic and imposing mountains dominate; yet, what is most remarkable is the city square. It is not so much a question of size or surface area, but rather of space—or better yet—of *place*. It is an *empty* place, marking out a perfect, even magical, square. There is nothing in the center but a small fountain; there are no trees, no statues, no monuments, no barriers. Simply nothing and nobody, save on those special holidays when one can find a flea market—then there gleam irridescent and splendorous colors, and the space comes alive with people. Ordinarily, the inhabitants prefer to walk around the square, under the covered arcades that trim its borders; so that thus they need not expose themselves to the openness. For this place almost seems to unveil—or, rather, to cause vertigo: far from enhancing the value of those facades that enclose it, the square appears more like a crude asteroid fallen from the sky. With its ore-ish tint, it seems to be extraneous to itself. It shimmers with a sparkle come from far away; with the sparkle of night—if, in fact, it is true that the night is a Stranger: the "Giver of Wonderment" (Hölderlin, "Bread and Wine"). *Nothing will have taken place but the place—except, perhaps, a constellation.*[25]

Always horror and wonder; always of emptiness. Yet, can we compare this square with the excess of Speer's Grosse Platz? Impossible. For the square of Speer is the result of a will to produce, simply by size, an *effect* of fascination and the annihilation of the human person. It does not *mirror* the infinite of celestial emptiness, but rather reflects an image of hypertrophied human power subsequently rendered inhuman. It proceeds from a totalitarian project wherein exclusion functions as a deadbolt to the security of the totality. Grosse Platz was purposely designed to be filled with an obedient multitude, obeying "as a single man." The superhuman Nazi was the inhuman totality and cumulation of individual beings counted as homogenous quantities—and whose singularity was, in advance, reduced to zero. Even the SS can be accounted for in terms of pure numbers. While the small square in Villa da Leiva opens itself up to destitution, void, and wonder, the architectural project of the Nazi's was enclosed within itself and there became fixed in an unbearable and sterile crispation. Its enormity was merely the result of a normalization that had been maximized.

Yet, Villa da Leiva is nothing more than a survivor apart from modernity. The city itself is a museum; but then, many of Europe's cities are becoming museums, beginning with Venice (and even Paris in certain respects). This becoming-museum grows in proportion to those centers that are solidified and fixed in their "history"; for, by such fixation, they leave open spaces only to the outskirts or new cities. Consequently, inasmuch as suburbs have no history, growth is generally anarchical—or given over to the whims of developers and urban planners! Thus the choices seem to be limited to a chaos (which is living), or a harmony (which is dead). It is this that Leon Krier explains in another text: historic city centers suffer from an overdevelopment in height (oddly enough, on account of the high cost of land), which leads to a congested and crowded architectural fabric.[26] Conversely, the outskirts or peripheries are excessively spread out horizontally, thus creating an urban fabric that is too loose. And this, in consequence, contributes to the congestion of the city centers. This schema, although somewhat simplified, is nevertheless well founded. Still, we are well within are rights to wonder whether or not the disharmony between the overdeveloped center (the vertical) and the excessively spread-out outskirts (the horizontal), constitutes an absolute evil? For, by what law could the modern city grow "harmoniously?" By what reason must we prefer Classical harmony to modern chaos? (Historically, this vision has been somewhat simplistic; for Paris, in the seventeenth century, was much more chaotic than it is today!) Must we then choose between chaos and harmony? Or, rather, might we not let them peacefully coexist? Might we not allow them to mutually interpenetrate (without creating some sort of obstruction), in a world that is both pluralist and decentralized, synergic and nontotalitarian?

The Classical model is one that propounds a program of "natural" growth for cities. Naturally, modern development is seen as a cancerous overgrowth that is *against* nature. Here I would merely point out the presupposition that presupposes a "naturalness" to a city that, by definition, is a historical "object." Furthermore, this naturalness itself is disseminated in its very "nature" (or essence). Yet, this organic model is nothing more than a *historical* construction. It remains wholly rooted in an Aristotelean conception of art. The three golden rules of Classical architecture that Krier mentions (*venustas*, *firmitas*, and *utilitas*) are directly drawn from good old-fashioned metaphysics. More precisely, they are derived from the Platonic-Aristotelean determination of *techne* as the *mimesis* of nature. This definition is perverse because it overtly propounds nature as *the* model; when, in point of fact, art constitutes the underlying model by which a *meaning* of nature is apprehended.

Here I shall break from this line of thought, for it carries us too far from the main point. However, according to Aristotle's double definition of human nature, a *petitio principii* is already evident in the harmonic model. If man is an animal endowed with a *logos*, then it is because he is a political animal and vice versa. In other words, a *logos* is erected in nature to better hide the human "technical" character. The result is such that politics is given out as an effect of nature. Similarily, with Plato—who takes architecture and *techne* in general as the model of natural order—we can detect the same flaw: "Well now, the good man who speaks for the best surely will not say what he says at random but with some purpose in view, just as all other craftsmen do not each choose and apply materials to their work at random, but with the view that each of their productions should have a certain form. Look, for example, if you will, at painters, builders, shipwrights, and all other craftsmen—any of them you choose—and see how each one disposes each element he contributes in a fixed order, and compels one to fit and harmonize with the other until he has combined the whole into something well ordered and regulated (*kekosmenon*)."[27]

Let us beware of examples, for they are exemplary; that is, they are normative. Architecture, under the bold banner of being nothing more than one example among others, determines, in advance, the demarche of logos. More precisely, it constitutes the *archetype* of true knowledge as order, precision, and harmony. In the preceding paragraph, the very order of the discourse assigns the "natural" order of things. Indeed, the eidetic syntax is of the same order that orders "art" and "nature."

Traditionally, Classical architecture is thought to be the very paragon of order. At the same time, this order is supposed to imitate the natural order of the *cosmos*, such that such architecture constitutes a microcosm. That the edifice is an imitation of nature hardly signifies that nature produces houses nor that architecture is limited to examples of "natural" homes such as caverns and caves. On the contrary, *mimesis* presupposes an infinite separation with the "natural" inasmuch as—from the very bosom of this separation—there surges forth a relationship of "harmony" wherein nature itself appears to be constructed "like" a temple. Every architectural theorist, from Vitruvius Pollio to

Palladio to Speer himself, has obeyed this demon of analogy: that Nature is imitable only because, according to Nicomaque de Gérase, it alone has been *produced* "as if from an architectural blueprint."[28] The world itself, like the *cosmos*, is an architectonic harmony of homogenous elements. Unfortunately, the metaphor tends, fatally, to become literal: the world was not merely constructed *like* a building—not according to an architectural blueprint—but *by* a Supreme Architect: the Demiurge, God. The human architect—by imitating the divine order of the Creator as expressed in the physical world of nature—creates a symbolic microcosm of the divine macrocosm.

But what takes place after God is dead?—at least, after the death of the metaphysical God that philosophers have hitherto conceived as the Great Clock Maker of Creation, the *architectus maximus*, and Keystone of their architectonics? What will become of architecture—hitherto revealed as metaphysical—in a "postmetaphysical" epoch? Shall it become chaotic? Yet chaos, understood synonomously with anarchy (as the counteressence *logos* and of *arche*), is itself, fundamentally, a Greek word. So, still, unknowingly, we wallow in Greek heritage.

"From what perspective must we view Antiquity?" Hölderlin asks. His response is neither from the view point of Classicism nor from that of Modernity, inasmuch as each is under the influence of the *model*: the former as the will to return and the latter as the illusion of departure: "We dream of culture, of piety, etc. Meanwhile, we have none—it is indisputable. We dream of originality, of independence; and we think we say new things, when in fact, it is merely a question of reaction—a sort of sweet vengeance on our subjection as regards Antiquity."[29]

Today, these words remain true: perhaps the whole of modernity is nothing more than a sort of sweet revenge against the Greek model—a sweet vengeance, but a vengeance all the same. It is a "resentment against time" because it is only a reaction. Yet, nothing is more difficult than to liberate ourselves from such a model and from such an *impress*. And this is for good reason. It has, for two millenia, been dissembled and dissimulated as natural; and precisely this natural or "natal" must be uprooted from that which is second nature: from a culture overlayed with the sacred seal of tradition. It is this we find most fertile in Heidegger: the notion of a *preliminary* destruction of tradition—preliminary to any access to the "thing itself."

This destruction or deconstruction is not concerned with annihilation or brutality, but with liberation; thus it allows for the experience and *free* use of the Proper. It may be that, as much as we are imbibed with Classical culture, we have never truly found Greece.

Even though we believe ourselves to be free and to say "new" things, we do nothing more than repeat. And even that which we repeat is not original. The original is concealed; indeed, it *began* in concealment: the history of the West is that of a decline—from the very beginning. Or, rather, the Beginning itself is revealed as a catastrophe. It is not simply that the original escapes *us*; no, it began by escaping those dwellers of the beginning—from the Greeks themselves. Heraclitus spoke of an altogether different harmony than the cosmical-logical order of Plato and of an altogether different "nature" (*phusis*) than Aristotelean physics. Nevertheless, Aristotle was able to barely remember Hesiod's myth whereby chaos is deemed the origin of everything. But already he understood chaos as a disorder rather than as an opening-up, a primal fault or essential separation without which the world could not have come to be. Aristotle never seized the significance of this fault, principally because his *logos* concerned itself with a steady and replete presence. Later, chaos and emptiness would be marked with a negative sign, even if this negative would thereafter partake in essence as the driving force behind the dialectical process.

Andreas Loser is a professor of Classics at a school just outside of Salzburg. He lives in a suburb that sits directly on the opposite side of the city; and he inhabits a development whose street names are both flowery and poetic: names such as Birchwood Boulevard, Avenue of Pines, and Avenue of Willows. Everyday he must—as he has no car—pass through the city center to go to work. Yet, when returning home, he often circumnavigates the "downtown" area, choosing instead to walk haphazardly through the open fields. Finally, when he reaches the Alm canal he follows it, for it leads directly to his house. According to him, the city center is unbreathable. But that which burdens him in the city is not so much the crowd itself (for he equally dislikes it when the streets are empty), as it is the very idea of concentration: indeed, the physical sensation of obstruction and anguish. As he once described it upon returning from a card game: "Nothing here makes place." To make place is to create emptiness—an emptiness that lightens and makes possible the appearance of *places*. "With the light of that moment, silence fell. The warming emptiness that I need so badly spread. It was a brightening, a primordial rising, an origination, so to speak. My forehead no longer needed a supporting hand. It wasn't exactly a warmth, but a radiance; it welled up rather than spread; not an emptiness, but a being-empty; not so much *my* being-empty as an empty form. And the empty form signified: story."[30]

The story is the word rendered free to its places. Perhaps this "origination" or "brightening" corresponds to what Heidegger called *Ereignis*. And *Ereignis* is precisely that which permits the taking-place to *take place*. Yet such brightening is of no-thing; it happens by surprise, breaking through the obstruction. It is like the sudden irruption of *being-empty*—or of the desert itself. Obstruction is necessary for such brightening. As Loser explains, he needs the city center (however unbreathable and unbearable it may be) to free himself and so reach a state of grace. This latter could even be called a *state of time*. Therefore, contrary to Krier's assertions (and contrary to those of every purist), Loser likes the disharmony between an obstructed center and an empty periphery. Indeed, he spends his time between city and noncity, center and periphery, numerousness and scarcity—such that he is a being of the inter-ruption, of intermittance and *thresholds*. His understanding of the "state of time" corresponds to the traditional definition of the concept of threshold: the "transition between privation and wealth." Besides his professional career, Loser enjoys another activity: he seeks out archeological sites where he may study the thresholds of homes, churches, temples, and other ancient dwellings. By standing over the threshold, Loser remains ever on the watch. Even his name, Loser, seems to be in harmony with the verb *losen*—a popular Austrian expression meaning "to spy" or "overhear." (Needless to say, he too is a great admirer of the "old" language.)

So, between city and noncity—and always *on the lookout*—Loser remains open to the Dwelling Place. The Dwelling Place is nothing more than a threshold or open door, and thus—according to Hölderlin—a "life-dwelling." The earth dwells. Yet, such dwelling only appears as such when the earth happens upon the word. In the work of Peter Handke, for example, we find a constant concern for the geological narrative (here understood literally and *not* scientifically). One need only read his novel *Slow Homecoming* in which the hero, Sorger (the Worrier), travels from the original Chaos of the Great North to that of the great modern city (New York). However, it is a return that resists returning to the "native land" and that is made ever more slowly, with ever more delay and postponement. The concern for form subsists; yet, it does not wish to in-form or en-close. Rather, it pays its respect to Chaos: for it is nothing more than the *pathway* toward form that, according to Klee's succinct formula (repeated by the narrator), is the "empty possibility of the narrative."

The distance between the original Chaos of Nature and that of the big city is not very great. Today, we even speak of urban "jungles," whose interiors seem impenetrable and, a fortiori, impossible to inhabit.

Or perhaps, at the very limit, we inhabit the threshold. "Does not an ancient word like 'postern' reveal the threshold as a place of safety?" The narrator would cite an "almost obsolete" dictum: "The threshold welcomes." The threshold sustains; it is the first layer, the ground (the French *sol* originates from the Latin *solum*). "In the village it was said that during an earthquake, one must not run outside; rather, one should place oneself over the threshold and under the door frame. There, one was sure to be safe." To be safe or sheltered is to be *between*: it is to be neither inside nor outside. "My country: it has become the image of a hand painted on a sign whose index finger points away, under which we read the caption, 'To the Fountain.' The place in which we used to live signified a refuge where we once were able to defend ourselves." Yet to the question, "Would you defend your country?" Loser responds: "Perhaps not the Parliament—but I would this barn here and that cabin over there." And Heraclitus, who was quite familiar with thresholds, would have responded: "Perhaps not this city—yet I would defend this baker's oven." Indeed, we defend the *here itself* not because it belongs to us, but because we are *here*: we belong to it.

According to Valéry, the city is created out of disquietude and concern. To be concerned means to not find rest, to be unable to feel at home: *unheimisch*. Only one who seeks but *has no* place can be concerned. And only one can seek who, in the suspense and expectation of the taking-place, perceives the suffering and dispair of the place. This seeker seeks inasmuch as he or she dwells in the in-between. In the inhabiting of the threshold. Trakl writes, in a poem entitled "*Winterabend*," the following line: "Pain petrifies the threshold." It transplaces the juncture of the rending apart, of the fault. Pain *is* the threshold as the opening-between. According to Loser, the verb *rend*—in German—belongs to the word *threshold*. It is the hyphen that separates and joins together; that draws nearer and keeps a-part.

Without such concern there can be no being-at-home; such that to experience the strange or foreign opens the way to the Proper and to the "pathway toward form." The Land already opens up in the drawing nearer that takes place in the rending apart. Yet, we should not mistake the one who experiences the threshold for the modern adventurer for whom the Difference between the proper and foreign is absolutely abolished. (By *Difference* I understand the threshold that rends apart *and* draws together each allotment.) "It is at that moment that 'savagery' becomes the Absolute itself and is esteemed as the fullness 'of Being.' " Yet, continues Heidegger, "When we romantically ascribe to the adventurer a particular intensity and density of 'life,' we then forget that *where* danger is posited as the Absolute, it loses every characteristic of danger."[31] The earth can be neither hospitable nor inhospitable for the adventurer simply because one has either moderated the difference—or entirely abolished it. One is, in essence, everywhere "at home." Everywhere one goes, one carries one's own ground and land. Yet, this ground is merely that of a subjectivity that, because it wishes to be immovable and solid, is all the more a desolate waste land. In all actuality, nothing can befall the adventurer for that one is deprived of all "*adventura.*" In a way, one's life is as much without dwelling as that of a person who has never journied outside a room. Perhaps even less so.

Certainly, Loser is no adventurer, but a lover of thresholds and the journey "*aufs Land.*" He knows that he belongs to the land; yet the link is as obscure and invisible as that of the *mother* tongue. (We should not speak of the "fatherland," but of the "motherland": the land of the Earth-Mother.) Furthermore, the link is fragile. Twice, the "state of time" that Loser has seized, breaks: first, when the inhuman cry of a frail child rings out in the night; and again when, while walking through a park in Salzburg, he espies ominous markings on a tree—"two thick black bars bent into a square shape," the swastika. "This sign is the nonimage; the cause of all my malaise and the dispair of this land." The swastika was a sign that figured prominently in all of Speer's buildings; however, Krier ascribes only a decorative value to it: according to him, it was only a "detail."

Loser would destroy the "Obstruction without a face." Yet, at the same time, he is in no way solaced. Far from it, for he knows that he belongs to "a people of Evil doers: not one people exists that is more scattered or more solitary." Indeed, he would destroy the "Obstruction" not only to rid himself of a horrible sign—the horror of the "fatherland," of Waldheim's Austria—but also so that the mountain is finally able to be *empty.* "Finally, you have the right to be nothing at all," he says, bidding farewell to the "Obstruction." (Unless, of course, he speaks to himself.) To be nothing at all, nothing will have taken place but the place . . . save, perhaps, a word. And the word, once free, creates for itself an indraft—a whirlwind. It is full of an emptiness—of an Empty-Being that whispers with the song of the earth and the weight of the world.

Notes

1. René Descartes, *Discourse on Method and Meditations*, p. 11. All philosophers from the time of Socrates (who rarely ventured outside the walls of Athens) have preferred the city. Descartes himself, in a letter addressed to Guez de Balzac, declared to have found "among the confusion of a great people" more liberty and solitude than in the most removed country setting.

2. René Descartes, *Discourse on Method*, p. 10.

3. On November 9, 1989, the Berlin Wall became a relic from another time. That which took place—when thousands of East Germans freely and joyfully went beyond the "wall of shame"—cannot, even today, be measured in all its significance. All we know is that something decisive happened; something irreversible not only for Germany, but for the entire European continent. Already we have seen the reunification of a country absurdly sundered, and now we await something profound from the rest of Europe—something that cannot be amoebically reduced to the "European Union" as proposed by the Maastricht treaty, that is, a techno-structure without any political and social project. It might even be said that that which shall take place in 1992 risks creating new obstacles to the future. Perhaps we should beware of a new wall: this time constructed not out of iron and concrete—but out of capital. Will the West withdraw into its old "European fortress," thus refusing the removal of all walls, the call to disarmament and a *glasnost* that is valid everywhere from sea to sea? Shall it refuse this unique opportunity: this other beginning that has *happened* to us and that transforms us into a "New World" many miles from America? Might not History, finally, march forward and so bring to completion a Modernity that, for two centuries, has been deferred? [This note was added when the French edition was about to go to press, and followed by the mention: "Seattle, November 13, 1989."]

4. This is the same sort of amalgam as that which declares Scionism to be a form of racism. Scionism, like anti-Fascism, is a *political* attitude, whereas rascism cannot be supported by any consistant theory: it is viscerally *ignorant* through and through. (In addition, it is an exacerbated antiintellectualism.)

5. Krier adds the following: "The futile destiny of even the most powerful modern institutions expresses itself only too clearly in the ephemereal appearance of their construction. Is it not that the impotence and lack of vision and moral authority of the United Nations, the European Parliament, UNESCO, NATO, and so on, is only too clearly indicated in the architectural mediocrity of their headquarters?" But what if the (relative) weakness of the architectural appearance proper to democratic institutions constitutes their internal force and the very sign of their adaptation to an epoch of growing immaterialization (including that of political power), to the

bendability and liberty of action instead of to the postmortem rigidity of Cyclopean apparel? Already the visible has less power than the invisible; thus, in the domain of nuclear weaponry, it is better to have a single nuclear submarine—which is theoretically undetectable—than to have 100 warheads stationed at a single, locatable site, such as on the high plains of Albion (France).

6. René Char, *Oeuvres Complètes*, p. 732.

7. Leon Krier, in *Speer, Architecture 1923–1942*, p.18.

8. The expression is from Hitler himself who used it in a "fireside conversation."

9. Krier, *Speer*, p. 23. Speer himself said of modernity that it was a "romantic illusion." The accusation is, itself, the ne plus ultra of modernity.

10. Heinrich Tessenow, German architect and author of *The Small City and Artisan Class*, was Speer's mentor.

11. Friedrich Nietzsche, *Thus Spoke Zarathoustra*, "On Redemption:" "This, indeed, this alone, is what *revenge* is: the will's ill will against time and its 'it was.' " Yet resentment speaks ever so clearly at the end of Krier's essay where he extols the "word of stone" against the "electronic word." And this forbids any reversal pure and simple; in other words, to impugn the past in the name of electronics would be no less of a vengeful act.

12. Habitation à loyer modéré (HLM), is basically the French equivalent to our own department of Housing and Urban Development.

13. Francois Koch, *Le Monde* (Friday, May 22, 1987).

14. Heidegger, "The Turning," in *The Question Concerning Technology and Other Essays*, trans. William Lovitt (New York: Harper and Row Publishers, 1977).

15. Martin Heidegger in *Gesamtausgabe 53, Hölderlins Hymne "Der Ister,"* p. 38. "Etymologically, *Anfang* derives from *an-* (in, at, to) and *fangen* (to seize, take, catch) . . . Happily the English language has another word for 'beginning'—with an etymology corresponding to that of *Anfang*. That word is 'inception,' deriving from the Latin *in-* (in, at, to) and *capere* (to seize, take, catch)." Quoted from the Translator's Foreword written for *Parmenides*, trans. Andre Schuwer and Richard Rocjewicz (Bloomington: Indiana University Press, 1992).

16. Martin Heidegger, "Letter on Humanism," in *Basic Writings*, p. 220: "Whoever takes 'communism' only as a 'party' or '*Weltanschauung*,' is thinking too shallowly, just as those who by the term "Americanism" mean, and mean derogatorily, nothing more than a particular lifestyle." This is a good example of voluntary amnesia.

17. Heidegger, "Letter on Humanism," in *Basic Writings*, p. 218.

18. Heidegger would later assert this in an interview with *Der Spiegel*, which was published posthumously. See Chapter 9 in this book.

19. Heidegger, in *Gesamtausgabe* 53, *Hölderlins Hymne "Der Ister,"* p. 86.

20. Jacques Sicilier, "Pour la victoire finale," *Le Monde* (May 9–10, 1987).

21. Krier writes: "The Colossal is a quality that participates in the real world of the measurable and nameable. *Colosseum* is not a defamation, but an affectionate denomination."

22. Leon Krier, *Speer*, p. 23.

23. This sentence was written in 1949 by Heidegger who read it in an unedited conference on Technology. It was quoted only recently, for the first time, by P. Lacoue-Labarthe in 1987, before the "scandal": Heidegger and Nazism (see *La Fietion du Politique*, p. 58).

24. Chief Plenty-Coup, quoted from *Touch the Earth: A Self-Portrait of Indian Existence*, compiled by T. C. McLuhan (New York: Simon and Schuster, 1971), p. 136.

25. Mallarmé, *Oeuvres Complètes*, pp. 474–475.

26. Leon Krier, "Choosing Chaos or Harmony," in *Real Architecture* (the catalogue from an exposition on "classical" constructions at the Building Center Gallery, London. March 18–April 15, 1987).

27. Plato, *Gorgias* (503d) in *Plato: The Collected Dialogues*, p. 286.

28. Quoted by Daniel Payot, in *Le philosophe et l'architecte*, [Paris: Aubier, 1983] p. 68. "The model is always produced . . . the scene is never original."

29. Hölderlin, *Oeuvres*, p. 594.

30. Peter Handke, *Der Chinese des Schmerzes*, Suhrkamp Verlag, 1983.

31. Martin Heidegger, *Gesamtausgabe* 53, *Hölderlins Hymne "Der Ister,"* pp. 91–92.

8

Totalitarian Space

By the term *totalitarian space*, I understand the space of total mobilization; space that is itself totally mobilized. In other words, the word *totalitarian* as used here does not have an exclusively political significance. Nor is it to be taken in an ethical sense; rather, it must be understood primarily in metaphysical terms. In a certain sense, it entails that which Heidegger called *Gestell*: the instilling Apparatus that submits the totality of Being to the position-summons. This Apparatus transcends any political agenda, and therefore, there is no less a totalitarian space in a "democratic" regime than in a "totalitarian" one. Furthermore, that it does transcend any political agenda does not signify that it is "above" or "outside" of politics; no, it signifies that it crosses over and determines—from top to bottom—the political field of modernity that has subsequently been imprinted with its print. And it is to this that the theme of "Omnipotent politics"—shared by intellectuals as different in their positions as Ernst Jünger (who advocated the total State) and Jean-Paul Sartre (who hailed the "total Marxist man" and who, even after 1945, assigned a positive sense to the word *totalitarian*)—bears witness. However, despite their divergent paths, it is true that each began from an Hegelian conception of the Absolute Subject: both were opposed to the abstract individual as conceived by the bourgeois-analytical thinking that succeded from the Enlightenment.

In another way, Heidegger—to call this conception into question—would, in a lecture given on Hölderlin in 1943, reassert the primacy of politics as the determining moment (itself radically *out-of-*

question) of a modernity brought to completion. During his discourse he would implicitly refer to Hegel:

> Consciousness, wishing to be certain of History, must be a consciousness both in action and planning. The fundamental modern form in which the consciousness of self—which models everything upon itself and which orders all beings accordingly—is the State. It is for this reason that "Politics" becomes the normative self-certitude of "historical" (*historischen*) consciousness. "Politics" would determine itself from a History (*Geschichte*) conceived according to the norms of consciousness—that is, according to a "technological" experience. "Politics" is the completion of History. It is thus precisely because Politics constitutes the historico-technological and fundamental certitude of all action; such that "Politics" shall be characterized by the utter and unconditional absence of all questioning of itself. This unconditionality of "Politics" and its Totality go hand in hand. And the reason for this mutual embrace and its content hardly rests—as we would naively believe—upon the accidental arbitrariness of dictators; but rather, upon the metaphysical essence of modern reality in general.[1]

Here is certainly not the place to penetrate further into the remarkable disjunction that Heidegger effects between the modern character of political "totalitarianism" and the way in which the Greeks thought the *polis* as the "theater of Being." (This latter being radically other than the "unconditioned primacy of the 'Totality of politics.' ") This disjunction has nothing to do with that articulated by Krier: for the latter attempted to separate Speer's architecture from the National Socialism—to which it was totally subordinate. On the contrary, Heidegger's strategy was much more complex. On the one hand, he wanted to "ground" the totalitarian regime of National Socialism in the general movement of modernity's coming to completion. (It is true that in so doing, he would legitimize National Socialism strictly in terms of metaphysics.) Yet Heidegger would take another turn—the only one possible according to him—in order to liberate himself from a totalitarianism that had been completely assimilated to the completion of the metaphysics of absolute subjectivity. This turn, as we know, was a return to the Greeks; to the *polis*, itself assimilated to the very *site* of the "There." "There" was to be experienced as the most important and dignified question. Indeed, the question is one that goes beyond the Greeks to the extent that they did not satisfactorily interrogate the *polis* as the very "locality" of Being. Keeping this in mind, we can understand the strange occurences during Heidegger's course given in 1943, at which time he reduced to nothingness any assumed "collusion" of a Germano-Hellenic alliance or the naive belief that National Socialism would be the legitimate heir of the Greek *Anfang:* "In no way do we do justice to either current political thought (1943) or to the Greeks when, in our desire to put 'science' to work, we merrily confuse that which stands itself in its proper being and its historical singularity. In no way do we assist our understanding or valorize the historical singularity of National Socialism when we present Hellenism in such a way that we might believe that the Greeks were already 'National Socialists'."[2] We see it: however sharply the disjunction is effected, there is still an ambiguity in the discourse on "modernity." Is it even possible to be quits with any compromise, historical or historial, with National-Socialism—or political totalitarianism in general—by simply re-turning it to its place (in History)? And is not this historialism equivalent to the resignation of thinking (and therefore of acting?)—that is, to a more refined form of a dialectical reconciliation?

That which remains clear is the steellike link that links Modern metaphysics to the totalitarian principle. It is clear—but only if we agree to consider that which Heidegger isolated as the coming-to-completion of Modernity's conception of a total reality within the system of absolute knowledge and the self-deliverance of the will (to power). The True is All; and only the All is the True: we, insofar as we are subjects, cannot get away from this. Even Nietszche was unable to elude this circle of totality, which he later presented as the "world of the Will to Power"; *that is to say*, the world of Dionysus.[3] It was a world that was totally flat and marked by an almost "holy" horror of emptiness—of the interstice, of openness, and so forth—that was always destined to be *occupied* by the mass (or masses) and also to be obstructed, in advance, by the construction of space as total space; that is, totally blueprinted, prearranged, and settled. Such a blueprint was the principle or common "place" from which the highways and concentration camps were constructed: from Nuremburg's "Cathedral of Light" to the extension, on all borders, of bunkers, blockhouses, and barriers. (More precisely, these latter were constructed only in those areas where the threat of foreign invasion was imminent.) Yet, we must add, this principle was not the privilege of a specific regime—however spectacular its *staging* may have been during the millenary—though ephemeral—Third Reich. Perhaps it was even this character of "staging"—the spectacle of it—that ruined the Third Reich, for an invisible organization is always more powerful than an organization that is clearly projected.[4] To be sure, National Socialism contained an inherent contradiction: it was hardly the monolithic rock as has always been presumed. First, we find the political stage staged with a multitude of factions fighting for power. And then, at its very foundation, we find the simple personality of Hitler: the frustrated artist who wished to transform his Wagnerian-Romantic-and-antimodern aesthetics into the "construction" of the new State. Yet for such a State, Hitler finally realized—though much too late—a much more performative method was necessary—an absolutely modern method.

Here I shall discuss only those passages from Jünger's work *The Worker* that are particularly provocative and enlightening. To begin, I would call into question the assertion by Julien Hervier (the French translator) that this is a "descriptive work" without "any normative value." I do so primarily on the grounds that it is impossible to obtain a "purely" objective description (or supposedly objective) of a totalitarian phenomenon. At the very most, we might situate ourselves upon the "neutral" ground of the historian; and from there, describe the "mechanisms" of each totalitarian regime taken in its *historical* specificity. Yet, it is obvious that Jünger did not speak from a historical perspective—primarily because the book appeared in the autumn of 1932. Nevertheless, as he paradoxically notes in the Preface to the German edition of 1963, this book was "much too late with respect to the ensuing events," but still *ahead* of the turbulent tide of 1933. It is true that in this sense we cannot read *The Worker* as "the apology of an everyday ordinary totalitarian State" (Julien Hervier) and even less so when this "everyday ordinary" State evolves into the National Socialist State. There is yet another reason why the argument of "neutrality" of *The Worker* may be denied. (Incidentally, the argument of neutrality has much in common with Krier's argument that asserts the neutrality of architecture within the political arena.) Yet, this other reason also denies any reading of an "apology" for National Socialism; more precisely, Jünger placed himself beyond the historian such that his project was endentured neither to the services of a cause nor to the neutrality of a clinical and objective perspective. Rather, his project was primarily that of meta-physics, and therefore of meta-politics. It is useless to cite the numerous passages in which Jünger explicitly opposes Nazi ideology (i.e., anti-Semiticism)—and that his book was subsequently unwelcomed by the Nazi intelligentsia. It is just as useless to try to "save" Jünger by delineating his differences with the aforementioned ideology; for, in so doing, we place ourselves in a position that he—like Heidegger—objected to. As regards this thorny question, Jünger comes very close to Heidegger. Indeed, if there is no historical or objective *description* of totalitarianism in either Jünger or Heidegger, it is precisely because a normative viewpoint is constantly deployed. However, it must be noted that each had his own unique normative vision. Metaphysics articulates the law of that which is but never enters into any detail—of course, this itself is nothing but a detail.[5] Quite simply, metaphysics is incapable of describing "details" or particularities because it immediately assumes a position of totality. It formulates its principle in a totalizing fashion, or rather, in a "totalitarian" fashion—and this in much the same sense that we speak of a "totalitarian regime"—though this latter, for the global viewpoint of the former, is also only a detail. Hence the hesitation and malaise we feel when reading *The Worker* and, certainly, when reading certain pages from Heidegger, a malaise that emerges precisely from the "particularities." For example, did Jünger describe State-sponsered communism? Was he a "National-Bolschevic" as was his friend Ernst Niekisch? Or, on the contrary, did he foresee the rise to power of the National Socialist State? And why did Heidegger amalgamate, seemingly without concern, Americanism and Communism? To us, today, this seems rather outrageous. For, in reducing everything to such sameness—"as regards essence"—we thumb our noses at that which is essential: at the differences and immeasurable singularities—at everything that describes History *not* as a teleological process whose goal is assured, but as the coming of unforseeable *events*—most of which are aber-rational. Though I should say, these events are no less aber-rational than life itself which, according to Science, had but a small chance to happen here on earth.

Totalitarianism is, in essence, metaphysical; and this, in turn, implies that every absolute metaphysical position is totalitarian. Yet, is this not so only because every absolute position posits "being in totality" within a representation or "image of the world"? Consequently, Being is posited as a simple position, which was precisely Kant's position. And for this reason (in view of the rise to power of the totalitarian principle that is unshakable insofar as it is founded upon itself), there is only one tenable "position," which, as it were, may very well be untenable as a position. Here I speak of the *Deposition*. From the very beginning it contends with the totalitarian principle that has been inscribed—from the very beginning—as the *arche* or principle of architecture. We might characterize it as an-archical in the same radical and paradoxical sense that Reiner Schürmann ascribed to it in his book *From Principles to Anarchy*: anarchy and anarchitecture. Yet, might this not be just one more structure composed of "principles," whereby we fall once again into metaphysics—though this time, de-totalizing?

To return to Jünger's book, it would be very interesting to show in detail just how much it inspired Heidegger's formulation of "The Question Concerning Technology." We know that Heidegger had studied the text during a "private" class in 1939 and that Heidegger's own fundamental text appeared some 15 years later. For both thinkers, technology was in no way a neutral instrument used for either noble or ignoble ends; rather, technology was considered to be a—or perhaps even THE—power that governs the totality of that which is. Even more than Hitler, it was "the present and future of (German) reality and its law."[6] The power of reasoning and installing had expanded its hold on the totality of the real and had subsequently transformed it into simple material. The material war, in the first World War, which profoundly influenced Jünger and signified for him the collapse of a bourgeois world, served as a sort of prototype or projection of what would be in the future, a "total-all-out-war" for the Domination of the planet. But more, this war would in itself establish the Reign of Domination-for-Domination's-sake.

From this point of view, it is clear (at least from Heidegger's perspective) that total war was not brought to an end with the surrendering of the *Reich*. Rather, it was carried on by other means. Here we might reverse Clausewitz's famous formula: is not the world economy (inasmuch as it is the pursuit of total war by other means) our only "political" space? As for such structures as the bunkers and camps, they have been abandoned—the Movement has left them behind—and total mobilization, which never ceases to change its appearance, continues to spread out and hold the four corners of "reality."

Whenever the question of art and its *place* in total space emerges in *The Worker*, there reappears a preoccupation with architectural order; such that architecture rediscovers the statute that has been inscribed in its very name—one that we might describe as archaic and hegemonic. According to Jünger, during the nineteenth century, literature was supreme and architecture was hardly even considered to be an artistic genre. Notwithstanding, "in certain epochs, such as when the great cathedrals were constructed, architecture emerged as the queen and mother of every other art form and even established their rank."[7] Conforming to the double meaning of *arche*—of beginning and rule—architecture is that art which is nearest to the Origin and which, accordingly, dominates all other arts. And once again, Jünger's discourse seems to overlap Heidegger's: first, he rejects bourgeois aesthetics inasmuch as it is founded upon the exaltation of the individual genius (which represents the beginning of the "decline" of art). Art is no longer a historial power able to put truth into play or impose it upon an entire people. Art no longer belongs to an epoch dedicated to the mobilization of the masses and to the movement of energies; it no longer lies upon a *massive* foundation as did the temple of Zeus (which Heidegger duly notes in "The Origin of the Work of Art"—a text contemporaneous with *The Worker*), but is diluted by the "lived experiences" of the aesthete and individual genius. If, on the contrary, nineteenth century architecture was truly despicable, it was because bourgeois architecture simply could not be. For architecture derives from a *will* to put one's mark upon the most refractory, terrestrial, and "obtuse" materials to the spirit. The elemental is the place of *departure* for all architecture, just as for Nietzsche chaos precedes the Will to power and the will to create a world.

Jünger regards architecture as that which institutes the most intense and strict relationship with the State—that is, with the organic totality of Being. The State is an "organic structure," of which architecture (inasmuch as it totally organizes space according to the technical means that have been appropriated) is the "figure" or the most tangible and *present* form. Inversely, according to the antiquated analogy of philosophy-architecture, architectural construction is the reflection of this total State insofar as it requires the coming together of every Worker—from the economic advisor to the most specialized laborer. This, of course, is in accord with the hierarchical and technocratic model that discloses the resanctification of global space.

The total State—of total mobilization—implies, therefore, a total art. "Art must show that life, in all its grandeur, is conceived as a totality. Furthermore, there is nothing that is removed; nothing that possesses validity in itself and by itself. On the contrary, there is no part of life that cannot be considered as the material of art."[8]

According to Jünger, this becomes clear "if only we consider that the greatest task which presents itself to the artistic will consists in shaping the shapes of sites." Obviously, between each of the "great sacred sites" that Jünger cites—from the rocky Tibetan walls to the grand city of the Incas later destroyed by the Europeans, from the bunkers of World War II that vaguely resemble the Great Wall of China to the wall constructed by the Myceneans and even the wall authorized by Hadrian in the north of Scotland—there exists an abyss. There is an abyss not only because the gods which inhabited the bunkers never fled (in fact, they were never able to be present), but also because the means and ends of the Atlantic Wall already excluded, from the outset, such a sanctification of sites.

To be sure, the German bunkers derived from totalitarian space—however, they were in no way the denouement of its perfection. For, as regards the expression *the perfection of technology*, Jünger gave special significance: indeed, it was the conclusion or fulfillment of such perfection in a determined Figure (that of the Worker). The bunkers, while forming an integral part of what he called *the landscape of work-in-progress* (which characterizes the transitory phase before the Completion), merely belonged to a preparatory phase. In the end, this landscape is nothing more than an industrial park—but one that has already become planetary and that "has already uniformily covered the terrestrial globe with its various constructions and structures: with its industrial zones and cities. No region exists that hasn't been enclosed by a network of roads and railroads, cables and radio frequencies and both jet and maritime travel. It is more and more difficult to determine in what country or even, in what part of the world any given photographic image was taken."[9]

This homogenization of space by networks—and the transformation of the earth into more or less equivalent "images"—is a direct result of the modern conception of the world conceived by Galilean physics. Space—or at least that space so theorized by modern mathematics and physics—is itself totalitarian insofar as it admits of only one homogenous and infinite continuum that subsequently, and in a single stroke, destroys any singularity of place or *topos*. Even today we can calculate with an uncanny and "mathematical" precision the trajectory of a meteorite without it seeming to go "against nature," such as the Physics of the Aristotelean place so designated it (even to the point of being ignorant of the word *space*). Certainly, military architecture did not begin with Vauban, but the uniform inclided planes of his fortresses—which prefigure the aerodynamic bulk of the bunker—would not have been thinkable without a mobilization of space: without a rational and calculating conception of "physical" movement in a sense that was absolutely non-Greek.

This space—which is so total and compact and which effaces from the outset every difference between every place (beginning with its separation from the *templum* or sacred place)—is entirely desanctified. Its characteristic of incessant mobilization "resembles the monstrous workshop of a blacksmith" out of which no lasting work—that is, no work confined in its contours—ever emerges. Stability itself is quickly dissolved into its sign of "work-in-progress;" and even the notion of "work"—understood in its Greek sense—loses all authority. This landscape of work ever in progress—however planned it appears to be and however much it responds to imperative needs and commissions and norms of security and of production—remains abandoned. For more than a century, it has surrendered to an octopuslike anarchy and to an image of our cities beyond the city walls: "cities constructed like ant hills, confused and entangled with various architectures and with ever new novelties which confer upon their facades an uplifted look." Under such conditions (that of overorganized improvisations), the question of form or style—whether it be modernist, Baroque, neo-Classical or postmodern—no longer has any importance. For the essential is to have at one's disposal a reserve of stock that is renewable every ten years: it is to have on hand novelties, newness and inventiveness that, within ten years, will be out of fashion but that, in the ten years to come, will become fashionable once again.

It is clear that such a state of things would not settle well with a mind as permeated with metaphysics as was Jünger's. Under the terms of his Nietzschean conception of the world as "an enclosed and perfectly delimited totality," where "no evolution whatsoever could extract from Being (i.e., from the totality of beings) more than there actually is," the technological process must one day come to an end; such that the apparent anarchy of forms merely masks an accelerated standardization of *the* Form.

If this form "so coincides with the trait of our time (of 'work-in-progress') in such a way that today we cannot risk to build anything that might endure 1,000 years," it must be possible to one day—according to the rate of technological standardization—reconstruct "in the monumental style." But this will not happen until the first phase of the mobilization of the world by the Figure of the Worker will have been surpassed. It shall be a destructive phase, but above all, transitory; it shall be distinguished by an inadequacy of technological means that, according to the ends in sight, will be ever more enormous; it shall be marked by a difference between the technological state and the state of the world at hand—the latter of which shall remain caught within such decrepit old structures as Christianity. (As a typical example, Jünger offers the contradiction between the means and ends involved in the "construction of *Sagrada Familia* in Barcelona." According to him, it is a "romantic monster" that is mendacious "even to its last brick," insofar as it attempts to build a *cathedral* with modern technological means—"means which are typically anti-Christian.")

We might ask ourselves, then, *when* will this transitory phase be surpassed? When will we be able to build, once again, in the monumental style and for 1,000 years? More particularly, does the architecture of Albert Speer—which was constructed for an Empire that was supposed to last 1,000 years and which was purposely monumental—correspond to the final phase of the process? Or, on the contrary, was it not somewhat untimely and premature? Did it not overstep the characteristic "work-in-progress" while all the while remaining (and for obvious reasons) in a state of simple and continual progress? Furthermore, was it not quite simply an unrealistic project—especially at a time when a state of total war had barely just begun? Or, rather, did not the National Socialist revolution already constitute the coming to an end of the Movement, at least in the sense of a total mobilization whose ends were to establish a world Empire?

According to *The Worker*, the final phase—understood here as a completion or *telos*, where the Figure happens to stabilize within its contours and limits (and therefore, its place)—constitutes a symbiosis or total correspondence between the state of technology and the state of the world. Consequently, this final phase implies a sort of uniformity on a planetary scale. Yet, this uniformity is not limited to nation-states: total war can only come to an end with the institution of a new world order—one that is imperialistic but that, in no way constitutes a European Reich. Moreover, the very idea of an Empire remaining in a defensive position fortells its inevitable defeat insofar as an offensive move is the only movement that corresponds to the total mobilization by which technology may come to dominate. It is for this reason—in addition to the fact that it belongs to the preparatory phase of "work-in-progress"—that the architecture of the bunker is condemned, in advance, as already having been surpassed. The Atlantic Wall is one of many "structures in ruins" that technological modernity shall not stop producing as long as it refuses to yield to its completed Figure.

In returning to that style of monumental architecture that corresponds to the completion of technology, we could call forth another factor that may have prohibited Speer's project from being its prefiguration. Not only did such architecture encroach upon the end of the process, but it also constituted something that Nietzsche would have called a *grand style regression*. A regression because it would impose an antimodern architectural *type*—that is, an imitative neo-Classical style that in no way corresponded to its instrinsic nature. Without a doubt, German bunkers were more modern than Speer's colonnades. And yet, strangely enough, these bunkers have never been judged "works of art," nor have their fabricators been called "artists." Had Speer's conception of a "*gross* Berlin" succeeded, it would have been nothing more than a monumental caricature of Imperial Rome. The bunkers were that much more *signifying* of an absolute modernity—in motion—precisely because they did not pretend to transmit artistic—that is, romantic—values. Rather, they were marvelously adapted to their purely technological function.

Finally, could we not say that that which was characteristic of the aesthetics of National Socialism was in no way its totalitarianism, in no way its modernism, in no way "the encounter between modern man and technology" (for certainly Americanism would have been better situated to carry out such an encounter); rather, was it not its "aestheticism" and "retrograde culturalism" both of which pushed National Socialism to prefer the effect to efficaciousness, representation and expression to an effective presence, and finally, the myth to "work-in-progress"?

According to Jünger, the "work-in-progress" nature of our world—which is the sign of our time—demands that we renounce the "presumptuous language of progress" as well as "the fallacious illusion of being in possession of unattackable values."[10] These values, whether they be those of the cult of the Chief or the belief in the privilege of blood and birth or whether they be those values that pursue social awareness and cohesion and beneficence in the marketplace, can only disillusion with respect to the state of the world. At the very least, such values can only postpone the catastrophe—and, at the very worst, precipitate it. To be entirely conscious and aware, the modern must know that "the question of value is in no way decisive."[11] Value merely pertains to that romantic attitude which Jünger denounces as "an affair for museums, an occupation for collectors, romantics and revellers in the grand style."

❁ ❁ ❁

It now remains for me to situate the Bunker within totalitarian space. Yet, such a task has been rendered practically impossible insofar as the Bunker has already been withdrawn from this space—protected from its domination—and thus, destroyed—even though it remains relatively intact on account of its monolithic bulk.

The principle of *armament*, which belongs essentially to totalitarian space (Jünger uses the German term *Rüstung*), does not carry primarily a military significance. Rather, according to Jünger, arms in themselves are nothing.[12] In fact, we speak of "arming" a ship—signifying that it has been provided for, supplied, and equipped and thus ready to be sent upon the sea. In this way, armament constitutes an important component of the movement of total Mobilization—and total Mobilization an important component of the technological Apparatus. Surely, this armament cannot be reduced to the simple rearmament characteristic to the lull between two wars. On the contrary, it deeply determines the "landscape of work-in-progress" inasmuch as it intensifies the notion of work for work's sake (or will for will's sake). The fact is that the Bunker—at precisely the right moment—was inscribed within that process which covered the totality of space with a sort of "scaffolding" (primary meaning of the word *Gestell*)—scaffolding that was later supposed to be removed as soon as the front line itself had been moved. Yet the Bunker—on account of its purely performative function—was surpassed by a "wave" that was much more performative in technological terms. Here I refer to the landing of the Allies in 1944. Yet—even here—we might say that that which overcame the Reich was its deeply entrenched archaism, symbolized by ill-adapted technological means and antimodern ends. The Bunker *remains* hard upon the earth and ground; and there it pretends to *stop* movement and impose an insurmountable limit upon a wide expanse that is nothing but movement and chaos—that is, the Sea. As Nietzsche wrote concerning the Will to Power, it dwells fast instead of "becoming" the Sea itself.

Today, the bunker remains—but it has been deposed. It has been mutilated inasmuch as it has been disabled—in a way, put out of order—and unmoored from its Dwelling Place: subsequently, it slides slowly toward the spacious Sea—space that it was supposedly supposed to stop and restrain. Today, we must enter upon a path of disarmament—but not that hypocritical path which the Super Powers have followed. Though perhaps as of late, they have come to realize that which Jünger wrote some fifty years ago: "An excessive arsenal of destruction in no way ensures security." Such an arsenal is simply a ruinous and useless colossus. Nevertheless, it is maintained and even enlarged with other arms and with other destructive apparati.

Therefore I say again, "disarmament"—but in what sense? The bunkers have already been disarmed (both in the material and literal senses) insofar as they no longer *serve* their intended purpose; they have been dispossessed—not only of their machine guns, but also of their gunners. At the very most, we can only vaguely see the machine gun sites, the placements for antiaircraft artillery and the turrents used for other arms. We should remember that tools which are obsolescent—and out of use—often times reveal themselves better than when they were actually in use. They disclose the "nature" of the world in which they were integrated—forming an almost organic "totality" of essence. We might say that the Bunker formed one body with its "gunner," molding him, shaping him—offering him the ideal carapace and proffering him the ideal clothing and "habits" (in the original sense of *habitation*). Let us think of Hölderlin's famous fragment that begins: "But man inhabits a hut and he enwraps himself with the cloth [habit] of his shame; for his Being is more intimate and heedful."[13]

Let us also keep in mind Hans Bellmer's portrait of Max Ernst. The face has been constructed out of carefully assembled bricks—such that we are reminded that Bellmer was imprisoned (along with Max Ernst and other Germans) in a French concentration camp situated near the city of Aix. Indeed, he was enclosed within a building that was itself an old brick factory . . .

Do not the Bunkers already constitute the "organic constructions" of which Junger spoke? For Bunkers—insofar as the body is reduced, within that which can appear as only a mausoleum, to its final cadaverous state on account of its imprisonment and its total separation from the open world outside—can only, at bottom, reappropriate, at millenary intervals, the immemorial tradition of the tumulus and dolmen from which they differ only in terms of raw material. That they, at present, are empty and therefore devoid of any threat brings them only that much closer to most megalithic constructions. But Bunkers do not only bury—they themselves are buried. Of course, there are exceptions: every now and then we come across concrete, crooked, and displaced lookouts, the majority of which blend in splendidly with the natural landscape. But here, too, bunkers no longer belong to the space of total mobilization. For, for total mobilization, the proper site or place proper, is nothing—nothing more than one of the many factors taken into account in the total organization of means and ends.

Thus we find bunkers strewn upon the ocean shores and shrouded upon a hillside: from the Atlantic to the foot of Mount Olympus and the flown gods, they are everywhere in Europe—they are the prefigurations of the earth's total encrustration in concrete. Stranded, or rather contemporarily transformed by History's considerable and caustic irony into incinerators, these bunkers are used "pacifically" to burn domestic garbage and the refuse by which our world is suffocated. Stranded, or rather given over to the ground, to the earth—to the original chaos from which art finds its source, these bunkers have become signs without any signification; or more precisely, they are signs that signify nothing more than the failure of that imperial and imperious will to give form and meaning to space, a content to emptiness.

Furthermore, we must not be led to believe that, with the demise of all the old bunkers, we shall be forever freed from totalitarian space. At every moment throughout the world new bunkers arise, all of which are as uninhabitable as those of the Atlantic Wall. Yet, these "new" bunkers are everywhere disguised to satisfy the needs of "rational" urban planning: they constitute the new "democratic" cities that demand the deportation of entire populations—so that such populations may be regrouped into the "socialist" variations of our sinister camps. And all of this seems to signify one thing and to obey one principle: that of the bunkerization of the planet. This is why we urgently need to depose every bunker. Indeed, the need is even greater when we realize the number of new structures constructed everyday. And while these structures never admit of being as organic as the bunkers, they nevertheless prohibit any access to the sea; they still enclose, enwall, and bury the bodies of their inhabitants—or servers.

Perhaps the Figure of the Worker has come to an end. For the executor of the blueprint—the very one who imposes it upon the totality of all that is—has reduced this Figure to a simple state of given fact and materiality. This Figure—which, like a universal mold, has projected the world into thin air and which has disintegrated it better than the atomic bomb—may have come to an end. And yet modernity has in no way come to an end: like the bunker, it lies dilapidated, derelict, and deserted by its own gods. For the gods fled the very day they discovered their own true face and countenance: chaotic, shapeless and sanguine. What, then, remains?

What can we do? Is there nothing to do? Or rather, must we not rid ourselves of this will to do? Of this will to produce meaning? Of this will to signify and to command? Must we not abandon this principal principle of architecture and philosophy? And thereby accept—once and for all—to be *unarmed* and, therefore, soldiers of nothing? Soldiers who have no arms with which to hold nothingness and who might only behold the emptiness as that which renders us free? Between the fissures and cracks of the (un)armed concrete, the Sea spreads out beyond our sight.

Notes

1. Martin Heidegger, *Gesamtausgabe 53, Hölderlins Hymne "Der Ister,"* pp. 117–118.

2. *Gesamtausgabe 53, Hölderlins Hymne "Der Ister,"* p. 106. "*Science*," which Heidegger himself encloses within quotation marks, designates "political science" in the National Socialist vocabulary. That is, it was no more "scientific" than was the vulgar Marxism at the time.

3. "This world: a monster of energy, without beginning, without end; a firm, iron magnitude of force that does not grow bigger or smaller, that does not expend itself but only transforms itself; as a whole, of unalterable size, a household without expenses or losses, but likewise without increase or income; enclosed by 'nothingness' as by a boundary; not something blurry or wasted, not something endlessly extended, but set in a definite space as a definite force, and not a space that might be 'empty' . . . this, my *Dionysian* world . . ." Quoted from Nietzsche's *The Will to Power*, trans. by Walter Kaufmann, p. 550.

4. It is for this reason that the concentration camps—necessarily hidden from onlookers and destined to disappear entirely after their use—demonstrated a technical efficiency far exceeding any propaganda or any ordinary production or staging.

5. This passage—as well as every other that concerns itself with "detail"—seems to be a tacit rebuttal of Jean-Marie Le Pen's assertion that the Nazi death camps were nothing but a "small detail"—Trans.

6. This is a much cited sentence from one of Heidegger's political "calls" of 1933.

7. Jünger, *Le Travailleur*, trans. J. Hervier (Paris: Christian Bourgois, 1989) p. 263.

8. Jünger, *Le Travailleur*, p. 268.

9. Jünger, *Le Travailleur*, p. 270.

10. Jünger, *Le Travailleur*, p. 236.

11. Jünger, *Le Travailleur*, p. 118.

12. Jünger, *Le Travailleur*, p. 243.

13. Hölderlin, "In the Forest," fragment 37 in *Oeuvres*, p. 927.

9

A Past That Will Not Pass Away

A German historian once described Auschwitz as "a past that will not pass away" and deemed it less original "than the archipelago of the Gulag."[1] In fact, the entire history of Nazism could be rewritten according to this perspective: "the so-called [*sic*] extermination of the Jews under the reign of the Third Reich was a reaction; or rather, a deformed reproduction and not a first action or original act."[2] Undeniably, this argument made quite a sensation and immediately caused a public outcry—even eliciting a response from the German philosopher Habermas who spoke of "apologetic tendencies" and "revisionism."

Nevertheless, this *past that will not pass away*—in addition to characterizing the German past in general—could very well characterize Heidegger's own personal history. The quarrel among the German historians remained unknown to the French public until the "scandal"—*Heidegger and Nazism*—exploded onto the intellectual scene. At present, seven years after Victor Farias's boisterous publication of that book, the scandal seems to have withdrawn into itself: perhaps from lassitude, but also because "current affairs" must continually seek new scandals. Yet there can be no novelty or newness in this "past that will not pass away" precisely because it bears witness to what Hölderlin called a *caesura*. Within the caesura, one's relationship to time and to one's "passing" is radically severed; even in such a way that both "before and after no longer allow themselves to be reconciled like rhymes."[3] We can no longer be the same "after" Auschwitz, as we were "before" it; nor can we be the same "after" Heidegger. Neither Auschwitz nor Heidegger allows itself to be presented and, therefore, neither can be represented. Subsequently, we can no longer think as we thought before; and even, in a way, we can no longer think—at all. At the very least, we are in need of "changing" our way of thinking, although this change is itself unthinkable; or rather, it is unthinkable as a simple change, such as a change of opinion or article of clothing. Just as we cannot rid ourselves of metaphysics as we might a pair of old socks, we cannot rid ourselves of Heidegger by simply invoking "Nazism" or "Auschwitz."

Yet, why does this "subject" always seem to return? What good does it do to dwell upon "Auschwitz" and Heidegger's "error"? Can we not forget—having now erected monuments to the ill-fated and having now raised an accusatory finger at Heidegger—and go on, without more ado, to something else? But it is precisely in this way that an impotent understanding reasons; that is, as said Hegel, one incapable of looking directly upon death. And, in fact, we wonder whether death is capable of being looked upon—calmly?

No, this past that will not pass away is not merely the obsession of those who are maniacs of memory and resentment. Something resists not only this will to forgetfulness and for-giveness, but also the will to memory and remorse. It is not an obsession; for there is nothing by which we are obsessed—and nothing that appears before us to be absolved of its right of way. In the same way, no return whatsoever is possible; for to what could we return? And how could we return to that place which is swallowed up even by itself? It is a place where no one, at present, is able to go; and yet, where millions of human beings have gone never to return? There is a point of no-return—a caesura—that forbids us even of speaking of a return: of a return to places and to a before that has somehow evaporated. At the same time, this point—which is infinite, unthinkable, and unable to be placed—orders everything. It is a point that points out that we do not think *yet* and that points out not so much another History (other than that of Being), but a beginning other than the Inception itself, that is the Inception of the End, of History. Rather this point is another beginning that re-quests a dispossession or deposition of that first possession constituted by the Greek (or German) *Anfang* (Inception).

Today, that which can be said of the caesura, of Auschwitz, and of Heidegger seems obscure; for, insofar as such relationship cannot be articulated in terms of causality or analogy, it has become quite invisible. Indeed, all this is immeasurable because the shadow of the incalculable—of Auschwitz as it was—is spread thoughout and over our present and not *only* over Heidegger's thought. Anyone who pretends to escape such shadow and to radiate apart from the caesura, without taking any part therein and thereby remaining intact, has either bid farewell to History or is playing the part of a forger.

The "scandal" has passed away, but not this past that never was a past—the reason for which it will not pass away. For such a past to pass away, it would need a passageway. Yet, every passageway has given way: something has come to pass, but this coming-to-pass has surely not been the passing away of History; for not only would this be too phenomenal, but finally, we could forget and pass on to "something else." Thus, what has come to pass is not the end of History, but its becoming-a-deadend or aporia and, in this same movement, its becoming *apolitical* (*aporos/apolis*). The *polis* that Heidegger called the *site*—the There of Being—has been swallowed whole; and, as it were, all hands have been lost—both in spirit and in body. Only indifference remains: only the devastation that has been rendered so vast that none can walk within or experience it; such that, in truth, we are become with-out pain. We have lost language not so much in a foreign land, but in a place, or rather in a nonplace (utopia) that has dissolved all strangeness and all propriety. It is a place whose silence suffocates—suffocating even to the silence of the word.

Perhaps these words are too intense. Nevertheless, they are the only words I can speak when faced with such ruin—a ruin that is still in keeping with the beginning: with that moment of solemn and shocking shock from which a thought rises like a star rising in the night sky. Yet we know no more about stars than do the *stars* themselves. Heidegger became a *star* at the very moment he passed away and so became removed from a philosophical vault that was already in disrepair.

It would seem the page has been turned. And it was turned all the more quickly because it has not been read—at least not properly read. During the "scandal" many had their hands full: while some tried to re-collect the refuse, others tried to terminate the entire affair. And what an outrageous spectacle! No sooner was the curtain drawn than the scene turned to more pressing affairs! Nevertheless, it shall be observed that intellectual polemics cause fewer deaths than "real" wars, and moreover—on the whole—most were able to satisfy their various grievances; that is, while some were able to settle their accounts, others were able to turn the circumstances to account. However, all in all, the risk was next to nothing; for the interested party—"him"—he had disappeared. Heidegger could be condemned only in absentia or acquitted for want of any present. We could dissect his cadaver (his books) just as we might anatomize the scandal, yet neither would be of any importance.[4]

Have I yielded, then, to an offensive instinct? Have I howled with the rest of the wolves? Or brayed with the rest of the asses? Have I failed to keep the law of silence by writing—*et tu quoque*—what I think regarding the whole Scandal?—especially because no one solicited my opinion? But then, my voice had no chance whatsoever to overcome such uproarious noise. And finally, who am I to judge Heidegger, Nazism and the rest of the whole horrid affair? Nothing. Yet no one is so "well placed" that one might speak: for here, there is no "good" place nor any indisputable site or point of view. Notwithstanding, there is a word—from Rimbaud—that I believe speaks the truth. Yes, the *truth* about what took place: "Any vision of justice belongs to the pleasure of God alone." Have we then become God's equal, that we too might appropriate this pleasure?

Surely, what is desirable is to do justice to History. Yet, at the same time, this task is both arrogant and impossible insofar as it is a question of this "past that will not pass away" or of the History that we have authorized and written. For, indeed, we are the delirious authors—in a sense out of our senses—who have written the death of God. "Lightening and thunder require time; the light of the stars requires time; deeds, though done, still require time to be seen and heard. This deed is still more distant from them than the most distant stars—*and yet they have done it themselves*." Thus spoke the madman in Nietzsche's *Gay Science*. Today, he still speaks to us and to our "present." And yet, perhaps we shall need more time to have "understood" Heidegger and to have "seen" Auschwitz.

Thus I have spoken—in my name; yes, *me* in spite of the philosophical interdiction that demands impersonality and that insists on a "we" without face. I have spoken because there has been no other way; because a "we," a community, perished within the walls of Auschwitz—perished from the final solution. I speak though I myself am not Jewish: I speak in my name, or rather for want of any name and for want of being able to speak in the name of whatever "Heidegger," "thought," or "man" may have been. I have spoken in the name of everything that has withdrawn its visage; yes, I have spoken and written about that which, at bottom, must remain beyond the word, for want of any appropriate name or present.

To begin with, I have spoken of the beginning, of the shock (*Stoss*, another Heideggerian word; in fact, they all belong to Heidegger—he took them all, stole every word from us). I have spoken, therefore, of the shock that constituted the encounter with this "calm chunk of earth, fallen from an obscure disaster"—Heidegger once again rummaging through Mallarmé's tomb! I have spoken of the reading—if, in fact, it is one; if, in fact, it can be read—that has made unremovable marks and indelible stigmas.[5] I have spoken—no doubt while thinking of the infernal machine of the *Penitentiary Colony*, but also of Nietzsche, who wrote: "Of all that is written I love only what a man has written with his blood. Write with blood, and you will experience that blood is spirit."[6] But even more, I was thinking of some Other Thing—of History or Auschwitz (for want of any name)—written in blood instead of the Spirit that supposedly should have guided it. No, blood is not always spirit; but when it becomes spirit, it is better to be bloodless in advance. Lautréamont once wrote that a spot of "spiritual" blood could stain an entire ocean.

Thus I speak of stigmas—yet stigmas of what? Marks of infamy? Or perhaps of preference? Some saints were marked with stigmas that designated those places on the body where Christ had been wounded; in other words, the five wounds of Our Father. The stigmas designated the wounds precisely by re-marking them. Yet, Christ's wounds were themselves already written—that is, already heralded by the Bible to be Christ himself. Therefore, such stigmas or written traces re-mark the Mark; as if writing (the marking out of the Mark, the original wound, and the very point of *now*: *stigmè)* were the origin. Yet it is an origin that always already came to pass, that has already been written and marked-out and become, in this way—and only this way—historical. Yes, History itself is nothing more than this re-mark, this re-writing of a mark that has already been written—but that must always be re-inscribed, recharged, and overcharged—upon the eternally innocent and punishable body of the illiterate who has nothing but his living flesh to offer as a text. Now, the stigmas I refer to were those that marked the people of the Scripture.

Let us replace this word *stigma* with the word *imprint* and suddenly an image of virgin wax—upon which a seal or *typos* is stamped—would impose itself. Yet this imprint not only has the same stigma of anteriority that characterizes the Mark upon virgin "matter" but also an anteriority that is that of a past that will not pass away, of an essence having-been (*Wesen-Gewesen*) and of an Origin that has always already come to pass and that, for that very reason, has always yet to come. The Letter is Spirit or Being—but, like Being, it has always already been stamped with a seal. Both have been thus sealed from the very moment of their first fore-wording, *ousia*, and presence; and neither have any addressee other than its Self, and so must remain forever unreadable. It is a Letter that, according to Mallarmé, "does not request the quest of a reader." No one—nobody—could be such an addressee; for to be so, one would have to be *other than* Being—and therefore, nothingness. Yet *Dasein* has to be no-thing: the very place open to Nothing and so the "*lieu*-tenant of Being," that is, literally, the one who takes place in place of Being.

Heidegger's reading goes to such extremes that today it has been stigmatized as a mark—of infamy. Though "before such aggression I would merely respond that my contemporaries do not know how to read; or rather, they only know how to read newspapers."[7] However, whatever the power of the Mark or Letter, it is impossible to reduce, to nothing, nothingness, and that blankness, always haunting the text, will always return "in order to say, in the end, that [there 'is'] nothing beyond and so, to authenticate silence."

Is this simply the "jargon of authenticity"?, as stigmatized by Habermas or is this the undecipherable scrawl scribbled in a definitely foreign language—even though this language happens to be our "maternal"? Was this not an insane undertaking, an aberration of youth, to keep reading, abandoned by everything, even by language, pages and pages filled with words that were solemn, formal, and sometimes repetitive, sometimes academic and sometimes obsolete? Yet these pages were always breathless—written—explosive, brilliant: here I speak of *Sein und Zeit*. Question of jargon? Yes. Question of authenticity? Yes. Yet it is of a kind that, with each page, a hole of sorts is dug between the two—a hole that opens up into an abyss. Jargon, we read it from morning 'til evening, even through the late hours of night; and in the darkness we ruined our eyes—reading by lamplight—reading a text that was impossible to read. Surely, the text was all the more unreadable inasmuch as we carried no key to unlock its treasures; there was no key with which to open it—in fact, we were disposed, only, of a somewhat unfaithful English translation and an incomplete German dictionary. However, the latter was of no great use because in those cases where the fundamental terms were not neologisms, they underwent such a transformation that they were no longer recognizable. But nonetheless, the Book emerged, *a total inflation of the letter*: a resistant, indivisible, and literally impenetrable whole.[8] It was a whole whose hardness only helped to exacerbate our desire: we had to enter or forever desist not only from reading, but from being; in other words, from Being and, quite simply—as we say in jargon—from any authenticity.

It is impossible to separate the reading of this "treatise" from the place in which it was treated—or rather, from the place into which it retreated. It was a place apart and in retreat from the world. It was a place that had been accepted as a "spiritual" retreat; a place of meditation that was not only apart from but also the very place of the a-part: the a-part of the word and of silence. This place was a Dwelling Place that dwelled more within us than we within it. The house hardly had liveable living quarters; yet we worked on the ground level—within a single and obscure room that was open to every wind: open, yet, without windows. "It is he that opened the house."[9] He, the Genius of the place. It was a communal house: an old elementary school that the community had rented to us at a modest price on account of the want of children to whom they could teach reading. Or rather, they had only us—we foreigners, vowed to a foreign language; we were withdrawn inside, far from any civilization, without any contact with the "rest" of the world. We had no telephone, no electricity—not even a road, only a slender path worn into the hillside, surrounded by the oaks and the black desolate sheaths of shale. Is this dereliction without a name? Or is it a gift given by the only present that is still inhabitable: the deserted deserts of solitary and communal thought?

In short, the dreamed place is dreamed that we might read from its obscure retreat *the* Treatise and that we might conclude with it the sealed pact of both Being and the Letter [*de la Lettre, de l'Etre*]. Such a relationship—or union—would, without difficulty, interact with the "situation" of the thinker; for the latter was withdrawn within his *Hütte* wherein he wrote the treatise of an existence that has also been abandoned, that has been handed over to a nullity without bottom, but that is still capable of having an impact even on the anxiety of nothingness, even on the poverty of silence without name: an impact with an unheard-of splendor. I might add that even the altitude of these places—namely, Todtnauberg and Marie-Haut—was in agreement: some 3,000 feet above sea level.

Need I point out that we hardly ventured to these high places to bathe in rejuvenating sources and springs? Nevertheless, there were two such sources: one (which was behind the mountain) we canalized in order to form a sort of basin in which we washed ourselves each morning. The other, which was undrinkable—and which could hardly satisfy our parched throats—kept us at a distance; indeed, it seemed to keep us apart from all such association—whether good or bad. Yes, the Book (*Being and Time*) was as unfit to associate with as the place.

The idea (or ideology) of a return to nature or to mother-earth in no way crossed our minds. To what could we have returned? For that arid earth was able to give way to only an "inept, obstinate and mysterious" work (Rimbaud): to a clearing rather than a deciphering of a treatise that was just as mysterious. It was only to that end that we had come—to *entomb* ourselves within the tomb of nothingness or Being-there. And, as for the landscape, we left it to those few wanderers who may have wandered within its embrace. According to Heidegger, he himself never observed the landscape: he was a sort of countryman, a peasant of a land that had become invisible—that had entered into *us*. He was a "monster of innocince," as Rimbaud would have said.[10] "What shitiness! What monsters of innocince these peasants are! In the evening, one must travel six miles just to get a drink. Here, *Mother* has placed me in a sad hole." Yet, the sad hole of Marie-Haut was worth as much or more than the hamlet of Roche, "Laïtou, my village," even though it lacked the resource of a restaurant some six miles away.[11] To drink, we had to satisfy ourselves with the source—or with the original. (Here I mean to say the original text.)

Peasant . . . , and the rough reality to be embraced—even Rimbaud was so impelled. Of course, this was also his loss; that is, his quest for gold. Yet, what was this salt of the earth that we were so persistent in seeking in a book as hard as *rock*? And precisely what *mother* threw us into such a hole? What necessity necessitated the retreat of every everything? "When deep in a winter's night—when a snow storm rages round one's cabin, lashing out and re-covering and dissimulating everything—such is the time for philosophy. It is precisely then that its questioning must become simple and essential. And the elaboration of each thought can only be but difficult and essential. Indeed, language's difficulty in articulating itself is similar to the withstanding of the pine tree during such upheaval."[12] It is thus that I have always envisioned philosophy; and it is thus that I have confronted the language of Heidegger's thought: as a hard and rough rock resistant to erosion and the elements—because it itself is sprung from the elements. It is elementary in every sense of the word, including that of a disconcerting and volcanic simplicity. The first philosopher, Plato, once remarked that "All greatness resides in the storm." And Heidegger, the last philosopher, repeated it at the end of his "Rectorate Discourse."[13] To be sure, it was at the very center of such a storm that Heidegger's thought took shape—thought that, like every philosophy, was unique to its time. Having said this, I shall not overlook the fact that the text just cited regarding the "snow storm" and the need and urgency of philosophy, was first printed in a newspaper (*Der Alemanne*) on March 7, 1934. Such a "deep winter's night" and such a "raging snow storm" speak not merely of the inclement weather that a wanderer in the mountains might have to confront; for they also speak (without speaking) of the inclemencies of the present and of the seasonable—if not indispensable—winter's night: *the epoch*.

Accordingly, is it time to philosophize when the storm rages? Should we philosophize even when the storm storms with winds of madness—indeed, of Nazism? Yes, and especially at such a moment. Perhaps even Heidegger never thought enough. Perhaps his fault was to have had a period of time (it hardly matters how much time: ten months or ten years), in which he "acted too much and thought too little."[14] In fact, he wrote the preceding statement some time later, in a courtyard, where he asked: What is it that gives us to think? To which he responded: *Most thought-provoking is that we are still not thinking*. And when Heidegger wrote *we*—"we still do not think"—this was not his usual figure of speech. For he includes himself within this *we* and within this want. This want itself is, in a sense, an *entreaty* of thought.

We must remember that to read Heidegger is, primarily, to learn how to think and to learn how to read other thinkers. Almost all of Heidegger's written works are readings, sometimes of a single sentence such as Nietzsche's "The desert grows!" And sometimes they are of a single Word. Without these readings on "traditional" texts, thinking would simply fall, once again, into oblivion—or what is worse, into academic routine. And those who would dwell upon Heidegger's "want" must also recognize the enormous debt that all thinking to come shall bear as regards the Heideggerian "lesson." Here I understand *lesson* in the philological sense of "reading" (of a corrupted text, for example).

❁ ❁ ❁

It is a simple setting—a group photograph of rather poor quality—presenting a table around which various bureaucrats are assembled. With his head thrown slightly backward, his appearance is one of constipation, of crispation. But here he is: Heidegger. And on his chest we see the infamous insignia: "In his capacity of *Führer* (rectorate) of the University of Freiburg, he bears upon his chest the swastika, emblem of sovereignty of the Nazi party." Such was the manner in which the newspaper *Libération* exhibited or exploited the actual picture. Certainly, it was a photograph that had been known for quite some time; yet, here, one read the following caption: "Heil Heidegger!" What a wonderful greeting. Notwithstanding, if we look closely at the picture, we can hardly distinguish the so-called emblem—hardly, but also the shock is hard when we finally have to admit the fact.

However, whatever role "malevolence" may have played in the launching of the scandal, it is undeniable that the picture does *exist*, such that, not only was it not tampered with, but there are others that reveal the same insignia. Furthermore—and contrary to what he has asserted—Heidegger ended his classes with the Hitlerian greeting: *Heil!* A sacred name insofar as it already dwells within the very name that signifies the sacred: *Heilige*. How should we *see* this picture? How can we reconcile it with the inner picture depicted by his *texts*?—or that of a solitary and interior man who meditated apart from organizations, institutions, and bureaucracies and who stated that a man who wears no uniform, *today*, is like a phantom? It would seem that the two images have nothing in common; and that the "inner" picture is the only true one. For only it is in agreement and *accord*—accord, which has always been taken as the very definition of truth; that is, as the adequation between a thing and its mental image. Heidegger as *Nazi* is an unimaginable thing and therefore not true with respect to his *essence*. And those who would assert the opposite are seeming imposters, moved only by their "hate of philosophy" and of truth. To be certain, there lurks, somewhere behind their every recourse to "facts" and documents, a resentment toward authentic thinking. It is a pity that we are not in possession of any "document" dating from Plato's time—one representing him at the tyrant's court in Syracuse—for such representation would have allowed us to avoid 2,000 years of philosophy (if, of course, this be the desired end).

This similarity with Plato's Sicilian adventure is not entirely accidental. Let us remember those unforgettable pages that Hannah Arendt consecrated to Heidegger on his eightieth birthday. If she was able to characterize Heidegger's involvement in 1933 as "ten short months of fever" or as a brief and "youthful indiscretion," then how can we be so unwilling to pardon him? How can we be less forgiving than she who, with an incredible lucidity, denounced the "banality of evil" and the "terrifying phenomenon erupted from the sewer"?

Yet, to pardon someone is to imply that one has prior knowledge of culpability. Furthermore, if Arendt pardonned her former Mentor, it was simply because she judged his error minimal with respect to the essence; which is to say, with his work (thought) that, according to her, did not belong to the common everyday occurences of the time. His error was not so much *this* well-determined participation in Nazism; rather, it was participation as such, contrary to the calling of a thinking that is necessarily withdrawn and *in retreat* from politics. Just as evil evolves from sickness—so Heidegger, after ten months of fever, was able to relinquish his "moral" responsibilities and return to his high—and healthy—spheres, never to descend again. At least, this was the version disseminated by Jean Beaufret and most of us adhered to this dogmatic explanation if only because the contrary seemed impossible, unthinkable: "His [Heidegger's] relationship with Nazism was limited to ten months of administrative cooperation and a publicly proclaimed agreement. Perhaps we might think this to be already too much. Yet, we must not forget that these ten months were followed by twelve years in which his professional teaching and his writer's silence rendered him rather intolerable to the powers in power. Such that, in 1944 he was alienated from the university—an alienation that was continued by the new occupying authorities [i.e., the French]."[15] But here we leap from a simple pardonning to a complete washing of the affair: Beaufret, hardly satisfied with simply minimizing Heidegger's culpability, would nullify it, turning it into a sort of heroism that was misunderstood and unjustly punished. We are to believe that Heidegger would have been "persecuted" by those "powers"—with whom he was forced to associate for ten months—on account of several inoffensive signatures signed to some old academic papers. Power being what it is (or was), Heidegger merely bore the burden of human stupidity. He endured a "conspiracy of mediocrity and men turned sour," such that his "Nazism"—in this hagiographic perspective of "rehabilitation"—emerged only from calumny and insipid propaganda. Thus, the misadventure of 1933 was nothing but an "enormous indiscretion" and act of foolishness.[16] But who, in youth, has not done something foolish? (Perhaps youth is relative, for in 1933, Heidegger was forty-three years old and his major work, *Sein und Zeit*, had already published.) Furthermore, did not Heidegger write. "Whosoever thinks greatly must also go astray greatly?" (The important point being that to every "great" error there corresponds a "great" thought.) However, such an argument leads to a fatal flaw insofar as it implies a relationship of *correspondence* between "error" and "thought"—even at the precise point where we have strived to keep all such error absolutely outside of thought. Moreover, this sentence asserts the necessary character of the thought-error relationship: it is even extracted from *the very experience of thought itself*—which, at bottom, demands that there be no thought without errantry.[17] As was indicated in his conference (contemporary with his "error") entitled *On the Essence of Truth*, it demands that history exist *only* as errantry. Here Heidegger stated that errantry, insofar as it was an "essential component of the opening of Being-there," dominated all of *historial* humanity insofar as it itself was the theater—the place or scene—of history. Errantry was "not a happenstance fault or occurence, but the empire of this history wherein all modalities of errancy confusedly intermingle."

Upon serious examination of this "error" we find that it is not simply *accidental*. Rather, it constitutes the very sign that signals the opening of thought to the wind of history. Subsequently, thought could do nothing but go astray. Arendt might very well believe the opposite: that "the tempest that elevates the thought of Heidegger does not have its origin in this century. It [Heidegger's thought] hails from the immemorial and that which it leaves behind is an accomplishment which, like every accomplishment, returns to the immemorial."[18] This elevated vision (of a *philosophia perennis* beyond all historicity) seems little in conformity with the intrinsic tenor of a thought that—even if it refuses to be current—still considers historicity as an essential constituent of *Dasein* and even of *Being itself.*

Of course, Heidegger would assert that "philosophy is essentially 'untimely' because it is one of those few things that can never find an immediate echo in the present."[19] Yet, *untimely* in no way signifies that which is immemorial or outside of time. According to Heidegger, philosophy—as *un*-untimely as it is—*is,* in this sense, our history. (However, to see it as such, the turning would be necessary; and, in a way, one would have to be situated *outside* of history—or to have declared it ended.)

In any case, it becomes impossible to leave unmentioned—in the Freudian sense of denial—a past that has been reduced to an "enormous indiscretion"—especially when it has been so rationalized simply from a seeming desire to save "Germany." For did not he who sought to save the German university also declare: "We have the new Reich and we have the University. . . . In Germany, a revolution is occuring; yet, we must ask ourselves: has a revolution come to the University as well? No. The fight still consists in preliminary skirmishes . . . "

We could quote from other texts from this period, beginning with Heidegger's "call" to vote "yes" on the plebiscite of November 12, 1933: "Only the Führer himself *is* German reality, both present and future. He is its law."[20]

Certainly, these texts had become well known before the publication of Victor Farias's book; but even then, as Hegel once said, that which is well known often goes unrecognized. In fact, the known remains unknown even when we recognize the blindness *of others*: "In short, according to the logic of the 'kettle,' we were aware of everything and still there was nothing of which to be aware. And thus, without hindrance, we shall continue to manage our inheritance: nothing has come to pass, nothing could have come to pass, and this is why your daughter is deaf."[21]

In effect, nothing came to pass; and yet we continue to manage our "inheritance" without alarm—quite simply, we prefer the inheritance of 1789 to that of Mao's Red Guard handbook. For why did we storm the Bastille if it was not to celebrate its Bicentennial? I hold no grudge against anybody: nonetheless, it is always a bitter experience to realize that one has come too late, that one knows nothing, and that there are no blind, only those who are "non-seeing", as expressed by the new "political correctness", that is, the universal euphemization.

Nothing happened, nothing came to pass—nothing but a scandal. And it hardly went unnoticed. But if nothing happened—that is, anything in any of the camps—it is only because we were too intent on obtaining (or retaining) our "inheritance." We had to inherently pass on a past that would not pass away. Still, all those walking corpses that refused to die were rather encumbering. What should we do with Heidegger? And what shall we do with Auschwitz? Shall we ignore them? Shall we abandon them to silence? No, for this is the best way to keep them coming back—like ghosts from the grave. Surely, ghosts (*revenants*) of this magnitude are not healthy for our modern habitat. So—we are better off speaking about it. Yes, we must speak—about it. That is, we must interrupt these ghosts; though I suppose they are already inter-rupted.

Once and for all, let us leave any so-called inheritance to those "children of current affairs" who harass us. For, in truth, there is no "inheritance"—and above all, no "Heideggerian" inheritance! Sorry! We shall not get our hands on anything! We must be absolutely modern: we must be disinherited. On the other hand, perhaps there is no other inheritance than an in-co herent word and a forbidden thought. Though, in this knowing-how-to-be disinherited, in this disappropriation and deposition, there is a flowing forth and fulguration: a freedom without equal. And yet, it could be that that which we have inherited from Heidegger has been a will to inherit nothing: to deconstruct every inheritance by delivering it over to itself and thus to its own freedom. Such is the "free use of the Proper" that, according to Hölderlin, was so difficult to learn, properly. What is proper to learn, is learning to unlearn, even the Proper. If Heidegger was never able to accomplish this ultimate gesture, he yet bequeathed it to us as "the task of thinking" in the age of the end of metaphysics.

But now, let us return to the "scandal." *We have known about it for a long time*, could it be we have always known . . . ? At least, we have known since the undeterminable "moment" of the caesura—undeterminable because it has determined itself as decisive. Thus from that "moment" on, what good has it been to construct bunkers and dig trenches? What good has it been to fortify a fortress called *Heidegger* (as they once fortified a fortress called *Europe* and as "they" once entrenched themselves along the Atlantic coast), precisely when (or where) the enemy was already inside? Precisely when the walls were already cracked and already wide open and gaping? Precisely when the walls of the edifice—of the house of Being—were already ruptured? To know the abyss, one need only know how to read Heidegger—for he is nothing more than the fore-bidding and bidding abyss.

Only later did Farias come, dressed in his boots, riding his big horse, and brandishing his big lasso. He came to tell us that he told us so: that God (Heidegger) is dead! Incredible news! Mind boggling! Sensational! Never before seen! How could we have passed by without seeing the Letter (Being) stolen? Perhaps, it was precisely because it struck our eyes and blinded us? But then, maybe there are eyes that are able to see such a thing—that are able to discern that which has nothing to do with nothing? Heidegger—*a Nazi*? No! Are you serious? I thought he was a philosopher. Ah! Now I know!—you were speaking of the other one, the *sozi*?[22] Good God! Tell me I am dreaming! Somebody please wake me up!

But Farias—he knows. Of course, he never read Heidegger, but then, he did not need to—to uncover the traitor!

One is well within his or her right to deem this reading (if it is one) as "insufficient or debatable, and even, at times, so offensive that we wonder whether the inquisitor hasn't just begun reading Heidegger an hour ago."[23] In all actuality, there has been a misunderstanding: Farias did not "read" Heidegger to learn how to think. In fact, he did not "read" at all as a philosopher, but as an Inquisitor. He already knew what he was looking for—evidence of blame. He sought an inescapable culpability. That Heidegger happened to be a thinker was of no importance to this Inquisitor inasmuch as he simply sought to label him as a "Nazi," indeed, as a "militant Nazi." Such terroristic tactics can cause quite a scandal, especially when it reduces the horizon to a series of "facts" and when it is accompanied by some serious deformations of perspective (an example would be that of Abraham a Santa Clara or that of Sachsenhausen). However, it is just as childish to reproach an Inquisitor on account of his "will to harm" (Fédier). Yet, what should we expect from such an accusation—Indulgence, or commiseration?

For the most part, most of the facts assembled by Farias are secondhand, but indisputable—unless, of course, one could prove the contrary; which, up to this day, has not been done. What is overwhelming here is not so much the force of Farias's accusation, but the poor arguments used by the defense. And therefore, the principal effect of Farias's book will have been "to consider the scandal 'put aside,' at least for a certain period of time and to form a certain *doxa* about the thing judged. Already we have seen the question arise: 'Can we still read Heidegger?' Such that if such was the intended effect of the book—to dissuade reading and questioning—this would be a catastrophe. However, we should not despair of our ability to read."[24]

If we should not despair of our ability to read, then we must understand why the "non"-reading of Farias forbids us to read the very one who taught us how to read and how to think. (To accuse the "media" of manipulation would be to fall, once again, into the paranoic fear of a plot or of a "conspiracy of mediocrity," as Beaufret wrote. As it were, the media only magnifies the actual trauma.)

Yes why this storm?

Could it be because the accusation touches a sensitive nerve; it puts pressure on a wound that is hidden and therefore invisible to the naked eye, an inside wound that continues to bleed if only because it is an untreatable scission. Somewhere, Nietzsche wrote: "Only lately have we had the courage to face that which we know. Only recently have I dared admit to myself that I have been a complete nihilist." And Heidegger, did he have this courage? Is it not strange that he who spent an essential portion of those somber years of Nazi rule engaged with Nietzsche (to overcome European nihilism, no less), never once spoke a word about the awful event? That is, about Shoah and the Extermination of the Jews?

And upon this silence every defense of Heidegger breaks down. Well, perhaps not every defense, for there is always someone who will find some explanation and some justification: "I think there is an element of dignity in Heidegger's behavior that must not be underestimated. In effect, if he had made (I take the worst possible scenario) a statement consistent with the expectation of public opinion, then the public would have said: it is not with such statements that he is going to be excused for what he did—he shall not get off so easily. Furthermore, we must not forget that, during Nazi rule, Heidegger did not remain silent. Of course, he could have left Germany, but once again, Heidegger was not a hero."[25] There is something laughable about these lines. Yet, as Hannah Arendt once remarked: "The good of laughter has not, as of yet, been visibly revealed to mankind. Perhaps this is so because thus far every thinker has spoken ill of laughter and, in effect, abandoned the very question of laughter . . . "

But let us be serious. And let us begin at the lowest level: Beaufret presented Heidegger as a sort of hero, as one who resisted Nazism with a "silence" that made him "intolerable" to the "authorities." Fédier would then explain to us—in a less unreasonable manner—that "during Nazi rule, Heidegger did not remain silent." Notwithstanding this, not all of Heidegger's remarks concerning Nazism were critical. How can we forget the famous passage from his course given in 1935, when he spoke of the "internal truth and greatness of the [Nazi] Movement"? Also, in this same course, he wrote: "From a metaphysical point of view, Russia and America are the same; the same dreary technological frenzy, the same unrestricted organization of the average man."[26] How can we believe, even for a moment, that Heidegger *was able* to leave Germany? And to what country would he go? How could he leave his people ("the metaphysical people"), especially when it had been so taken by the vice of what he called the *demonic*? How could he leave when he never even wished to leave his province, and this on account of his faithfulness to the "land" of the only *Heimat*?

Shall we say that he actually criticized the "philosophy" or rather, the official ideology of Nazism—indeed, the racist biologism of Rosenberg? Yet, to attack an ideology is not the same thing as to fight a regime. In another interview, "the Master of Heidegger studies in France" (in fact, Fédier was simply the mortician or minister or administrator of "heritage") would cite a passage from Heidegger's course on Hölderlin (1934) in which the philosopher found fault with a Nazi poetaster named Kolbenheyer. Yet, is this proof of Heidegger's resistance? Especially when all of these virtuous defenders take care to not quote from those texts in which Heidegger rails against "Americanism" and "liberal democratic" ideology and from all those texts in which Heidegger celebrates the grandeur of the Germanic sacrifice (most notably, at Stalingrad)? And shall we believe that it was more *honorable* to remain silent that to join the general chorus of voices that arose, after the war, to recall this *Andenken* with which thought (*Denken*) is in intimate relationship? We might say that, in light of the enormity of the disaster, Heidegger had his breath taken away—that, in a sense he had been inter-rupted. But is it possible to have one's breath taken away for thirty years? Even when one continues to speak in public before students? Even when one continues to give ones opinion on "real" everyday matters, such as the atomic bomb, genetic manipulation, and German "prisoners of war"? To be sure, these were serious matters, but hardly as serious as the Genocide of the Jews.

Of course, we never expected a public statement from him, at least not in the form of an autocritique. Indeed, the *Schuldfrage* (the question concerning culpability) did occasion some pitiful discussions: a "clear conscience," according to *Being and Time*, is not a conscience at all. Certainly, no one asked Heidegger to exculpate or justify himself; yet, at the very least, he could have offered a word—nothing more than a word. "The most humble and most difficult thing to articulate . . . that single word which the Whole of the West—in its pathos of redemption—was never able to say: *sorry*."[27] This word for which Paul Celan waited so anxiously but never heard while at Todtnauberg. It is a word that can even be said in silence—in the form of a prayer.

Perhaps every "sacred name" is wanting. Yet this one little word—*sorry*—cannnot be wanting "As long as Kindness, / The Pure still stays."[28]

❁ ❁ ❁

"He who does not speak, gives consent." Doubt is more than uncertainty: it is a slow poison, a venom that slowly paralyzes one's body. Did Heidegger hold anti-Semitic beliefs? No, it is almost impossible to give evidence of anti-Semiticism without saying, at least once, the *word Jew*. Yet, Heidegger spoke neither a word for nor against the "Jews": for him, the word simply did not exist. The "Jewish question" was not in need of a solution, if only because, for him, the question never arose. As if a "thing" could exist without a name: "Where word breaks off no thing may be"—or so reads a line by Stefan George upon which Heidegger commented.[29]

(Let me give an example of such "silence."[30] We often speak of a "Judeo-Christian civilization." Although this expression is somewhat imprecise and confusing, we cannot deny that Judaism has played an important role in the formation of the Christian West. Greece is not the only source of our world, though it has been of our philosophy. However, for Heidegger, History was simply the History of Being. And because *Being* is not a word stemming from Hebrew, the Jew "is" not; or rather, is, in no way, historial. And, insofar as one is deprived of historiality, one "is" the Other: one is deprived from any identity.)

"Where word breaks off": by *word*, we must understand the Word or *das Wort*. *Jew* in no way constitutes a proper noun or even, properly speaking, a simple noun insofar as it does not name a language. (What is Yiddish when compared to the "ontological" and untranslatable profundity of the "native" tongue?—and, as for Hebrew, Heidegger never learned it; instead he preferred the *New Testament in Greek*.) Furthermore, *Jew* does not name a country or a land or a people if only on account of the Diaspora that, in a way, contradicts any rootedness or logocentricism. Perhaps it does name a religion: but then, is not God dead? Even so, where—in God's name—within the Parthenon would we place YHWH (the Unpronouncable)—especially because both the structure and the word are Greek? At the very least, *Jew* is that noun which contradicts all identification. Indeed, it constitutes the pure contradiction to the principle of Identity that has thus far ruled Being. *Jew* is the Difference—one that can not be spoken *as* such, for it passes neither through Being nor nothing . . .

Can we have a word for that which we cannot say? And how can we understand that which is unable to say anything to us? We shall not find escape from this typically hermeneutic circle in the form of "facts"; for these latter can appear only within a clearly defined horizon. Nothing is there where a word is in want: there is no word for Auschwitz, it is that which is without name. Even today, the death camps remain outside of any word: they are unimaginable no matter how many facts we possess, no matter how many accounts we have heard from those who survived. *Nacht und Nebel*, Night and Mist—such is the German translation (which is somewhat faulty), of that thing which "is" in want of a word; of that thing which "is" in the very fault of the word—and of Being.

Thus, we have silence on both sides. Indeed, we have the silence of a thought that has no word for the silence of the final solution, for such a silence that every thought has gone up in smoke or receded into the mist—every thought for Being is the first and last word. Everyone is familiar with the following famous lines by Adorno: "Auschwitz proved, in an irrefutable way, the total failure of culture. . . . All culture consequent to Auschwitz, including the urgent need to criticize such a disaster, is nothing but so much refuse."[31]

These sentences still ring true; yet, the commonplace that they have become is hardly recognized if only because there is no way of *saying it*: in the name of what could anything be said? In the name of the Unnameable? Yet, if all discourse—including all critical discourse—only adds to the disaster, it is precisely because it is of the same order as that culture which has, in a sense, "scuttled the ship"—such that, according to Adorno, "not even silence escapes this circle." It would seem we come against a total impasse; unless, of course, we take as our point of departure this very impasse; unless we begin from the caesura that has interrupted both the word and silence. According to Jean-Luc Nancy, the evil is unjustifiable, untenable, and unpardonable—yet, above all, it is a formidable positivity that can no longer be adorned with the sublimity of the satanic "black sun." "For us, the night can no longer radiate; rather, it sinks into the dissolution of a mist that makes it still darker: *Nacht und Nebel*."[32] Such mist effaces every sign; then comes oblivion that, according to Pindar, removes the ground of every thought. Oblivion: *lethè*. The withdrawal of *alètheia*. The radical fore-wording of Being is such that it itself is obliviated in the totalitarian organization of being. Perhaps what we can think—thanks to Heidegger—is the Extermination as a Term in the History of Being and Western nihilism—even though he himself was utterly silent upon the whole process. Was not the Extermination merely a minute detail in the obfuscation of the planet? Yet, I am not willing to admit that Heidegger even *thought* that; for, to think that is to not think at all: it is to fall into a total absence of thought. No, it is even more than an absence or failure: it is a refusal, a black hole. Not only does the "mist" overspread the essence of modern science, but it has also spread over into the foul air of the charnel houses wherein it seems to forever swallow up any possibility of the Western "Spirit."

In an interview with *Der Spiegel* (dated 1966, but published only after his death), Heidegger declared that, "Only a God can save us." What God could this be? The same type of god that tried to "save" the German nation? How could Heidegger believe, even to the end, in this type of Messianic—and historical—salvation? Did he learn nothing from history? More precisely, did he not learn that history is unable to save anybody and that any salvation (by history) is, in itself, the absolute loss of Spirit? It may be that we have misunderstood Heidegger's declaration—that nothing and nobody can save us—and so, accordingly, we must "wander through the unthinkable." Such was the way in which Hölderlin described the modern tragedy of slow death to which Oedipus was condemned: blinded and deprived of any presence and any god. However, if it is possible to tie Auschwitz to Western nihilism (and the Extermination to the Determination of Metaphysics and its "closure"), then can we go so far as to write, as did Philippe Lacoue-Labarthe, that Auschwitz is "the horrible revelation of the essence of the West?"[33] Is there a particular "logic" that has lead directly to Auschwitz? Has there even been a pathway—either direct or indirect—that has linked Western thought to the concentration camp? Did this latter emerge from some sort of "essence" or "historial determination?" Is it not, rather, the abyss that swallows up all "historiality"?—thus precipitating the absolute destruction of all "logic," all "essence" and so on?

"European thought must take into account, absolutely, Auschwitz. And this is a never ending task. However, it would seem that Heidegger's thought is the least qualified for such an undertaking."[34] So be it; but then, what thought is capable of taking into account the Incalculable? And in whose name is it necessary? What categorical imperative could be so imperative as to demand that? Is not our most important duty simply to know how to think—to think a thinking that cannot itself be reduced to a "simple taking into account?" For upon whose account would we draw—especially when every such account has been discounted?

What Auschwitz has "revealed" about thought is its radical inability to think this past that, not only "will" not pass away, but escapes the very laws of historial (and rational) representation. Quite simply, this past is not at all something of the past. Hitler not only destroyed the German reality (with which Heidegger identified for a period of time), but also the Historial itself. He, in one singlehanded stroke, destroyed any faith one might have had in the salvation of human essence. Now, here, we are—without any essence; and perhaps we shall be so "for 1,000 years." (We wonder whether Heidegger thought the reign of Technology in the fashion of a Millenary Reich?) Only the "last man"—that "functionary of Technology" who is committed to a process of pure exploitation and the management of accounts—only he is determined by, and provided with, an essence. The planet has left its axis forever; but more, it has been removed from the Word and handed over to the unfettered machination of Power. And because the human being (the subjugated "subject") is rendered that much more important and unable by this Power, one is subsequently that much more intent upon a total and unconditional control of everything, beginning with the Incalculable. Auschwitz is an exemplary example—just as is the build-up for a nuclear "apocalypse." For this latter, we simply need push a button and . . . And, in the same way—with nothing but an administrative memorandum—6 million Jews were liquidated—but is this still a concern for "European thought," inasmuch as these terms do not hide some horrible void?

Once again, we always seem to return to this hole: how can we learn how to think when thought, thus far, has been unable to find any word for annihilation? The forbiddance of thought, in the name of Auschwitz, would be a (final?) "solution" if only we were in possession of a thought *other* than that which has revealed its horrible void. By this, I in no way intend to exculpate Heidegger or to justify his horrible silence with respect to the Extermination. In fact, such silence should not be taken as insignificant, especially when we remember that only he can be silent who has something to say (*Being and Time*, paragraph 34). Yet I hardly see a "way out" by simply returning to those old European "values" or to a humanistic ethic that—it too—failed to account for Auschwitz.

The work is endless—particularly the work of mourning: for we must overcome, not only the traumatic experience of the Extermination, but also, that of the silence of thought. Even, we must overcome the loss of thought's voice—and, along the way, we must remain vigilant; we must take care to avoid any identification between the two "phenomena." For—between Auschwitz and thought—there can be only an abyss. We cannot say that the concentration camps "arose" from European thought (even if the latter were to be identified with

Metaphysics or Heidegger); nor can we honestly believe that the Gulag "arose" from Marx's thinking. Nevertheless, the abyss calls for thinking the relationship: the abyss itself (or the impossibility of going from one side to the other, the heterogeneity of two dimensions) constitutes a relationship. It is that relationship which must be thought but which always eludes thought.

Identification ends in confinement and sclerosis. Consequently, in my opinion, it constitutes the greatest danger as regards the scandal "Heidegger and Nazism." Even Heidegger himself succumbed to this danger—which may be reason enough to prohibit our following this same maddening process. Yet, such identification took place on both sides; that is, on the side of those who accused and those who defended. As for those guardians of the Temple, they identify Thought in general with Heidegger's thought and subsequently reject, as a necessary and logical consequence, any identification of Heidegger with Nazism. (This latter is held to be a prime example of nonthought.) Moreover, any relationship between Heidegger and Nazism can be only an aberration insofar as that which is pure cannot ally itself with that which is impure. Thus, according to this argumentation, all of the denials would be justified; for example, Heidegger once argued that one had no right to judge National Socialism "while observing 1933 from the perspective of 1937."[35] Yet, we might object that Nazism was already viciously anti-Semitic in 1933, and that one need only read *Mein Kampf* to realize there was no place whatsoever for a Jewish Settlement in the new Germany. Of course, Heidegger would respond that he never read *Mein Kampf* and that it was fundamentally Hitler who deceived him, that it was Hitler who pushed the "Movement" out of its true and original direction, and that, once again, it was Hitler who betrayed the Revolution and who sold out the country to its worst enemies: capitalism and the "madness of Technology."

Perhaps Heidegger would have done well to read *Mein Kampf*. We might even laugh at such a book were it not so atrocious—laugh because oftentimes it is useful to read the most illiterate "literature."

The hiatus remains, if I might say, athwart the gorge. And for us, *Mein Kampf* shall always remain unreadable. Nevertheless, I shall continue to read Heidegger's "Rectoral Discourse," even though it still causes me to tremble from an inflamed rhetoric that eulogizes the duty one owes to the military, science, and work and from its bannishment of "academic liberty" by the university's *mise au pas*. But then, I stay terrified upon reading these so-called *Political Texts* precisely because I almost hear the thundering voice of the Führer. In all these lectures and proclamations, we hear the same words: indeed, Heidegger uses the same "Heideggerian" language in celebrating Aryan law and its inflexible will. Today, such texts cannot be re-called without a shudder. If Heidegger had changed his tone of voice, his vocabulary, or "style" in which he expressed his new found faith, this could be of concern only to the "little man," and we know what little value he accorded to "biography" and to "life" in general. Yet, Heidegger always speaks a Heideggerian language precisely by saying something else—something radically other: a "Heil Hitler!" of sorts that is also an absolute *Unheil* for thought. Yet, by using the same language in a radically different way, did he not subjugate his own thought (and perhaps even all thought) to the "filthy beast"? The only way to escape this black hole will be to play "Heidegger against Heidegger."

It would seem that this is not at all sound, that it is even a diabolical strategy. At least, this is the opinion of Luc Ferry who (in the accusatory camp) admits, rather frankly, that Farias's book is only a "pretext" to destroy every French school of "Heideggerians" and their deconstructive dispositions. In effect, I would hardly dwell upon this sort of argumentation, except that it shares the same insane logic of identification—and therefore of blindness—as that logic which seems to be at work on the side of the defense. Here—or there—it is written, tacitly—silently—that we are forbidden to read a thinker in a way other than he read—and understood—himself. Now, even though Heidegger never ceased, in both his writings and his classroom lectures, to call for a certain vigilance and emphasize the need for thought to think against itself and even though he *actually* "set Heidegger over and against Heidegger" (for example, in the Turning), it would seem that this call has remained nothing but *Greek* to those on both sides of the debate. Moreover, it would seem that, on account of a certain inertia or entropy or even a natural liking for comfort and tranquillity, Heideggerian thought has been set into a rigid and sclerotic body of doctrine, from which there is no salvation. This solidification has served both sides well, for it is always easier to find fault with and dissect a corpse than a living body of thought. Today it seems more necessary than ever to think "Heidegger against Heidegger;" but because the liberty of thinking—even against itself—is very much inherent in the "essence" of thought and its liberating power, we can substitute any proper name we like (for example, "Marx against Marx"). I find nothing shocking in Lacoue-Labarthe's interpretation—on the contrary. Still, it does appear to be more problematic than ever as regards the "logic" that would be deployed in the West's history of nihilism.

The heart of his interpretation resides in his clarification of the process of "identification." This latter term, which he explicitly borrows from Freud, is used "to designate that which is at stake in the mimetic process" and that which revolves around appropriation. Hence, we find that politics "emerges from the *enfictionment* of beings and of communities."[36] For example, the very question concerning the formation of a people—perhaps we might speak of its "autoformation"—implies that we question how a national "identity" is forged. This is essential when questioning Heidegger's Nazism and "nationalism"; and this question is not dependent upon the past, even if today it is termed in terms of "cultural" identity. The point at which identification as such ensues from *evil* is precisely the point Schelling had already clarified in his essay *On Human Freedom*. Essentially, it is the will to rise up *toward and against everything* as a Self. For, the *Self* is able to determine itself as such only in relation to an "other." It is a determination that is itself determined by exclusion whereby the identification of the other is identified as a nonself. The "example" par excellence of the other—at least since the advent of Christianity—is the Jew. It is somewhat unjust to find fault with Heidegger on account of his visceral anti-Catholicism. The Catholic Church—or at least those who were high in the hierarchy—never hesitated to close their eyes to the Extermination that surrounded them. (Not until recently the Church has established official relationship with Israel; furthermore, the proceedings of Carmel at Auschwitz have proven to be—at best—an ambiguity that is difficult to maintain).

According to Heidegger, it is good to bring meditation against the "pernicious temptation to take those phenomena, which are nothing more than the consequences of nihilism, as nihilism itself." We must not "consider the reign of Technology and the uprising of the masses as the causes of our century's historical situation." (Here, not only Christianity, but everything that can be called *culture* must be considered as part of these "historical determinants.") Yet, such meditation is cruelly in want from the very moment we relinquish the experience of thought and its abyssal liberty for the adoption of a position—even if this latter is critical, prudent, involved, or indifferent. It is not so much a question of not taking any position at all (this would always be a position), but to put that "taking of a position" to the test. Any de-position shall appear to be untenable and intolerable—and even inhuman—as long as we abide by the measure of humanism that, because it already knows who and what humankind is, abstained from any further questioning. On this head, any further questioning shall not be sufficient, for this might very well constitute a sort of sanctuary of last resort. However, for us to venture beyond—to experience that which shall certainly appear only as a divagation and incoherence outside of reality (at least as long as we continue to take such reality as *the* unquestionable measure and norm)—we must stand without any point d'appui and without regard to either Being or humankind. Hölderlin once wrote that, "On this earth there is no measure." In translation, this might mean there is no measure by which we can measure "evil." Nonetheless, Auschwitz seems to have achieved an absolute degree of it. But what—on earth—is an *absolute* evil? And how can we recognize and know it? And more, we wonder whether such absolute evil ensues from an absolute knowing and knowledge?

At the end of his Transcendental Analytic, Kant gives the metaphysical (logical) measure of "nothingness": "The object of a concept which contradicts itself is nothing, for the concept *nothing* is impossible." Perhaps "nothing" is inconceivable; and yet, such an impossibility has already taken place. Indeed, the event of this taking place ought to be able to be conceived—conceived, though, in a way other than by the work of the concept. To think nothing "itself" as not being "anything," but rather as that which "nihilates" demands a certain "meditation." But who, today, still wishes to take the time and effort to meditate that? Especially when it is easier to label Heidegger as a *nihilist* and his works as *nihilism*—that thus we need not read him, discuss him—think him. But what is it precisely that we call reading? And what is it to read? Let us let Heidegger respond:

> What is it that we call reading? That which, in reading, carries forth and guides (our gaze) is the gathering. Yet, around what does reading gather? Around that which is written, and around that which, in the written, is said. Properly speaking, reading is the gathering around that which, without our knowledge, has already laid claim to our being, whether or not we wish to respond to or elude such a request.
>
> Without such a proper reading, we cannot even see that which concerns us; nor can we consider that which peers forth and appears.[37]

This brief text already contains and implicates all of Heidegger; everything, that is, that calls for such a proper reading (*eigentliche*) of the Word—but implicates, also, the hermeneutic experience. The hermeneutic circle is present in every reading, in the form of this preliminary request (*Anspruch*), anterior to all knowledge, which has already addressed its word to us—and thus our "being." This word not only precedes but makes possible all seeing and therefore the very gift of presence. Without reading, we would be unable to see that which appears, for such appearance could appear only as such—as "seen." Thus, one can read only that which has already been "spoken" to the reader, though this word is hardly satisfied with the deliverance of some sort of "message"—indeed, it seems to remain before all utterance; and yet, it speaks to us only inasmuch as we let-it-be-said. But then, perhaps, we might refuse such word.

A trained eye has no difficulty discerning in the Heideggerian determination of the essence of reading, a certain twist in logocentric thinking—if only because already reading (*Lesen*) is ascribed to the gathering (his translation of *logos*). Yet, such logocentrism is not merely an inheritance from Metaphysics, but rather refers to what Heidegger calls the *Anfang*, or the initial sending off of Western thought.

I must confess that to read Heidegger I was obligated to learn German. A certain critic from *Le Monde* has complained about the "Germanization" that Heidegger would have made the Spirit undergo—as if Heidegger had been the first thinker to have made philosophy speak German. Who can deny that thinking has hitherto dwelled in Germany for some 200 years! It is true: only Heidegger asserted that the German language is the sole depositary of the "original signification" of the "Spirit." It is said that Heidegger "maintained until his death that thinking is only possible—both for today and tomorrow—in the German language. Not only is this position irrational and unbearable, but it constitutes an extreme violence in its symbolic import." It is Violence—yes. But then, Thinking (in the West) has never appeared as anything but an "unbearable" violence. For quite some time, it was possible to think only in Greek, even to the extent that "thinking" was articulated with the Greek word *philosophos.* Strangely enough, the Greek language never had a word to say "language"; it only had the word *logos*, which signified much more than our word *language*, or "reason" or "spirit." To be sure, logocentrism derives from the first sending off of Being—and therefore, of Thought; and in the Greek world, anyone who did not understand the *logos* was considered, quite simply, to be a barbarian rather than human. (In this sense, even Heraclitus was "logocentric.")

Perhaps this privilege of the Greek—as *logos*—seems somewhat exorbitant and unreasonable—and, it is, obviously. *Philosophy*, as a Greek word, speaks Greek. Such that, in this original and first sending off, "all" has already been set into motion: in other words, *Anfang*, though this latter word speaks German. But this is of little importance insofar as German (philosophy) is nothing but a repetition of the original sending off that deflects it towards "another" such sending off—another, but one that is, at bottom, the same. The Gathering around One and the Same: could it be here that we must situate Heidegger's thought? But then, we would have to admit that all Western thought—at least, all that goes by the name of *philosophy*—dwells upon this same principle, which is precisely the principle of identity, and that, subsequently, this gives rise to an abyss with the Extermination—even if this latter consitutes a totalitarian process.

❁ ❁ ❁

Despite all the respect I have for Emmanuel Levinas, I can in no way hold Heidegger's adherence to Nazism as a mark of the Evil One. This reference to the traditional demonic figure is simply an easy way to disencumber oneself of that which must be thought and relieve oneself of the "disquietude" (*Unheimliche*, Heidegger's translation of a line from the *Antigone*, characterizing the human being). If God died at Auschwitz, then the devil did as well. And Hannah Arendt is correct when she speaks of the "banality" of Evil: the Nazi functionary who, with zeal, applied himself to the extermination of the Jews was in no way extraordinary; rather, he, by definiton, was anybody, simply the first comer. But does this justify the "explanation"—the only one that Heidegger gave publically—of Nazism as the "encounter between modern man and planetary technology"? Of course, this explanation, given a posteriori (it has been shown that he neither wrote nor said this parenthetical remark in 1935, but added it to the publication of his course in 1953), tends to justify the aberration of Nazism within the historial scheme of things. But more, this explanation tends to erase everything that constitutes the singularity of Nazism: for it can be said that not only Nazism, but "Americanism" and "Communism" as well constitute this encounter between modern man and planetary technology. Were we to take this argument to its extreme, then we too—we promoters of democracy—would be Nazis inasmuch as we are "modern" and inasmuch as we deal daily with technology! In much the same way, we might say that agriculture has become "a motor-driven alimentary industry" (and thus a technological business), *similar* to the "manufacture of corpses in the concentration camps and gas chambers"—but then, we must admit this is not quite the *same* thing . . . Or perhaps are we to understand that, in the eyes of a Heidegger filled with the nostalgia for the peasant world, the destruction of peasantry was a crime equal to that of the Extermination? And furthermore, when he speaks of "corpses" *in general*, Heidegger "forgets" to mention that they were these of the nonpeasant "people"—the *Jews*.

No, this is not at all the same thing. Certainly, it is too easy to invoke, as Alain Finkielkraut has done, a certain "kinship between the manufacture of corpses and the more or less general health of the world"—and to thus exculpate Heidegger while slandering the defenders of "modernism." (In effect, this does a great disservice to the thinking of Being by making it seem both nostalgic and antimodern. Much to the contrary, Heidegger was never quite so *absolutely modern* as in his "withdrawals" to the Greek past; for it was then that he *projected* it into the future and liberated it of every solidifying and sedimentary element.)

This is not the same thing; nor does it signify an eternal return of the same, for the "same" began—with Auschwitz, but already with Nietzsche—to become altered in a way—and the "universal" so often invoked by the humanists suddenly burst. The Extermination cannot be reduced to a "sort" of becoming-technological of the world, nor can it be classified as a type of symbolic event falling under the law of a higher essence. For who can be sure the Extermination had any essence in the metaphysical sense of the word? And who, therefore, can be sure that any discourse concerning (philosophical) essence can make sense of such a "thing," or even embrace it? Perhaps what is most disquieting in Heidegger's famous declaration concerning the Extermination—the only declaration in which he touched upon the camps—was not so much his saying they constituted a technological process—such being their "essence" and *quidditas*—but in limiting the Extermination to "that," to this "what" that it may very well have been, but only from the point of view of a discourse on essence. Indeed, he limited the Extermination merely to a discourse. Consequently, all that was unsayable and inexpressable with respect to Auschwitz would evanesce as inessential; but it is precisely this and only this—the Inconceivable—that must become "essential" if we are not to shut our eyes to that which concerns us at present: the want of any Present.

Only from the point of view of the visible, of the representable and calculable, does Auschwitz become but one more example of the becoming-technological of the world. Yet, that it was *the* triumph of *Organization*, the coup de grace of the planning and rationalization of the reduction of the human being to a state of stock, of raw material, and means of production and so on—this can be only a commonplace and, thus, a nontruth. Rather, let us say, a *half*-truth. It is true that the Organization and the Planning of beings constitute the "oblivion" of Being; and from here, it is not too difficult to delineate the Absolute Evil in Technology, or even the "failure of thinking" therein (I have in mind that thinking thought in memory of Being, its origin and its various epochs—which Heidegger unfolded for all to see—and not that thinking thought only in terms of norms and universals). This is a somewhat safe reading inasmuch as it fails to think the essential ambiguity of European nihilism as well as the "Janus head" of Technology. As regards this latter, we might imagine one face turned toward beings and their exploitation or administration according to the plans of the will to will; but the other face, toward what would it be turned? Precisely toward the want of any "what," such that we cannot imagine any face at all. Simply turned toward the invisible and the incalculable. At the end of "The Turning," Heidegger would ask, "Will we see the lightening-flash of Being in the essence of technology?"—a conference that belonged to that same course of studies in which he declared his famous declaration concerning the concentration camps.[38] The whole of these courses was entitled *Look into That Which Is.* That which is—is it simply beings or Being? Or is it neither of the two? Being rather the space between—the Difference?

Thus we see that nothing is simply one-way; for even in the Same there is the Other—an "other" beginning. And thinking, of itself, is overcome and defeated only by itself, when it becomes reductive. If Technology is a menace—even the Menace—it is not because of some malevolent and satanic power, but because it is a form of *thinking* (in this case, that of calculation and strategy) and because it imposes this form as the *only* form, without any regard as to its origin (reason for which Heidegger would always translate *techne* with the word *knowledge*). It has often been said that Heidegger sought to escape modernity by returning to the Greeks; yet such an assertion ought to give us pause: is there even such a thing as a "pure" modernity or is not modernity simply an imitation (in the form of a reaction) of the Greek way? Practically—literally—every word we speak bears testimony to this: in politics—a Greek word par excellence—every concept conceived therein was "originally" Greek, beginning with that little word which, today, seems so indispensable: *demokratia*.

This past that will not pass away includes Ancient Greece as well—this sudden sending off, this Inception of thought, in short, Being. If the Turning is not simply a simple word—if it is the injunction erupting from the want and inability of thought nearing its end—then it can hardly signify a mere change of position, but rather, the utter abandonment of every position, and even the abandonment of Being as position: a Deposition. But what want could so compel us to explicitly renounce and abandon every foundation, every ground—even Being itself, or at least whatever remains of it—that thus we might enter into "Evan-essence"? Only the shock of Technology can awake thought from 2,000 years of sleepiness. In the midst of Danger, will we find the saving power? Perhaps—but only on condition that we renounce the Same—and renounce as well the same—old—form of thought. Simply to repeat or interpret our (past)"heritage" is no longer permitted.

It needs a translation in the way of thinking. And yet, this is not at all a revolution—which ultimately always translates into a catastrophe. Rimbaud, who experienced the utter impossibility of any return, once wrote: "My spirit, take care; beware of any violent resolution for salvation. Stand ready!"[39] In other words, a nonviolent salvation void of any will to purify and void of any tragic or heroic pathos. Such a salvation would be characterized by a careful and constant watchfulness over every sign—over every subtle mark and remark—of a turning—even within the want itself—which hands us over to this "wide-open and exposed face." Yet what face? The face of God? Of Him—the only one who can save us? "Already the expression—'may a god come'—has lost its meaning." There remains only the want; there remains only the "wide-open and exposed face" of which Jean-Luc Nancy has spoken (*Des lieux divins*).

What remains is to make a stand within this want wherein thought—now fundamentally disarmed—cannot make itself respected in a way other than by its bare exposition. And respect—this philosophical virtue par excellence—is its only power: to attract our thoughtful gaze (and not merely a brief glance, after which we may quietly pass on to something else). Notwithstanding this, the "thing" is always there; it would hardly relinquish its grasp so easily. Such a thoughtful gaze allows one to respect one's friend while keeping one's enemy at a respectful—distance. With respect to Heidegger, and equally with Auschwitz, we might ask, have we had enough respect?

To be sure, respect is possible only if one pays respect to that which gives itself over to being seen—and which subsequently regards us. Heidegger saw nothing, of Auschwitz; and therefore, it never regarded him. However, is this alone sufficient in bearing testimony to his thought? And can a thought that has no regard for *that* still be regarded as thought? And therefore can we have any respect for that—for that which has no respect whatsoever for Auschwitz?

Before responding—if any response is possible—we must take a closer look. But is this possible? What would we see at Auschwitz? Nothing. And what would we hear? Perhaps only the silence of the land. Auschwitz is a name that cannot be pronounced—it does not name a being. It is something that never should have been; indeed, it was something that was ultimately scheduled to disappear, for in the end, the camps with their Organization and their corpses were to be removed from sight.

> The crime against humanity was practically perfect. Though it wanted something—but what?—in order for it to have never taken place. Without corpses. Under "the lake of ashes," glistening peacefully; in the rebel forest of Vilna. . . . Look: these places are still called Treblinka, Belznec; the train station is there. The names are pronounceable, peaceful, not prohibited: like Bois-Colombes or Newport Beach.
>
> Crime that was never named, specified or called by its present! Always silenced, and still pseudonymous: unnamed; euphemized with conviction, without intrigue without actor without witness, without remains, without motive, without narration. No one thought about it; believed it; and many, not only don't believe (the "revisionists"), but accuse the latest tellers of the horrible tale of lying. Still euphemized today, in the new age of euthanasia.
>
> It is for this reason that the Jews of Warsaw only demanded that it be known; that it be uttered: that an entire portion of "humanity" had been exterminated, *vernichtet.*[40]

Michel Deguy articulates the essential that gives itself over to be seen in *Shoah*, the film by Lanzmann. Oedipus saw the horror—and then blinded himself. But Heidegger, he saw nothing. We cannot even speak about his "silence"—no more than we could speak about the silence of a man who has never been able to speak. Auschwitz changed even into silence; and this silence was not that of humanity, but of the Word itself. That there has never been a *proper* name for the Extermination—that is, nothing other than an euphemism—simply says that here the Word (the Proper, Being, and everything else toward which Heidegger groped) has been swallowed up, has been, itself, annihilated within a disappearance that has gone so far as to effect its own disappearance—as if nothing (happened; in effect—nothing, once, was). "It happened once upon a time"—the Incredible, something more horrible than non-Being . . . But there is no word for this, no more than there is a word for "the buried treasure" in Stephan George's poem on which Heidegger commented: Being disappears and the Word becomes the Legend (*Sage*) of "Once upon a time there was Being" (impossible to say, *to say* meaning "to bring into being," *poiesis*). And from that time on, as Heidegger has written in *Unterwegs zur Sprache*, it is necessary "to carry out silence upon silence . . . "

Finally, we might ask ourselves if silence was Heidegger's last word, in much the same way that the Extermination was the last gasp and word—even apo-calypse, unconcealment—of Western nihilism: its revelation as nothing but nothingness, revealing its "truth" to be a desperate nonplace. It is in this way that we can read Georges-Arthur Goldschmidt: "It is true that Heidegger wasn't able to think Auschwitz inasmuch as Auschwitz was the very center of his thought: his center and unspokenness, his shadow within and his silence. Heidegger saw the essential and adhered to it and to the Extermination that was the *Wesen seines Grundes*, the essence of his groundwork."[41]

Decidely, non-sense draws forth non-sense . . . For, finally, how can we simultaneously assert that, on the one hand, Heidegger was unable to think the Holocaust and, on the other, that he saw it and adhered to it? Cannot a thinker think that which he has seen? But what, exactly, do we understand by the term *to think*? Do we mean a total blindness—founded upon an absolute clairvoyance?

Once again, what is it that we call *thinking*? And how could we make Auschwitz (or the programmatic annihilation of the other) the center of a thinking that never really had a word for that? And even the center of a thought whatever it may have been? For, if we speak of annihilation—of *Unheil*—we speak not simply of a word: indeed, annihilation spares nothing; it annihilates everything, beginning with the very thought that would constitute its "center." Yet, what is the "center" of this thought? What is its *thing itself*?[42] Is it not Being "itself"—of which the Nazis literally had not the slightest idea? It is true that Heidegger included "nihilation" (*nichten*, a word that does not exist in German and not *vernichten*, "to annihilate") in the allotment of Being and its "truth." How else could we understand Western nihilism? And how, from this nihilation, could we not see "the shadow within" of Auschwitz that was not an event without origin, coming from "nothingness"?

Notwithstanding, there is nothing and, then, there is nothing. There is ordinary nihilism—according to which "everything in every respect is nothing"—and then there is an extreme nihilism that concerns not only the nothingness of beings but also that of Being. And, to think this latter, "neither the political nor the economic nor the sociological, nor the technological and scientific, nor even the metaphysical and the religious perspectives are adequate to think what is happening in that age."[43] What, then, is necessary to think this "ontological" nihilism? Nothing else but thinking: an experience of thought must have taken place—which is to say, a translation in thinking must occur that retreats far from Being, though neither for something else (what else could there be?) nor to give itself over to the "real." No, this retreat brings us nearest—within proximity of the retreat that is itself in retreat—whereat Being offers itself each time. Within the thought of withdrawal and retreat, Being takes place as the event of this withdrawal; and thought takes place as the experience of this event. And this is in extreme distance with the Extermination, even though it hardly saves us from the present confusion.

More to the point, the thing itself of thought is in no way measurable and, in this sense, is nothing "real." Thus, we can say it is blind precisely because, in a way, it has everything to do with that which presents nothing "to see." No one is able to leap above one's own shadow, only others are able to do so—and these others are quite unable to leap above their own. Perhaps Heidegger was blind—yet if we are able to *see* it, it is on account of his enlightening thought. Moreover, if he was blind, it was in the same way that Oedipus was blind—indeed, for having had one "eye too many pehaps"; for having had an eye for that which does not allow itself to be seen: Being itself in its "clearing." Oedipus, after his downfall and self-mutilation, learned to "love the long time" (*Oedipus at Colonus*, v. 7). And Heidegger, after the collapse of the Reich, caught his second wind; though he never stopped seeing the disaster: for, as for the disaster, he remained ever more lucid than us. And we—we believe ourselves saved inasmuch as we have come "after," upon this land that, every day, is ever more devastated and somehow miraculously healed.

If Heidegger was blind, it was not for want of judgment; nor was it on account of some stupidity (which, as Kant has stated, is an "irreparable vice" to which even men of knowledge succumb), but rather, on account of being caught by want: by the want of sight, of knowledge, of thought—even, by want of everything. Being "itself" is nothing; it cannot be identified with anything whatsoever: neither with the Idea nor absolute knowledge nor the will to power nor planetary technology. And yet, it makes possible all identification and therefore all annihilation. The retreat shall be seen precisely in the calling into question of both the identity of Being and the identity of identity. Also, it is a calling into question of the identity of thought: from the first beginnings of philosophy—from Parmenides to Plato—to the last—from Nietzsche to Heidegger. In the end, Being returns to nothing more—than itself. It disappears within the tautology. For perhaps there is no other way for it "to be" (nothing but a tautology saying nothing: Being as the Same—*logos*). And perhaps there is no other way to disappear: to a-void or/and to give out[44] itself.

To think the thing itself *as* this destiny of the Same would, in no way, be the same thing. However, at the same time, this would not be purely and simply something else—as if the page could be so utterly turned. What other word could come and so unsettle the dictum of the tautological logos? Surely not another—word—for it would only be the other of the same and therefore always the same. According to Celan, "The world [is] to be re-mumbled." Yet, if we perceive in this want of any word and want of any Present something more than a lack—in much the same way that the want of any god is an "aid"—and if we take care that such a want embraces presence itself, its sending off, as crossed by sign that is neither positive nor negative, neither concealing nor revealing, but simply making a sign, then we are already under the spell of the call, of that which calls us, by its very withdrawal, to think. To think: to exist under the spell of the unthinkable and within its clearing—however obscure it may be.

The gods are not infallible. Nor are thinkers. Yet their failure gives us courage: even, "Consider success of any kind a disastrous failure."[45] And in a somewhat different tone—though none the less poetic—Hölderlin would remember, before entering into his night:

> The heavenly powers
> Cannot do all things. It is the mortals
> Who reach sooner into the abyss. So the turn is
> With these. Long is
> The time, but the True comes into
> Its own.[46]

Notes

1. Ernst Nolte, "*Vergangenheit, die nicht vergehen will,*" *Frankfurter Allgemeine Zeitung* (June 6, 1986).

2. E. Nolte, "Between Myth and Revisionism: The Third Reich from the perspective of the 1980's." Quoted by Joseph Joffe in "The Battle of German Historians," *Commentaire* (January 1988).

3. Hölderlin, *Remarks on Oedipus* in *Oeuvres*, p. 958.

4. This makes reference to the "anti-Farias" book by François Fédier entitled, *Heidegger: anatomie d'un scandale* (Paris: Robert Laffont, 1988)—Trans.

5. The text from which this chapter was taken first appeared in the *Nouvelle Revue de Psychanalyse* (no. 37, Spring 1988), dedicated to *The Reading*. The text itself was entitled "Turn the Page?" Yet, initially it was entitled "The Stigmas of Silence."

6. Nietzsche, *Thus Spoke Zarathustra* in *The Portable Nietzsche*, trans. Walter Kaufmann, p. 152.

7. Mallarmé, "*Quant au Livre,*" in *Oeuvres Complètes*, p. 386.

8. Mallarmé, *Oeuvres Complètes*, p. 380.

9. Rimbaud, "*Génie,*" in *Oeuvres Complètes*, p. 154.

10. In a letter, Rimbaud wrote in the dialect of his mother-earth (the Ardennes), thus we find *innocince* with an *i*. I would also point out that the English word *Mother*, in the text of the letter, was the strange surname of Rimbaud's mother, as if the poet had wanted to put a-part the trivial origin.

11. Laïtou = some stupid song. In French, *Roche* signifies "rock" and was the name of the farm owned by Rimbaud's mother.

12. Heidegger, *Aus der Erfahrung des Denkens*, p. 10.

13. *Alles Grosse steht im Sturm*, Heidegger's translation of Plato's *Republic*, 497 d. 9 in *Der Selbstbehauptung des deutschen Universität: L'auto-affirmation de l'université allemande*, ed. and trans. Gérard Granel (Mauvezin: T.E.R, 1982), p. 22. Hugo Ott notes (naively enough) that: "Heidegger was familiar with Greek and knew, in reality, that Plato had said: Everything that is great is fragile" (Hugo Ott, *Heidegger: Unterwegs zu seinem Biographie* (Frankfurt: Campus Verlag, 1988, p. 172). In effect, Heidegger never ceased insisting upon the *exposed*—and consequently, the precarious and preparatory—character of thought.

14. Heidegger readily admitted that he too was one who "acted too much and thought too little." See his "Lecture I" in *What Is Called Thinking.*

15. Quoted from Jean Beaufret's interview with Roger-Pol Droit, in *Le Monde* (September 27, 1974).

16. This is what Heidegger would have said *in private*. This is precisely the type of "enormous indiscretion" one commits in a private conversation.

17. Heidegger wrote this "biographical" text (*Aus der Erfahrung des Denkens* "From the Experience of Thought"), immediately after the collapse of the Nazi *Reich*.

18. Hannah Arendt, *Vies Politiques*, p. 320.

19. Heidegger, *An Introduction to Metaphysics*, trans. Ralph Manheim (New Haven, Conn.: Yale University Press, 1959), p. 8.

20. These texts were originally assembled in *Le Débat* 48 (January 1988), and translated by François Fédier. We must remember that these "political" texts have been known since 1962 (Schneeberger) and have been subsequently quoted and discussed (J.-P. Faye, J.-M. Palmier, etc.). Notwithstanding, these were the only texts that Heidegger explicitly *repudiated*—he never repudiated his *Rectoral Discourse* and his "Creative Landscape."

21. Alain Renault, "*La déviation heideggerienne?*" *Le Débat* 48: 172.

22. Michel Deguy, "Le sozi de Heidegger," in *Le Débat*, 48. In French, *sosie*, pronounced *sozi*, signifies "double."

23. Jacques Derrida, "*L'enfer des philosophes*" in *Le Nouvel Observateur* (November 6, 1987). Reprinted in *Points de suspension*, *Entretiens* (Paris: Galilée, 1992), p. 194.

24. Philippe Lacoue-Labarthe, *La Fiction du politique*, p. 188.

25. François Fédier, "Un national-socialisme privé," in *Voir* (Lausanne, December 1987). In his book entitled *Heidegger: anatomie d'un scandale*, Fédier reexamines his previous assertions, but only to reenforce them. If one disregards these three possibilities to explain the silence of Heidegger—namely, (1) indifference, (2) ressentment and bitterness after Germany's defeat, and (3) philosophical pride—then there remains only the following hypothesis: "It is quite possible that there exists a very dignified form of respect: for example, after martyrdom—when so many cries have been uttered—silence—a long, profound silence—is not at all improper." However, it is improper (to continue along this euphemistic path) to speak this way: not only because Heidegger hardly deemed it improper to speak about other "martyrs"—that is, of *German* prisoners of war—but also, because the very word *martyr* is improper, when used to qualify the genocide of the Jews (with some others) in the gas chambers. Originally, a martyr was the tortured Christian who died as a *testimony* to his or her faith. And more generally, only he (or she)

is a martyr who dies for a cause; who self-sacrifices for The Cause. Here, I agree with Lacoue-Labarthe as regards this subject: we have spoken improperly about the "Holocaust." "There was no sacrificial aspect in the *operation* of Auschwitz." Those who were gased—though they bore testimony to a faith and to a God other than that of the Western-Greco-Christian-Modern world died *for nothing*. They were not killed, properly speaking, but liquidated as a sort of refuse and garbage. This was done without the slightest cry. It all took place as a banal and technological operation and process: in effect, it was as routine as the work of garbagemen gathering garbage. It was a technologically perfect process—and perfectly silent.

26. Martin Heidegger, *An Introduction to Metaphysics*, p. 37.

27. Philippe Lacoue-Labarthe, *La poésie comme expérience*, p. 58.

28. Hölderlin, "In Sweet Blueness . . . ", quoted by Heidegger in 1951, ". . . Poetically Man Dwells . . . ," in *PLT*, p. 228.

29. Stephan Georg, quoted by Martin Heidegger in "Words," *OWL*, p. 140.

30. All of Heidegger's important commentators (Derrida, Levinas, etc.) have commented on the "foreclosure" that he effected on the Hebraic inheritance of the West. Marlene Zarader has attempted to show—though unconvincingly—that such inheritance could have been the very source of Heidegger's thought (*Heidegger et l'héritage hebraïque* [Paris: Seuil, 1990]).

31. Quoted by Jean-Luc Nancy in *L'expérience de la liberté*, p. 157. It may very well be that all "culture" is nothing more than "so much refuse." Notwithstanding, I would say that all thinking (or all poetry) does not necessarily constitute "culture." And therefore—following Christopher Fynsk's line of thought on Paul Celan—it has been only after Auschwitz that the poem (or thinking according to ex-perience)—inasmuch as it is marked by such an impossibility—remains the only possibility.

32. Nancy, *L'expérience de la liberté*, p. 160.

33. Philippe Lacoue-Labarthe, *La Fiction du politique*, p. 63. The entire question revolves around what "meaning" we give to the word *essence*. The caesura "resides" precisely in this: in the transformation of essence—in the metaphysical sense of *quidditas*—into an *inessential* essence; not an essence that is subsidiary or accidental, but one which is deprived of any "substance" (therefore, of a subject). This transformation also demands a turning in the essence of thought—which Heidegger outlines in his conference *Vom Wesen der Wahrheit*. Here, transformation refers to an "original inessence of truth as liberty"; and, in effect, demands such a turning to think the enigmatic "essence of Technology" that, itself, is not technological. So it was with Auschwitz. While seeming to be a simple technological process, it fundamentally transgresses the genre of metaphysical "essence"; and it is for this reason that Lacoue-Labarthe speaks of it as a *spiritual* event.

34. Michel Tibon-Cornillot, "*Heidegger; le chaînon manquant*," *Libération* (February 17, 1988). Indeed, there is a hiatus or missing link in the connection "Heidegger *and* Nazism" that is restricted to a juxtaposition of heterogenous elements. Yet, it is somewhat deceptive to *reestablish* the missing link by invoking Heidegger's doubtful "friendship" with Eugen Fischer who, as it were, was the director of the institute in charge of a radical (and racial) "hygiene." The want here is not a simple lacuna, but a true *abyss*.

35. Heidegger wrote this in a letter dated January 10, 1969, to Jean-Michel Palmier (published in *Cahiers de l'Herne Heidegger*, p. 116). Heidegger also compares the student uprisings of 1968 to those "already formulated in 1933." Perhaps this bears witness to a certain historico-political blindness on the part of the thinker—one necessitated by a "historial" clairvoyance that was much too clear?

36. Lacoue-Labarthe, *La Fiction du politique* p. 125.

37. Heidegger, "Was heisst Lesen?", in *Aus der Erfahrung des Denkens* p. 111.

38. Martin Heidegger, "The Turning," in *The Question Concerning Technology and Other Essays*, trans. William Lovitt (New York: Harper and Row Publishers, 1977), p. 49.

39 Rimbaud, "*L'Impossible*," in *A Season in Hell*.

40. Michel Deguy, "Une Oeuvre après Auschwitz" in *Au sujet de Shoah, film de Claude Lanzmann* (Paris: Belin, 1990) p. 42.

41. Georges-Arthur Goldschmidt, "*Rappel! Heidegger et le nazisme*," *Allemagnes d'aujourdhui*, 93 (July–September 1985). Goldschmidt goes even further inasmuch as he judges—with respect to a sensitivity to language or to "jargon"—that *Being and Time* is a terrifying book and thus perfect for the SS. In reality, this is simply to forget the majority of the SS were practically illiterate and preferred to drink beer than to read a treatise on fundamental ontology. Similarly, when Farias (following Adorno)—writes that paragraph 74 of *Being and Time*, under the pretext of appealing to "heros," brings into play "properly fascist elements"—the ineptitude falls on Farias: for are there only fascist heros? Indeed, was Homer a fascist?

42. It is for this reason that I have entitled the second volume of *Solitudes* with "*La chose même*" ["The Thing Itself"] (Paris: Galilée, 1992). This expression must be understood in the same sense as when Heidegger spoke of the *Sache des Denkens*.

43. Heidegger, "The Word of Nietzsche: 'God Is Dead,' " in *The Question Concerning Technology and Other Essays*, p. 111.

44. "Se dis penser": the French can be understood either in a negative way (to avoid itself, becoming no-thing) or in a positive way (to dispense

itself, in the *Es gibt Sein*). The word is undecidable and overdetermined by the presence of "penser", thinking.

45. John Cage, "Rhythm Etc.," in *A Year from Monday, Lectures and Writings*, (London: Calders and Boyars Ltd, 1968) p. 132.

46. Hölderlin, "Mnemosyne," quoted by Martin Heidegger in "What Are Poets For?" in *PLT*, p. 92.

Bibliography

Arendt, Hannah. *Vies politiques*, trans. B. Cassin and P. Levy. Paris: Gallimard, 1986.

Badiou, Alain. *Manifeste pour la philosophie*. Paris: Le Seuil, 1989.

Barthes, Roland. *The Pleasure of the Text*, trans. Richard Miller. New York: Hill and Weng, 1975.

Baudelaire, Charles. *Oeuvres complètes*, ed. Claude Pichois. Paris: Gallimard, 1976.

Benjamin, Walter. *Charles Baudelaire: A Lyrical Poet in the Era of High Capitalism*, trans. Harry Zohn. London: Verso, 1983.

———. *Illuminations: Essays and Reflections*, ed. Hannah Arendt. New York: Hill and Weng, 1975.

———. *Reflections: Essays, Aphorisms, Autobiographical Writings*, ed. Peter Demetz. New York: Schocken Books, 1978.

Berman, Antoine. *L'Epreuve de l'étranger*. Paris: Gallimard, 1984.

Bonnefoy, Yves. *Rimbaud par lui-même*. Paris: Le Seuil, 1961.

Cage, John. *A Year From Monday: Lectures and Writings*. London: Calders and Boyars, 1968.

Camus, Albert. *L'Exil et le royaume*, in *Théâtre, Récits, Nouvelles*, ed. Jean Grenier. Paris: Gallimard, 1962.

Celan, Paul. *Paul Celan: A Bilingual Edition*, trans. Katherine Wasburn and Margret Guillemin. San Francisco: North Point Press, 1986.

———. *Poems of Paul Celan*, trans. Michael Hamburger. New York: Persea Books, 1986.

Char, René. *Oeuvres complètes*. Paris: Gallimard, 1983.

Clair, Jean. *Considérations sur l'état des Beaux-Arts*. Paris: Gallimard, 1983.

Deguy, Michel. "Une Oeuvre après Auschwitz," in *Au sujet de Shoah: Le film de Claude Lanzmann*. Paris: Belin, 1990.

Derrida, Jacques. *Of Spirit: Heidegger and the Question*, trans. Geoffrey Bennington and Rachel Bowlby. Chicago: University of Chicago Press, 1989.

———. *Points de suspension: Entretiens*, ed. Elisabeth Weber. Paris: Galilée, 1992.

———. *Psyché: Inventions de l'autre*. Paris: Galilée, 1987.

Descartes, René. *Discourse on Method and Meditations*, trans. J. Laurence. Indianapolis: Bobbs-Merill Educational Publishing, 1960.

———. *Oeuvres et lettres*, ed. André Bridoux. Paris: Gallimard, 1953.

———. *Règles pour la direction de l'esprit*, trans. J. Sirvin. Paris: Vrin, 1966.

Farias, Victor. *Heidegger and Nazism*, ed. Joseph Margolis. Philadelphia: Temple University Press, 1989.

Fédier, François. *Heidegger: Anatomie d'un scandale*. Paris: Robert Laffont, 1988.

Ferry, Luc and Renaut, Alain. *Heidegger et les Modernes*. Paris: Grasset, 1988.

Finkielkraut, *La Défaite de la pensée*. Paris: Gallimard, 1987.

Froment-Meurice, Marc. *Tombeau de Trakl*. Paris: Belin, 1992.

———. *La chose même: Solitudes II*. Paris: Galilée, 1992.

Fynsk, Christopher. *Heidegger: Thought and Historicity*. Ithaca, N.Y.: Cornell University Press, 1986.

Haar, Michel (ed.). *Martin Heidegger*. Paris: L'Herne, 1983.

Handke, Peter. *Der Chinese des Schmerzes*. Frankfurt: Suhrkamp, 1983.

———. *Slow Homecoming*, trans. Ralph Manheim. New York: Macmillan Publishing Company, 1985.

———. *The Weight of the World: A Journal*, trans. Ralph Manheim. New York: Macmillan Publishing Company, 1985.

Hegel, G. W. F. *Phenomenology of Spirit*, trans. A. V. Miller. Oxford: Oxford University Press, 1977.

Heidegger, Martin. *Aus der Erfahrung des Denkens: Gesamtausgabe* vol. 13. Frankfurt: Klostermann, 1983.

———. *Basic Writings*, ed. and trans. David Farrell Krell. New York: Harper and Row, 1977.

———. *Being and Time*, trans. John Macquarrie and Edward Robinson. New York: Harper and Row, 1962.

———. *Erläuterungen zu Hölderlins Dichtung*. Frankfurt: Klostermann, 1971.

———. *Existence and Being*, trans. Douglas Scott. Chicago: Henry Regnery Company, 1949.

———. *Hölderlins Hymne "Der Ister": Gesamtausgabe* vol. 53. Frankfurt: Klostermann, 1984.

———. *Hölderlins Hymnen "Germanien" und "Der Rhein": Gesamtausgabe* vol. 39. Frankfurt: Klostermann, 1980.

———. *Holzwege*. Frankfurt: Klostermann, 1957.

———. *An Introduction to Metaphysics*, trans. Ralph Manheim. New Haven, Conn.: Yale University Press, 1959.

———. *On the Way to Language*, trans. Peter D. Hertz. New York: Harper and Row, 1971.

———. *Parmenides*, trans. André Schuwer and Richard Rojcewicz. Bloomington: Indiana University Press, 1992.

———. *Poetry, Language, Thought*, trans. Albert Hofstadter. New York: Harper and Row, 1971.

———. *The Question Concerning Technology and Other Essays*, trans. William Lovitt. New York: Harper and Row, 1977.

———. *Die Selbstbehauptung der deutschen Universität: L'auto-affirmation de l'université allemande*, ed. and trans. Gérard Granel. Mauvezin: Trans-Europ-Repress., 1982.

———. *Sein und Zeit*, 11th ed. Tübingen: Max Niemeyer, 1967.

———. *Textes politiques*, ed. François Fédier, trans. Nicole Parfait, in *Le Débat*, 48, [Paris: Gallimard] 1988.

———. *Unterwegs zur Sprache, Gesamtausgabe* vol 12. Frankfurt: Klostermann, 1985.

———. *Vom Ursprung des Kunstwerks: De l'origine de l'oeuvre d'art*, ed. and trans. Emmanuel Martineau. Paris: Authentica, 1987.

———. *Vom Wesen der menschlichen Freiheit: Einleitung in die Philosophie, Gesamtausgabe* vol. 31. Frankfurt: Klostermann, 1982.

———. *Vorträge und Aufsätze.* Pfullingen: Neske, 1954.

———. *What Is Called Thinking?*, trans. J. Glenn Gray. New York: Harper and Row, 1968.

Hölderlin, Friedrich. *Oeuvres*, ed. Philippe Jaccottet. Paris: Gallimard, 1967.

———. *Poems and Fragments*, trans. Michael Hamburger. London: Routledge and Kegan Paul, 1966.

———. *Sämtliche Werke*, ed. Friedrich Beissner. Stuttgart: W. Kohlhammer, 1953.

Janicaud, Dominique. *L'Ombre de cette pensée: Heidegger et la question politique.* Grenoble: Jérôme Millon, 1990.

Jünger, Ernst. *Der Arbeiter.* Hamburg: Hanseatische Verlaganstalt, 1932.

———. *Le Travailleur*, trans. Julien Hervier. Paris: Christian Bourgois, 1989.

Kant, Immanuel. *Critique of Pure Reason*, trans. J. M. D. Meibelejohn. Buffalo, N.Y.: Prometheus Books, 1990.

Lacoue-Labarthe, Philippe. *Heidegger: Art and Politics*, trans. Chris Turner. Oxford: Basic Blackwell, 1990.

———. *La Fiction du politique.* Paris: Christian Bourgois, 1988.

———. *La Poésie comme expérience.* Paris: Christian Bourgois, 1986.

Lamblin, Bernard. *Peinture et temps.* Paris: Klincksieck, 1983.

Mallarmé, Stéphane. *Oeuvres complètes*, ed. Henri Mondor and G. Jean-Aubry. Paris: Gallimard, 1945.

———. *Poems*, trans. Roger Fry. New York: New Directions, 1951.

———. *Selected Letters of Stéphane Mallarmé*, trans. Rosemary Lloyd. Chicago: University of Chicago Press, 1988.

———. *Selected Poems*, trans. C. F. MacIntyre. Berkeley: University of California Press, 1957.

Mettra, Claude. *Bruegel.* Paris: Henri Screpel, 1976.

Nancy, Jean-Luc. *Des lieux divins.* Mauvezin: Trans-Europ-Repress, 1987.

———. *The Inoperative Community*, ed. Peter Connor, trans. Peter Connor et al. Minneapolis: University of Minnesota Press, 1991.

———. *L'Expérience de la liberté.* Paris: Galilée, 1988.

Nietzsche, Friedrich. *Ecce Homo*, trans. Walter Kaufmann. New York: Vintage Books, 1989.

———. *Thus Spoke Zarathustra.* In *The Portable Nietzsche*, trans. Walter Kaufmann. New York: Penguin Books, 1976.

———. *The Will to Power*, trans. Walter Kaufmann. New York: Vintage Books, 1968.

Ott, Hugo, *Martin Heidegger: Unterwegs zu seiner Biographie.* Frankfurt/New York: Campus Verlag, 1988.

Payot, Daniel. *Le Philosophe et l'architecte.* Paris: Aubier, 1982.

Plato. *The Collected Dialogues*, ed. Edith Hamilton. Princeton, N.J.: Princeton University Press, 1961.

Proust, Marcel. *A la Recherche du temps perdu*, ed. Pierre Clarac and André Ferré. Paris: Gallimard, 1954.

Rilke, Rainer Maria. *Where Silence Reigns: Selected Prose*, trans. G. Craig Houston. New York: New Directions, 1978.

Rimbaud, Arthur. *Complete Works*, trans. Paul Schmidt. New York: Harper and Row, 1975.

———. *A Season in Hell and The Drunken Boat*, trans. Louise Varese. New York: New Directions, 1961.

———. *Oeuvres complètes*, ed. Antoine Adam. Paris: Gallimard, 1972.

Schürmann, Reiner. *Heidegger on Being and Acting: From Principles to Anarchy.* Bloomington: Indiana University Press, 1990.

Speer, Albert. *Architecture 1923–1942*, ed. Léon Krier. Brussels: Archives d'Architecture Moderne, 1985.

Trakl, Georg. *Das dichterishe Werk.* Salzburg: Otto Muller Verlag, 1972.